Strong Commanders, Weak States

A VOLUME IN THE SERIES

Cornell Studies in Security Affairs

Edited by Austin Carson, Alexander B. Downes, Kelly M. Greenhill, and Caitlin Talmadge

Founding Series Editors: Robert J. Art, Robert Jervis, and Stephen M. Walt

A list of titles in this series is available at www.cornellpress.cornell.edu.

Strong Commanders, Weak States

How Rebel Governance Shapes Military Integration after Civil War

Philip A. Martin

Cornell University Press

Ithaca and London

Publication of this book was made possible by a generous subvention from George Mason University.

Copyright © 2024 by Cornell University

All rights reserved. Except for brief quotations in a review, this book, or parts thereof, must not be reproduced in any form without permission in writing from the publisher. For information, address Cornell University Press, Sage House, 512 East State Street, Ithaca, New York 14850. Visit our website at cornellpress.cornell.edu.

First published 2024 by Cornell University Press

Library of Congress Cataloging-in-Publication Data

Names: Martin, Philip A., 1988– author.
Title: Strong commanders, weak states : how rebel governance shapes military integration after civil war / Philip A. Martin.
Description: Ithaca : Cornell University Press, 2024. | Series: Cornell studies in security affairs | Includes bibliographical references and index.
Identifiers: LCCN 2024017848 (print) | LCCN 2024017849 (ebook) | ISBN 9781501779015 (hardcover) | ISBN 9781501779039 (epub) | ISBN 9781501779022 (pdf)
Subjects: LCSH: Civil-military relations—Côte d'Ivoire—History—21st century. | Warlordism—Côte d'Ivoire—History—21st century. | Insurgency—Côte d'Ivoire—History—21st century. | Côte d'Ivoire—Politics and government—21st century. | Côte d'Ivoire—History—Civil War, 2002–2007.
Classification: LCC DT545.84 .M37 2024 (print) | LCC DT545.84 (ebook) | DDC 966.6805/3—dc23/eng/20240605
LC record available at https://lccn.loc.gov/2024017848
LC ebook record available at https://lccn.loc.gov/2024017849

Contents

List of Figures and Tables	*vii*
Acknowledgments	*ix*
List of Abbreviations	*xi*
Timeline of the Force Nouvelles Rebellion	*xv*
Note on Sources	*xvii*

PART I. THEORIZING REBEL COMMANDERS

	Introduction: Rebels, Commanders, and Military Integration after War	3
1.	A Theory of Commander Embeddedness	22

PART II. CÔTE D'IVOIRE

2.	Rebel Rule in the Ivorian Civil War (2002–2011)	45
3.	Commander Embeddedness in Postwar Côte d'Ivoire (2011–2017)	67
4.	Ex-Rebel Commanders and the Ivorian State	85
5.	Tracing Commander Embeddedness in Four Case Studies	104

CONTENTS

PART III. BEYOND CÔTE D'IVOIRE

6. Commander Resistance after Rebel-Military Integration (1946–2019)   *137*

   Conclusion: Field Commanders, War, and the State   *157*

   Appendices

      A. Interviews   *171*
      B. Community Informant Survey   *174*
      C. Political Transition and Inclusion Survey   *177*
      D. Variable Descriptions   *179*
      E. Appendix to Chapter 2   *184*
      F. Appendix to Chapter 3   *186*
      G. Appendix to Chapter 4   *191*
      H. Appendix to Chapter 5   *196*
      I. Appendix to Chapter 6   *198*

   Notes   *201*

   Bibliography   *225*

   Index   *243*

Figures and Tables

Figures

2.1. Spatial patterns of rebel rule in northern Côte d'Ivoire, 2002–2011 — 62

3.1. Wartime rebel rule and postwar commander influence in sampled subprefectures — 78

3.2. The correlates of postwar commander influence in Côte d'Ivoire (OLS) — 79

3.3. Rebel rule and postwar civilian perceptions of ex-rebels — 83

4.1. Predicted mutinies over collaborative rebel rule — 93

4.2. Change in predicted probabilities of *Crime assistance choice* given a change in *Wartime services quality* from its minimum to maximum (multinomial logit) — 98

4.3. Effects of increasing *Postwar commander influence* from minimum to maximum on Ivorian household access to services in 2014 — 100

6.1. Marginal effects of selected variables on predicted probability of commander defection — 149

A.1. Covariate balance, adjusted and unadjusted samples (coarsened exact matching) — 189

A.2. Rebel rule, postwar mutinies, and ex-rebel protests in former FN zone capitals — 193

Tables

1.1.	A theory of commander embeddedness	23
1.2.	Variation in wartime rebel rule	29
2.1.	Practices of rebel rule in FN territory (2002–2011)	60
3.1.	Postwar commander influence in Côte d'Ivoire (2011–2017)	76
5.1.	Paths of commander embeddedness in four matched cases	105
6.1.	Rebel rule and commander defection after rebel-military integration	142
A.1.	List of interviews	171
A.2.	Comparing in-sample and out-of-sample subprefectures in FN territory	176
A.3.	Comparing collaborative and predatory localities (sample means)	184
A.4.	Determinants of postwar commander influence (OLS)	187
A.5.	Disaggregating postwar commander-community ties (OLS)	188
A.6.	Heckman selection models (probit)	188
A.7.	Matching models	189
A.8.	Rebel rule and postwar civilian perceptions of ex-rebels (negative binomial)	190
A.9.	Determinants of mutinies and ex-rebel protest events (negative binomial)	192
A.10.	Determinants of mutinies and ex-rebel protests (zero-inflated negative binomial)	193
A.11.	Rebel rule and postwar police-citizen relations (multinomial logit)	194
A.12.	Household-level visit to police commissariat (logistic regression)	194
A.13.	Determinants of ex-rebel commander defection since 1946 (logistic regression)	199

Acknowledgments

This book would not have been possible without the help of countless friends, colleagues, and complete strangers. Above all, I am grateful to the Ivorians who took time out of their lives to share their experiences, knowledge, and perspectives with me. With Côte d'Ivoire being a country recently at war, these conversations sometimes touched on a painful past. I cannot adequately repay this debt. I can only hope that this book—if it offers nothing else—will help readers better understand Côte d'Ivoire's political history and the complex legacies of its conflict. Giulia Piccolino and Jeremy Speight generously shared their contacts and expertise with me during the early stages of my research and became academic collaborators. Abel Gbala and Bakary Soro provided diligent research assistance. I probably learned more about Ivorian politics from them over countless meals of *poulet braisé* and *alloco* than anywhere else. Thanks also to Sebastian van Baalen, Manogodjon Binate, Justine Davis, Bernard Die, Krista Desgranges Elkhamri, Yvan Guichaoua, Kathrin Heitz-Tokpa, Joseph Koné, Touré Kougninlin, Benjamin Olagboye, Maxime Ricard, and Michel Silwé.

Roger Petersen, Evan Lieberman, and Fotini Christia at the Massachusetts Institute of Technology encouraged me to ask questions that mattered, even if those questions were hard to answer. They have offered support and practical guidance at each step of my career. Regina Bateson's scholarship and teaching on ethnographic methods were also an early inspiration. My cohort at MIT—Nina McMurry, Reid Pauly, Cullen Nutt, Andrew Miller, Tim McDonnell, Parrish Bergquist, Mayumi Fukushima, Megan Goldberg, and many others—became a second family in Cambridge and provided crucial feedback and support. During a fellowship at the Belfer Center for Science and International Affairs at the Harvard Kennedy School, I received helpful input from Erica Chenoweth, Rebecca Davis Gibbons, Kelly Greenhill, Mariya Grinberg, Dan Jacobs, Tyler Jost, Sean Lynn-Jones, Zoe Marks, and Steven E. Miller. Additional thanks to Erica De Bruin, Kristen Harkness, Jacqueline Hazelton, Adria Lawrence, Shelley Liu, Kai Thaler, and Sarah Zukerman Daly for engaging with early versions of this project.

I completed this book as an assistant professor at the Schar School of Policy and Government at George Mason University. I thank the Schar School faculty and staff for being excellent and supportive colleagues. Ana Arjona, Risa Brooks, Roy Licklider, Paul Staniland, Will Reno, and Yuhki Tajima generously gave their time to participate in a book workshop and provided enormously helpful feedback. Amelia Johnston provided superb research assistance. David Mendeloff facilitated a writing sabbatical for me at the Norman Paterson School of International Affairs at Carleton University. Years ago, Ian Spears at the University of Guelph inspired me to study the problem of armed conflict. I am also grateful to those who reviewed this work and to the editorial team at Cornell University Press for their many constructive comments and suggestions.

Some of the material in this book was published in earlier versions in the *Journal of Peace Research* and *International Security*, and I thank these journals for their permission. Parts of chapter 3 were published in "Commander-Community Ties After Civil War," *Journal of Peace Research* 58, no. 4 (2021): 778–793. Parts of chapter 6 were published in "Insurgent Armies: Explaining Military Obedience and State Formation After Rebel Victory," *International Security* 46, no. 3 (2022): 87–127. I received generous support from the Center for International Studies at MIT, the MIT GOV/LAB, the Bridging the Gap Project, the Social Sciences and Humanities Research Council, and the Belfer Center for Science and International Affairs.

Finally, I am grateful to my parents, Mary and Orval, as well as my family and friends in Canada who have offered unconditional support during my improbable journey from rural Ontario to a career in political science. The largest thanks belong to my brilliant partner and wife, Saskia. She has supported me in every way imaginable with patience and love. There is no aspect of my work or my life she has not improved. This is dedicated to her.

Abbreviations

ACLED	Armed Conflict Location Event Dataset
ADCI	Côte d'Ivoire Association for the Demobilized
ADDR	Authority for Demobilization, Disarmament and Reintegration
AFDL	Alliance des Forces Démocratiques pour la Libération du Congo-Zaïre
ANC	African National Congress
CAR	Central African Republic
CEI	Commission Électorale Indépendante
CREFDI	Center for Research and Training for Integrated Development
DDR	disarmament, demobilization, and reintegration
ENV	Enquête niveau de vie des ménages
EPLF	Eritrean People's Liberation Front
FAFN	Forces Armées des Forces Nouvelles
FAN	Forces Armées du Nord
FANCI	Forces Armées Nationales de Côte d'Ivoire
FESCI	Fédération Estudiantine et Scholaire de Côte d'Ivoire
FLN	National Liberation Front
FN	Forces Nouvelles
FPI	Front Populaire Ivoirien
FPRC	Front Populaire pour la Renaissance de la Centrafrique
FRCI	Forces Républicaines de Côte d'Ivoire
FRELIMO	Frente de Libertação de Moçambique
FROLINAT	Front de Libération Nationale du Tchad

ABBREVIATIONS

FRUD	Front pour la Restauration de l'Unité et de la Démocratie
FSLN	Frente Sandinista de Liberación Nacional
FUNCIPEC	National United Front for an Independent, Neutral, Peaceful and Cooperative Cambodia
GDP	gross domestic product
GSPR	Groupement de Sécurité de la Présidence de la République
HVO	Croatian Defence Council
ICC	International Criminal Court
INS	Institut National de la Statistique
IRA	Irish Republican Army
JFN	La Jeunesse Forces Nouvelles
KDP	Kurdistan Democratic Party
KLA	Kosovo Liberation Army
MINUCI	United Nations Mission in Côte d'Ivoire
MJP	Mouvement pour la Justice et la Paix
MNL	multinomial logit
MNLA	National Movement for the Liberation of Azawad
MNR	Revolutionary Nationalist Movement
MPCI	Mouvement Patriotique de Côte d'Ivoire
MPIGO	Mouvement Populaire Ivoirien du Grand Ouest
MPLA	Movimento Popular de Libertação de Angola
MPS	Patriotic Salvation Movement
MSF	Médecins Sans Frontières
NATO	North Atlantic Treaty Organization
NFL	National Liberation Front
NGO	nongovernmental organization
NLA	National Liberation Army
NPLF	National Patriotic Front of Liberia
NRM	National Resistance Movement
PAIGC	African Party for the Independence of Guinea and Cape Verde
PDCI	Parti Démocratique de Côte d'Ivoire
PLA	People's Liberation Army
RDR	Rassemblement des Républicains
RENAMO	Resistência Nacional Moçambicana
RHDP	Rassemblement des Houphouëtists pour la Démocratie et la Paix
RPF	Rwandan Patriotic Front
SPLA/M	Sudan People's Liberation Army / Movement
SSR	security-sector reform
SWAPO	South West Africa People's Organisation
TPLF	Tigray People's Liberation Front

UCDP	Uppsala Conflict Data Program
UDPCI	Union Pour la Démocratie et la Paix en Côte d'Ivoire
UFDCI	Union des Femmes pour la Démocratie en Côte d'Ivoire
UIFSA	United Islamic Front for the Salvation of Afghanistan
UN	United Nations
UNICEF	United Nations Children's Fund
UNITA	National Union for the Total Independence of Angola
UNLF	Uganda National Liberation Front
UNOCI/ONUCI	United Nations Operation in Côte d'Ivoire
USAID	United States Agency for International Development
USC	United Somali Congress
UTO	United Tajik Opposition
UWSA	United Wa State Army
ZANU–PF	Zimbabwe National African Union–Patriotic Front
ZAPU	Zimbabwe African People's Union
ZDF	Zimbabwe Defence Forces

Timeline of the Force Nouvelles Rebellion

1893	France establishes the colony of Côte d'Ivoire within the federation of French West Africa.
1960	Côte d'Ivoire achieves independence under the leadership of Félix Houphouët-Boigny and the Parti Démocratique de Côte d'Ivoire (PDCI), the sole legal political party.
1990–1999	Transition to multiparty democracy. Houphouët-Boigny dies in 1993 and is succeeded by Henri Konan Bedié.
1999	General Robert Gueï takes power at the head of a military junta.
2000	Laurent Gbagbo and the Front Populaire Ivoirien (FPI) win elections. Purges begin against ethnic northerners in the army and civil service.
September 2002	Army units linked to Staff Sergeant Ibrahim Coulibaly attempt a coup against Gbagbo. The mutineers, calling themselves the Mouvement Patriotique de Côte d'Ivoire (MPCI), are repulsed from the capital and seize control in the north.
December 2002	The MPCI merges with two smaller militias to create the Forces Nouvelles (FN), now led by Guillaume Soro. FN forces consolidate control in the center-west.
2003–2007	Peace talks fail to reunify the country. United Nations and French military forces monitor a cease-fire buffer zone.
2007	The Ouagadougou Peace Agreement is signed, stipulating military integration and new national elections. Côte d'Ivoire remains effectively partitioned.

November 2010	Alassane Ouattara is declared the winner in the second round of presidential elections. Gbagbo's camp disputes the result and refuses to concede.
December 2010–April 2011	Renewal of rebel-government combat in multiple areas. One-sided violence against civilians occurs in several regions.
April 2011	Gbagbo is arrested. Rebel forces capture Abidjan and install Ouattara into power. FN army becomes the Forces Républicaines de Côte d'Ivoire (FRCI).

Note on Sources

Quotations from written and oral sources in French have been translated into English by the author. Following an institutional review board protocol for the protection of human subjects, I refer to interviewees anonymously throughout the book with the use of pseudonyms. Exceptions include public figures or authorities who provided consent for attribution. Research for this study was approved by the Massachusetts Institute of Technology Committee on the Use of Humans as Experimental Subjects (COUHES), Protocol # 1606619582 and 1606619582A001.

I. THEORIZING REBEL COMMANDERS

Introduction

Rebels, Commanders, and Military Integration after War

In the fall of 2017, I traveled on a research trip north from Abidjan to Korhogo, a midsize city in the Poro region of Côte d'Ivoire. When civil war broke out in 2002, Korhogo was one of the first towns to fall under the control of the rebel group that later became known as the Forces Nouvelles (FN).[1] By the time I arrived, more than six years after the FN triumphed in the war and integrated into the national army, the Poro region bore few visible signs of Côte d'Ivoire's protracted civil conflict. Yet over the course of dozens of interviews with Korhogo's residents—from motorcycle drivers to local hunting groups to elites in the mayor's office and the home of Korhogo's canton chief—the picture changed. Almost invariably, conversations about the war circled back to one individual: the former FN zone commander, Martin Kouakou Fofié.

Like many ex-rebel commanders in Côte d'Ivoire, Fofié was promoted by President Alassane Ouattara in 2011 to a senior position in the national army—his reward for helping to install the new regime. Yet in 2017, the former zone commander (or *com'zone*) still loomed large over his northern wartime fiefdom. Unprompted, Korhogo residents pointed out the many contributions Fofié made to the community, such as funds to refurbish the local cultural center and marketplace. At Korhogo's major marriages, funerals, and religious ceremonies, Fofié was a regular presence. On a patio overlooking the town one afternoon, a business owner gestured in the direction of a new upscale subdivision, remarking about the houses: "Most of them belong to Fofié, or to his men."[2]

Whatever the merits of Fofié's community works in Korhogo, the field commander's deep roots in the north were a serious problem to the government back in Abidjan. President Ouattara worried about the many ex-combatants and unemployed youth who remained in the orbit of commanders like Fofié. In safe houses around the city, secret weapons caches remained under the commandant's careful guard. These assets provided Fofié and his lieutenants significant potential for violent mobilization. In early 2017, thousands of former FN fighters had taken to the streets to protest the Ouattara government in cities and towns across the country.[3] Mutinous ex-rebel soldiers seized control of police and gendarmerie barracks, demanded payouts from the government, and briefly detained the defense minister. When the government sent other military units to confront the mutineers, some officers refused orders to arrest their ex-rebel comrades. Rumors swirled in the capital that cabinet members were chartering flights out of the country, fearful that the regime might fall. While the Ouattara government defused the crisis by handing out cash payments to the mutineers, tensions between the government and its ex-rebel allies in Korhogo ran high through the summer. In July 2017, ex-FN forces in the city coordinated armed attacks on government facilities that resulted in multiple deaths.[4]

These episodes of antistate mobilization by ex-rebels in places like Korhogo appeared to me to bely the narratives told by Ivorian government officials and international donors about Côte d'Ivoire's model peacebuilding record. In June 2017, the United Nations Operation in Côte d'Ivoire (ONUCI) had closed shop and departed the country, declaring that the return to peace was "irreversible."[5] Yet the fact that thousands of former rebel soldiers and their commanders—many operating from *inside* the national army—were willing to violently challenge the sitting government raised troubling questions about the kind of peace that rebel-military integration had delivered. The very same rebel forces who had won the war and installed the Ouattara government into power were now seen as a fundamental threat to regime security and national stability.

This book explores one of the fundamental challenges of politics in war-shattered states: creating obedient national militaries from the remnants of insurgency. I focus on a set of actors who are rarely analyzed in studies of postwar reconstruction: the field commanders of nonstate armed groups. When civil wars end through rebel-military integration, these field commanders become crucial brokers of peace and state recovery. They decide whether to implement donor-backed plans for militia demobilization and security-sector reform (SSR) and whether cohesive security forces emerge to buttress the stability of postconflict regimes. Yet ex-rebel commanders sometimes resist the statebuilding ambitions of government leaders and choose instead to retain clandestine armed networks and challenge the authority of capital-based elites—even when commanders themselves installed those leaders into power. Why? And why, facing the same national conditions, are there different patterns of cooperation and resistance across individual commanders?

My central argument is that the likelihood of ex-rebel commander resistance depends on prior processes of rebel governance that unfold during armed struggles. When effective wartime governance practices of armed groups allow field commanders to become locally embedded in rebel-ruled communities and develop independent power bases that outlive civil wars—as with Fofié in Korhogo—these commanders become empowered and motivated to challenge postwar leaders and disrupt centralized statebuilding. By contrast, when rebel rule is predatory and field commanders fail to develop strong linkages to civilian communities, the likelihood of postwar resistance by commanders decreases. *Ironically, wartime institutions that are welfare enhancing can hinder state consolidation by creating locally embedded military actors that are difficult for the postwar regime to control.*

These issues are not of mere academic interest. Intrastate wars have been by far the deadliest form of political violence on the planet since 1945. Many civil wars produce protracted cycles of conflict that are difficult to end.[6] Rebuilding functional security forces that turn rebel field commanders into obedient military officers is among the most critical steps in the peacebuilding and statebuilding programs that international interveners often champion in conflict-torn societies.[7] When military commanders remain loyal to regime leaders, postconflict states can deploy their armed forces to deter internal and external challengers, increasing the resiliency of the governing coalition.[8] By contrast, when commanders resist or undermine centralized statebuilding, the result may be renewed violence, coups d'état, or the withdrawal of state authority from large pockets of national territory.[9] Even if regime leaders do sustain a fragile peace without obedient commanders, the price tag is often staggering levels of bribery and coup-proofing.[10] Explaining how rebel governance shapes ex-rebel commander resistance after military integration allows us to understand when civil wars generate states with consolidated authority and when peace instead turns out to be a chimera.

The Puzzle

Throughout history, rebel challengers—or insurgents or armed groups, as this book interchangeably refers to them—who fight their way into positions of power have shaped the political fates of nations. Rebels sometimes win decisive victories and transform their armies wholesale into national militaries, as occurred after the Ugandan National Resistance Movement's march on Kampala in 1986, the Libyan National Liberation Army's overthrow of Muammar Gaddafi in 2011, or the Taliban's route of the US-backed regime in Afghanistan in 2021. In other cases, armed groups force governments to agree to the integration of rebel units and commanders through military power-sharing. The United Tajik Opposition, for example, muscled their way into positions inside the Tajik military in the 1990s, as did the Resistência Nacional Moçambicana (RENAMO) in Mozambique. Of some 167 cases of civil war termination between 1945 and 2016, nearly half involved the integration of ex-rebel forces into the military.[11]

Yet rebel-military integration presents a puzzle: the field commanders of integrating armed groups do not always contribute to building durable regimes or effective postwar institutions. Field commanders—sometimes referred to as "warlords"—are the intermediary specialists in violence who connect regime leaders at the top of postconflict states with the rank-and-file fighters who control the means of coercion within some portion of the nation's territory.[12] These commanders can order their subordinates to disarm, rearm, or hide their weapons for later. They can cooperate with SSR blueprints that create a tidy military chain of command legible to capital-based elites and foreign donors, or they can keep armed networks obscure and difficult to monitor. Often, they control substantial parts of the postconflict economy. To consolidate centralized authority, regime leaders require the cooperation of at least some subset of these commanders. If ex-rebel commanders do not provide this cooperation, the risks of security-sector fragmentation and renewed instability are greatly magnified.

Consider the contrasting outcomes of rebel-military integration in Zimbabwe and Côte d'Ivoire. Though rooted in different national contexts, these civil wars had notable parallels. Both the Zimbabwe National African Union (ZANU) and the FN in Côte d'Ivoire waged insurgencies for nearly a decade against ethnically exclusionary governments, and both civil wars ended with rebel forces taking power after contested elections. When conflict ended, observers in both societies expressed hope that new eras of peace and democracy were within reach.[13] Yet the regimes of Robert Mugabe in Zimbabwe and Alassane Ouattara in Côte d'Ivoire turned out to be poles apart in the degree of loyalty that ex-rebel field commanders showed to their new governments. In Zimbabwe, guerrilla commanders affiliated with ZANU swiftly integrated into the Zimbabwe Defence Forces (ZDF) in 1980. The ZDF in turn became a cohesive military that maintained unswerving obedience to the emerging Zimbabwe National African Union–Patriotic Front (ZANU–PF) party-state.[14] Though ZDF commanders eventually turned against Mugabe in 2017, the ZANU–PF regime's tight control over the security apparatus enabled it to crush dissent against its rule for over three decades, notwithstanding Mugabe's dismal record on human rights and economic management.[15]

Côte d'Ivoire's postconflict transition, by contrast, was characterized by ex-rebel commander resistance to the ruling regime and fragmentation within its security forces. After defeating Laurent Gbagbo and installing Ouattara into power, the field commanders of the FN army became the nucleus of the new Forces Républicaines de Côte d'Ivoire (FRCI). Yet when confronted with demands from civilian leaders to disarm and dismantle their irregular units, many ex-FN commanders balked. Instead, commanders like Fofié sustained parallel armed networks outside of the regular army hierarchy and thwarted efforts to reform the FRCI's bloated force structure. Widespread revolts against the government in 2014 and 2017 staged by ex-rebel forces cast the very survival of the Ouattara regime into doubt.[16] One journalist summed up the essence of the situation: "The problem in this country [since 2011] is that you have a government that is afraid of its own military ... it controls some of the weapons and soldiers out there, but not all."[17] Whereas ex-ZANU commanders worked to create a powerful and centralized state in Zimbabwe, ex-FN commanders in Côte d'Ivoire resisted the extension of postwar state authority and maintained autonomous bases of power.

These varied patterns of ex-rebel commander cooperation and resistance are not unique. Some integrating field commanders help to build obedient and effective militaries that ensure stability and regime survival. The Rwandan Patriotic Front (RPF), for instance, built a fearsome regime that has dominated Rwandan politics for three decades.[18] In China and Vietnam, communist and nationalist insurgents forged cohesive states in the mid-twentieth century that reshaped the regional balance of power.[19] In other cases, regime control over ex-rebels inside the military deteriorates rapidly. Leftist revolutionaries in Bolivia in the 1950s, anticolonial Marxist rebels in Guinea-Bissau in the 1970s, and religiously motivated insurgents in the Central African Republic in 2013 all fought their way into the state, but in each case, the ruling coalition descended into renewed strife as field commanders resisted submitting to government oversight and retained armed networks outside of the armies they integrated into.[20] Coup attempts followed. And across Central Asia in the 1990s, political rulers installed by well-armed field commanders struggled to consolidate control over the security forces they nominally governed. Armistices were secured, but only with extensive bribery and blackmail.[21]

Just as striking as this cross-national variation in military integration outcomes is the significant *sub*national variation in commander behaviors. Though previous accounts of conflict termination via warlord coalitions have treated these violence entrepreneurs as interchangeable actors, ex-rebel commanders rarely act as a homogeneous bloc. In Côte d'Ivoire, some ex-FN commanders *did* dismantle their wartime armed networks and become obedient agents of the Ouattara regime, even as other commanders forged independent paths and sustained irregular militias. Postconflict military integration can produce coercive institutions that resemble a kind of patchwork quilt, where authority is fragmented and heterogeneous. Some pieces of the quilt tether the larger structure together; other pieces are tenuous and threaten to tear the polity apart under strain.

Variation in ex-rebel commander cooperation and resistance following military integration represents a conundrum. Prominent studies of civil war termination tell us that rebel military victories ought to yield strong and centralized states, not civil-military conflict and security-sector fragmentation.[22] For wars ending in negotiated settlements, meanwhile, rebel-military integration has been assumed to reduce the risks of renewed conflict by providing a symbolic model of national unity and by credibly signalling a commitment to peace among belligerents.[23] Why, then, do some field commanders who fight their way into positions inside the state's coercive apparatus become loyal agents of the postwar regime, while others resist centralized statebuilding?

The Argument in a Nutshell

This book provides a theory that explains patterns of cooperation and resistance by ex-rebel commanders after military integration in terms of prior processes of insurgent governance during war. The argument consists of two analytical steps. First, I argue that armed groups' governance practices in occupied territories affect whether field commanders become locally embedded in rebel-ruled communities. Second, commander embeddedness shapes the capacity and motive of these field commanders to resist statebuilding and openly challenge regime leaders in the postwar period. Contrary to much conventional thinking about wartime governance, this book argues that practices of rebel rule that are welfare enhancing during armed conflict can later hinder the consolidation of centralized state authority.

To wage rebellion successfully, armed movements must elicit obedience from civilians in rebel-controlled communities—that is, rebels must rule. Practices of rebel rule vary dramatically, however, from broad-based goods provision and local power sharing, on the one hand, to heavy-handed coercion and the imposition of martial law, on the other. Variation in the quality of rebel rule may be affected by many factors, including the nature of preexisting institutions in rebel-controlled zones, the level of armed competition faced by rebels, or the content of insurgents' political doctrines. Whatever its genesis, rebel rule that is characterized by inclusive goods provision, the creation of mechanisms for civilian input, power sharing with local elites, and restraints on violent abuse—a cluster of interrelated practices that I term *collaborative rule*—better positions field commanders to sustain ties in occupied communities that outlive the civil war. Specifically, collaborative rule allows field commanders to maintain autonomous mobilization power in hinterland areas of the country and local legitimacy as guarantors of order in places of limited statehood. Commanders remain politically embedded in these communities. By contrast, when armed groups adopt *predatory* practices of rule during war, field commanders struggle to stay connected to communities after relocating away from their wartime zones. In areas of predatory rule, ex-rebel commanders' mobilization power and local legitimacy are likely to wither away as state institutions return.

Commander embeddedness has profound consequences as the armed group integrates into the state. New regime leaders at the state core and ex-rebel field commanders who control regional networks of armed fighters face a thorny cooperation problem. In principle, both regime leaders and commanders would benefit by cooperating to control the state and enjoy the spoils of peace. Yet regime leaders have a hard time credibly committing to fulfill their promises to field commanders, and commanders must worry about being excluded after they dismantle their wartime military networks and commit to military integration. Ex-rebel commanders also want to maintain control over private sources of economic wealth. Facing these mixed incentives, ex-rebel commanders must make a difficult choice between cooperating with the regime's statebuilding agenda or resisting regime leaders by preserving armed networks outside of the official security apparatus.

The legacies of wartime rule and commanders' local embeddedness influence this critical decision. Where collaborative rebel rule existed during war, locally embedded field commanders with strong ties to hinterland communities possess more coercive leverage vis-à-vis postwar regime leaders. These commanders have good information about local armed networks and can easily remobilize armed followers outside of official structures. Regime leaders will be wary of punishing locally embedded commanders and provoking a destabilizing backlash. Resistance is therefore a viable option. At the same time, locally embedded commanders are more likely to view postwar statebuilding as a threat to their own parochial interests because the redeployment of regular law enforcement to former rebel zones reduces these commanders' abilities to collect income from informal protection rackets. Centralized statebuilding thus tends to provoke distrust and grievances against the regime among embedded commanders. For these reasons, embedded commanders are more likely to resist directives to disarm or downsize irregular armed units and are also more likely to push for concessions from regime leaders through brinkmanship tactics.

The degree of resistance that ultimately occurs depends on strategic interactions with regime leaders, who can soothe commanders' grievances by offering concessions or intensify their fears by making hostile countermoves. Commander resistance does not necessarily mean that coups or large-scale violence will occur. Indeed, commander resistance may sometimes be hard to observe from afar, even as it ensures that the security apparatus remains fragmented and unreliable. Commander resistance can either lead to a fragile negative peace characterized by regime accommodation, periodic mutinies, and persistent military fragmentation—as seen in Côte d'Ivoire—or trigger an escalatory spiral of countermoves from the regime that risks devolving into renewed violence, coups, or rebellion.

Commanders from zones of predatory rebel rule, by contrast, are less likely to sustain coercive leverage vis-à-vis the central regime after integrating into postconflict militaries. With noxious reputations in formerly occupied communities, these commanders cannot efficiently tap into local networks of supporters or present themselves as effective intermediary brokers for the state in peripheral areas. Disobedience is risky because nonembedded commanders are vulnerable to regime punishment. At the same time, nonembedded commanders have weaker motives to resist centralized statebuilding. These commanders rapidly lose their influence in former rebel zones, so they are comparatively unthreatened by the return of the regular state administration. Rather than developing antiregime grievances, nonembedded commanders feel indebted to regime leaders for granting them access to new sources of patronage inside the security apparatus. In short, nonembedded commanders are more likely to become loyal agents of the regime and to cooperate with centralized postwar statebuilding.

The core argument is summarized as follows:

Collaborative rebel rule → Embedded commanders → Postwar resistance to statebuilding

Overall, this book explains how processes of local governance and order making during civil war exert powerful and counterintuitive effects on state recovery after the fighting stops. In terms of scope, this book's theory covers a broad range of cases. It pertains to situations where a nonstate group challenges an incumbent government through armed mobilization, the armed group integrates its forces in whole or in part into the national military, and there is actual implementation of military integration plans. It excludes purely nominal peace settlements or cease-fires that act as cover for belligerents to continue prosecuting war. My argument thus applies both to cases of postwar reconstruction after rebel victories and of military power sharing via negotiated settlements. The framework is applicable across both ethnic and ideological civil wars as well as secessionist and nonsecessionist conflicts.

Main Contributions

This book bears implications for scholars and policy makers concerned with armed organizations and warlords, civil-military relations in fragile states, and the durable settlement of civil wars.

First, this book develops the burgeoning literature on rebel governance and the local ties of armed groups within civilian communities. This literature has unpacked the myriad variations of local political order found in war-affected societies and the effects of wartime institutions on outcomes like the military effectiveness of insurgents, spatial patterns of violence, and the ability of armed groups to generate support and obedience from civilians.[24] With a few notable exceptions, however, past studies of armed group–civilian relations have been concerned with wartime outcomes exclusively rather than with what happens after transitions to peace. To the extent the legacies of rebel governance have been studied at all, scholars have mainly stressed the positive legacies of insurgent institution building and have depicted rebel governance as a nascent form of "state making."[25] Reyko Huang develops this hypothesis most explicitly, arguing that "war-derived institutional capacity [by rebel groups] is likely to facilitate the creation of a stronger state."[26] Terrence Lyons similarly argues that rebels with experience governing territory will make more effective statebuilders, since governance provides opportunities to develop "trained, effective and disciplined cadres."[27] A similar perspective can be traced to the older literature on peasant mobilization and revolutions. Theda Skocpol, for example, argued that when "direct links are established between peasants and revolutionary political and military organizations," the results of armed mobilization are more likely to be "the building of new-regime social institutions and state organizations."[28]

This view is overly sanguine. The evidence in this book suggests that rather than preparing insurgents to be effective institution builders inside the state, rebel governance at the local level can hinder centralized statebuilding. Using rich new data on wartime governance and commander-community ties, I show that social linkages forged through civil war can empower ex-rebel military actors to tap into their territorial bases to resist central regime leaders, rendering postconflict states regionally balkanized and with fragmented authority.[29] In this way, the legacies of wartime governance recreate the problem of "diffuse social control" in weak states that Joel Migdal so perceptively diagnosed decades ago.[30] Just as colonial policies of indirect rule enabled powerful strongmen across Africa and Asia to consolidate local authority and defy capital-based rulers after independence, so too can rebel rule in modern civil wars create openings for local violence entrepreneurs to build durable power bases that later restrict the abilities of state leaders to exert authority uniformly across territory.

This book also sheds new light on the evolution of armed group–civilian relations in areas of rebel control. Past works have conceived of civilians' relations to occupying rebels and perceptions of rebel legitimacy as deriving primarily from the distribution of territorial control between the government and rebels, from prewar vertical ties between insurgent organizers and local communities, or from rebels' initial recruitment strategies.[31] Yet these frameworks leave significant variation in field commanders' local embeddedness unexplained. Even in zones where rebels monopolize territorial control—as in northern Côte d'Ivoire between 2002 and 2011—there are big differences in commander-community ties from one locality to the next. Theories emphasizing prewar vertical networks or armed groups' recruitment patterns, meanwhile, cannot easily explain variation in commander embeddedness or violent remobilization in cases like Côte d'Ivoire. Rebel commanders were almost always outsiders in these communities, while most rank-and-file fighters were recruited and deployed in the same areas. Thus, nearly all rebel units exhibited concentrated recruitment, dense networks, and proximity of combatants in their zone of deployment after demobilizing. Despite this, postwar commander embeddedness exhibited striking variation across former rebel-ruled areas. While strategic conditions and prewar networks matter, this book casts the community ties of rebel field commanders as a flexible variable that is shaped by highly localized patterns of wartime governance.

My findings likewise contribute to the growing body of research on field commanders and warlords in weak states. In an important study of mid-level commanders in Liberia, Anders Themnér argues that rebel commanders have strong incentives to remobilize followers when peace processes threaten their status as brokers between national elites and ex-fighters.[32] Other works inspired by the prominence of warlords in Central Asian states have examined the multifaceted military and political roles of warlords and traced how warlords frustrate the centralizing ambitions of state leaders.[33] Like these scholars, I conceive of rebel field commanders as political entrepreneurs who are primarily concerned with survival and who harness different types of authority grounded in material and nonmaterial resources. But existing theories of the political brokerage roles of warlords, even as they help us understand how field commanders mobilize collective action, do not fully explain why commander-community ties remain strong or wither away in the aftermath of civil wars. This book addresses this lacuna by demonstrating how and why field commanders acquire and sustain (or fail to sustain) the mobilization power and local legitimacy needed for them to continue to broadcast authority and challenge state leaders after armed conflict ends and wartime organizations are formally disbanded. Rather than treating warlords as interchangeable specialists in violence, I explicitly theorize the sources of field commanders' coercive power *after* postwar transitions and provide an argument to explain variation across cases.

Second, the evidence in this book refines our understanding of civil-military relations and coercive institutions in fragile states. Broadly, comparative research in this area can be divided into three camps—a first focused on material resources, a second on state's coup-proofing strategies, and a third emphasizing ethnic politics. For the first camp, civil-military cooperation reflects the balance of material resources available to state leaders versus military subordinates. A lack of funding for security organizations, in this view, is a proximate cause of military resistance.[34] In postconflict contexts, resource-poor regimes may find it especially hard to control ex-rebel commanders who have access to alternative revenues through their involvement in illicit commercial networks or local extortion schemes.[35]

Though there are some complementarities here with my argument, the pecuniary resources of regime leaders are not always a reliable guide to the behavior of ex-rebel commanders. Consider, for example, the divergent trajectories of rebel-military integration in Côte d'Ivoire after 2011 and postgenocide Rwanda after 1994. In the initial years following its war-to-peace transition, Côte d'Ivoire experienced a veritable postwar economic boom and outpaced Rwanda in gross domestic product (GDP) per capita, growth, and defense expenditures by a healthy margin.[36] Yet the superior economic resources of the Ivorian state did not translate into cooperation from ex-FN rebel commanders or more successful statebuilding. In Rwanda, even though the country was one of the very poorest in Africa at the time of the civil war and genocide in 1994, the regime of Paul Kagame enjoyed enduring loyalty from ex-RPF field commanders after their integration into the state military.[37] States' material resources thus only take us so far in understanding the puzzle of ex-rebel commander resistance.

For the second camp, civil-military cooperation depends on the coup-proofing strategies employed by state rulers. In this view, chief executives intentionally adopt coercive institutions that are either unified or fragmented ("coup-proofed") to maximize regime survival and reduce coup risks.[38] The creation of duplicate security forces is presumed to increase the practical difficulties of antiregime mobilization by military units and lower the expected payoffs. Commander resistance, therefore, will reflect the degree to which regime leaders create institutional barriers to antiregime collective action. Yet coup-proofing itself is a sign of underlying conflict between regime leaders and military commanders that requires explanation. It would be a mistake to assume that capital-based elites have unlimited agency to design coercive institutions as they please in post–civil war states. As this book demonstrates, a compelling theory of coercive institutions must also account for the local embeddedness of former rebel field commanders who hold enormous sway inside the postwar security apparatus. Rulers who wish to create a unified security apparatus may find themselves unable to do so in the face of resistance from locally embedded commanders. Fragmented coercive institutions that appear as a coup-proofing tactic may sometimes be a consequence of commander embeddedness rather than the cause of commander loyalty.

A third camp associates ethnic cleavages with civil-military splits.[39] If political and military elites are embedded in rival ethnic networks, each actor will have less information about the interests and capacities of the other and cannot rely on coethnic norms of reciprocity to uphold cooperation.[40] Non-coethnic commanders may be especially fearful of being purged from the postwar coalition and seek to mobilize against the state preemptively to lock in their access to power.[41] Though arguments concerning ethnic politics are powerful and, as I show in this book, find some support in the historical record of rebel-military integration, a good deal of unexplained variation remains. Ethnic cleavages alone are surely too crude a variable to adequately account for the striking subnational variation in ex-rebel commander behavior found in many cases. In Côte d'Ivoire, civil-military frictions emerged *despite* the existence of coethnic bonds between the ethnic northerners of the Ouattara regime and ex-FN commanders. Ethnic cleavages thus provide at best a partial answer to the puzzle of ex-rebel commander resistance. This book argues that a fuller explanation of rebel-military integration outcomes lies in understanding the local social ties and political resources of integrating field commanders, which in turn derive from processes that occur during civil war itself.

Third, this book challenges existing perspectives on civil war termination. Scholars have stressed two primary factors to explain variation in settlement outcomes: the presence of third-party interveners and the terms of conflict settlement. In the first view, local actors' compliance with the terms of war-ending settlements—and particularly disarmament and demobilization—depends on the willingness of external interveners to make credible assurances to risk-averse belligerents and assist with capacity building.[42] In the second view, durable conflict termination depends either on the emergence of a victor capable of monopolizing authority within a clearly defined territory or the redistribution of power within new power-sharing institutions.[43] Decisive military victories are presumed to lead to the emergence of stable regimes, states with high infrastructural capacity, and even democracy.[44] Power-sharing agreements with provisions for military integration, meanwhile, are thought to foster peace by sending costly signals of peaceful intent and creating communally representative forces that soothe belligerents' security concerns even in the absence of a decisive victory for one side.[45]

While valuable, these arguments struggle to explain the puzzle of ex-rebel commander resistance after military integration. It is not hard to find cases of rebel-military integration that failed to produce cohesive security forces even when robust external interventions were present. Western efforts to help rebuild national armies in South Sudan, Libya, or Afghanistan illustrate the problem. External blueprints for military reconstruction and security-sector reform in these countries came unstuck in the face of persistent resistance by field commanders and militia leaders, even when those actors were the direct recipients of foreign aid. Many security-force assistance missions in fragile states share similarly unhappy fates.[46] In Côte d'Ivoire, the presence of a large multidimensional UN peacekeeping mission did not stop ex-FN commanders from resisting the donor-backed statebuilding agenda of the Ouattara government.

Arguments focused on the benefits of decisive victories and military power sharing, meanwhile, overlook variation in behaviors across former rebel actors within integrated security forces. Analysts tend to assume that rebel armies can be merged into incumbent militaries in a straightforward manner. Yet even for rebel armies integrating into national militaries from a position of strength, sustaining the obedience of local field commanders is a vexing challenge. Irregular armed forces must be transformed into a conventional military, and clandestine armed networks must be either dismantled or brought under the authority of civilian-controlled institutions. As Kimberly Marten observed, armed groups and warlords who merge into state militaries through conquest often use their power "to fragment and corrupt the army rather than building its strength as a state institution."[47] This book helps to explain why. It shows that the legacies of wartime rebel rule affect whether postconflict regimes can build loyal and effective militaries or whether rebel-military integration yields a Potemkin security apparatus.

At the broadest level, this book builds the case for a bellicist view of state development that is grounded in processes of war and violent politics.[48] Though scholars of state formation have long recognized the importance of war, empirical research on civil wars and militant organizations has barely begun the work of connecting conflict processes to state and regime consolidation.[49] Perhaps this is because so much attention in the peacebuilding literature has focused on external interveners.[50] Third-party interventions during transitions to peace may influence some short-run outcomes, such as cease-fire enforcement or the conduct of postwar elections. But theories stressing international actors provide an incomplete analytical foundation for understanding more complex postwar outcomes that touch on domestic authority structures, such as rebuilding state security forces or the consolidation of stable regimes.[51] This book illustrates how, in many cases, these outcomes are rooted in the social and institutional legacies of war itself. These legacies play out among local actors who rarely follow the scripts of foreign interveners but who are adept at maneuvering for survival amid uncertain transitions from war making to peace.

The approach to statebuilding and military reconstruction offered by this book also diverges from that of many policy actors in the West. Great powers such as the United States are sometimes motivated by strategic and humanitarian interests to assist partner governments in conflict-torn states to rebuild their security institutions. Yet the empirical record of security-sector aid from Western interveners is mixed at best.[52] International actors are often caught surprised when the armies of aid recipients disintegrate during periods of crisis—as the United States was in Iraq in 2014, South Sudan in 2013, and Afghanistan in 2021.[53] Despite these seemingly meager returns on investment, interveners continue to spend large sums on advising, training, and arms transfers in the hopes of reengineering the militaries of conflict-torn states over short time horizons.

This book argues for a more restrained approach. Without condemning all forms of external intervention, it offers policy prescriptions that demand fewer top-heavy investments in technical capacity and more local intelligence about the social roots of military organizations in fragile states. Whether in Libya, Iraq, or the Democratic Republic of Congo, training and resources supplied from the outside are unlikely to produce cohesive security forces if military commanders remain locally embedded with incentives to preserve autonomy. Former warlords and field commanders in these states will decide the pace and trajectory of military reconstruction, and they are likely to resist or undermine externally imposed statebuilding models if those plans diverge from their own interests.[54] As external powers seek alternatives to putting boots on the ground in overseas conflict zones, the need to economize on peacebuilding and security-assistance resources will grow. Interveners who wish to support stability and avoid inadvertently exacerbating political violence ought to understand the game that field commanders in these states are playing and the cards they play with.

From a normative standpoint, it is important to remember that creating an obedient postwar military and building a peaceable society are not the same thing. As cases like Rwanda and Zimbabwe illustrate, military cooperation with the state may sometimes underwrite entrenched authoritarianism. Locally embedded field commanders, meanwhile, can play a central though informal role in the maintenance of basic civilian protections and property rights in conflict-affected communities.[55] As such, this book does not seek to define an "optimal" trajectory of commander behavior in all cases. Regimes with loyal commanders may be ineffective administrators, repress their own citizens in grossly unjust ways, or be bad at foreign policy and diplomacy. Regimes with unruly commanders, meanwhile, may sometimes sustain a fragile negative peace, either because coup-proofing is successful or because regionally embedded commanders blackmail capital-based elites in perpetuity. Ex-rebel commanders have far-reaching but nuanced implications for political order after civil war.

Methods

This book combines close-range research in a single country with comparative evidence across a broader historical and geographic sweep. The bulk of the empirics come from Côte d'Ivoire, where I spent fourteen months during multiple research trips between 2015 and 2018. Compared to a large-N cross-national approach, studying one country in depth allows for the collection of more precise data about patterns of rebel rule, commander-community relations, and ex-rebel actors' postwar behaviors. Existing intrastate conflict data projects tend to aggregate variables at the national level or, at best, the level of the armed group.[56] Datasets on military organizations and civil-military relations, meanwhile, tend to capture only a narrow slice of observable outcomes, such as attempted coups d'état or the size and number of state security forces.[57] These evidentiary sources are therefore inadequate on their own for studying my theory of commander embeddedness. Much of this book prioritizes tightly controlled comparisons, subnational statistical analyses, and process tracing at the micro and meso levels.

Côte d'Ivoire offers a sensible environment for this task of exploration. The Ivorian civil war (2002–2011) produced rich variation in local patterns of rebel rule, allowing me to trace my theory at a fine-grained level while holding constant national and group level factors like external intervention, state capacity, and rebel group aims. Côte d'Ivoire is also a relatively accessible research environment where it was possible—with enough persistence—to collect the types of data needed. The Ivorian conflict ended in May 2011, four years before my first research visit. This meant that while wartime events were recent enough to be readily recalled by the individuals who lived through them, I could mitigate some (though not all) of the ethical risks associated with conducting research in conflict zones. I conducted over one hundred structured and semistructured interviews with former rebel commanders, rank-and-file ex-combatants, government officials, academics, journalists, and community members in former rebel-held territory (see appendix A). I also fielded two original surveys in northern Côte d'Ivoire, one based on extended interviews with key informants in a sample of ninety-three localities and another measuring political attitudes and perceptions of armed actors among a representative sample of twelve hundred residents. Electoral and administrative data, existing socioeconomic household surveys, memoirs by political and military leaders, party documents, and contemporaneous media sources from the national library archives in Abidjan round out the research materials.

Studying rebellion and postwar politics in Côte d'Ivoire also posed unique challenges. With the civil war being a relatively recent event, the available historiography is sparse. While interviews and primary sources provided invaluable insights, there are important limitations to what can be known about the Ivorian conflict at the current time. Core members of the original leadership circle of the FN are no longer alive, and the narratives presented publicly by spokespeople for the movement tend to present a romanticized and sanitized version of events.[58] The archives of the rebel administration were largely destroyed, scattered, or hidden after the end of the war.[59] Moreover, the fact that the former president of Côte d'Ivoire, Laurent Gbagbo, was on trial at the International Criminal Court (ICC) for alleged war crimes during my field research no doubt complicated my ability to gain the trust of some interviewees. I have given priority to accounts that I find most credible, but there are inevitably some events that are marred by unresolved debates or a lack of high-quality evidence, and I attempt to flag such instances.[60] It is my hope that this book—if it offers nothing else—will help to improve documentation of this under-researched conflict.[61]

A final word on methods: Readers may reasonably wonder whether it is possible for outside researchers to observe the behaviors of rebel field commanders in conflict-torn states to an extent that is adequate for a work such as this. Admittedly, over the course of this project, I came to appreciate why few previous academic studies have analyzed these commanders systematically. Gaining insight into these actors' resources, networks, and decision-making is difficult. Ex-rebel commanders have obvious incentives to conceal parts of their lives from scrutiny. Many are reluctant to grant interviews to foreign researchers. Strong cultures of secrecy shroud some of the networks they belong to. Important facts are not written down. The obstacles for researchers in this context are perhaps akin to those of the sociologist trying to study the inner workings of an organized crime group.[62]

Much of what I came to understand and believe about the Ivorian civil war and ex-rebel commanders' role in its aftermath came from the time I spent in northern Côte d'Ivoire, in towns and villages formerly controlled by the FN. Early on, I sometimes asked the wrong questions. Direct inquiries about former FN commanders could trigger suspicion, cautiousness, or stony silence. In remote areas where few academics visit, I was sometimes mistaken for a humanitarian aid worker or a human rights investigator. This likely shaped the narratives that people told me. Yet once I better grasped and accepted these boundaries, I discovered that it was possible to collect meaningful information, often from people who might not be considered obvious subjects for my research—business owners, traditional leaders, youth league presidents, school principals—but who had a wealth of knowledge to share about the events I wished to study. Almost none of this knowledge was written down. As I developed tools to gather evidence in a systematic fashion, the histories of these commanders and the communities they were embedded in became more legible. Though there are limits to what outside researchers can know about the most sensitive details of these commanders' lives, I am confident that the evidence I present in this book is reliable enough to generate important insights about these understudied actors.

Plan of the Book

This book is divided into three parts. Chapter 1, which makes up the remainder of part I, lays out my theory of commander embeddedness, connecting wartime rebel rule, postwar commander-community ties, and commander resistance to centralized statebuilding. In part II, I illustrate each step of the theory in Côte d'Ivoire, with individual chapters focusing on a key theoretical process and probing observable implications of the argument using qualitative and quantitative evidence. Part III extends the analysis beyond Côte d'Ivoire and concludes the book.

Chapter 2 provides readers with historical background to the Ivorian civil war and establishes the variation in rebel governance practices that existed across northern Côte d'Ivoire between 2002 and 2011. The chapter argues that the Ivorian rebellion is best understood as a symptom of ethnopolitical exclusion. Civil war broke out in 2002, when a group of Ivorian military officers of northern descent attempted to depose the southern-based government of Laurent Gbagbo and reverse the perceived discrimination against ethnic northerners. Repulsed from the capital, rebel mutineers took control of wide swaths of the northern countryside. Though the FN rebels lacked an identifiable political doctrine, contingent conditions of the war allowed the FN to develop a variety of governance practices across occupied communities. In some areas, FN field commanders acquired broad-based social support by providing basic goods, facilitating participation, restraining abuses, and forging alliances with community elites. Elsewhere, rebel rule involved unchecked coercion and violent extortion. To illustrate these patterns of wartime rebel rule systematically, chapter 2 introduces an original dataset of rebel-ruled localities that I constructed based on a survey of community informants in rebel-occupied zones. I use this data to flesh out in detail the varied governance practices that existed under the FN. I also show that this variation is not easily explained by factors that might confound my argument, such as local ethnic demography or rent-seeking opportunities.

Chapter 3 analyzes the consequences of these varied governance practices for field commanders' ties to rebel-ruled communities following the integration of the FN into the Ivorian military in 2011. Consistent with my theory, the chapter shows that field commanders sustained mobilization power and local legitimacy to varying degrees as a function of prior wartime governance dynamics, even after relocating away from these areas. In areas where collaborative rule occurred, ex-FN commanders were more likely to sustain contact with community leaders and local social networks after integrating into the military, enjoyed stronger social support, and were more likely to retain informal roles in community governance and policing after the 2011 transition. By contrast, in areas where FN rebels invested minimally in civilian welfare, commander-community ties tended to wither away after war's end. A battery of statistical tests suggests this link is unlikely to be spurious.

With the wartime origins of ex-rebel commanders' local embeddedness after military integration established, chapter 4 turns to the relationship between ex-FN commanders and the Ivorian state. I examine variation in the choices of ex-rebels to organize collective resistance to the Ouattara regime through a novel subnational analysis of military mutinies and demobilized rebel protests. The chapter shows that areas of collaborative rebel rule—and hence areas of commander embeddedness—ironically posed the greatest threat to the postwar regime. Endowed with strong local ties in the rural hinterlands, field commanders in these areas were able to efficiently sustain parallel armed networks outside official military channels and were more likely to openly challenge regime leaders. Relying on the community-level data introduced in chapters 2 and 3 as well as geolocated data on military mutinies and ex-combatant protests between 2011 and 2020, the chapter shows that wartime patterns of rebel-civilian relations can help explain postwar military mutinies and collective protests among ex-rebel fighters.

To supplement this novel analysis of ex-rebel military mutinies, chapter 4 also explores the role of ex-rebel commanders in another domain of statebuilding—local policing and crime prevention. Here, I probe another observable implication of this book's theory: commanders endowed with strong local support bases will tend to "crowd out" the policing functions of the postwar state, resulting in a more fragmented security sphere. I examine this hypothesis by leveraging data from a survey that I designed and implemented among nine hundred civilians in former FN-held territory in 2018 and a nationally representative socioeconomic survey of over twelve thousand households. I show that in rebel-controlled localities with past experiences of collaborative rebel rule, civilians had less confidence on average in redeployed state police forces, while ex-rebels have tended to retain their informal policing functions despite the demobilization of the FN organization.

Whereas chapters 2 to 4 draw heavily on quantitative data, chapter 5 explores qualitative evidence from four in-depth case studies. Using a matching method, I selected two controlled comparisons of rebel-ruled localities: Korhogo versus Bouaké and Sangouiné versus Mahapleu. Drawing on fieldwork in each research site, I trace the processes by which varied wartime governance patterns emerged under the FN between 2002 and 2011 and in turn how the field commanders who controlled these localities were able to leverage (or not) their postwar ties to rebel-ruled communities to resist the authority of central regime leaders. In the towns of Korhogo and Sangouiné, collaborative wartime rule by occupying FN forces led to strong postwar commander-community linkages. Embedded commanders in these towns preserved access to large off-the-books militia networks following military integration. In both cases—and especially in Korhogo—the Outtara government viewed commanders' local ties as a threat to regime security and attempted to dismantle their local networks, initiating a spiral of distrust and grievance escalation that eventually culminated in widespread ex-rebel armed resistance. Predatory rebel rule and weaker commander-community ties in Bouaké and Mahapleu, by contrast, constrained ex-rebel commanders' room for maneuver, checked the emergence of antiregime grievances, and led to sustained commander loyalty to the regime in Abidjan. These structured, qualitative comparisons allow me to illustrate the intervening mechanisms that connect insurgent governance to ex-rebel commanders' postwar behaviors and address lingering concerns about endogeneity and alternative explanations.

A natural limitation of any single country study is that it is difficult to know whether the theory is generalizable. Chapter 6 therefore steps back to a broader vantage point. Using a wide selection of historical and secondary sources, the chapter explores how my argument travels to sixty cases of rebel-military integration from 1945 to 2019. I show that field commanders from rebel groups that engaged in goods provision for civilians during civil war have been significantly more likely to defect from central regime leaders after integrating into postconflict militaries, even after accounting for differences in the type of conflict termination, the presence of third-party interveners, state resources, ethnic cleavages, ideology, and regime coup-proofing. This book's theory of commander embeddedness thus offers insights that can benefit scholars of civil war and military politics across diverse geographic and historical contexts. Finally, I apply the book's theoretical framework to assess the prospects for rebel-military integration in contemporary Afghanistan and the Central African Republic.

The concluding chapter discusses caveats and scope conditions of the theory, directions for future research on the legacies of rebel rule and coercive institutions in fragile states, and policy lessons for those interested in shaping military reconstruction after civil war. As a practical matter, rebuilding cohesive security institutions after armed conflict is exceptionally difficult, and there are no magic bullets for success. Policy makers should be wary of peacebuilding plans that envision transforming ex-rebel networks into Weberian bureaucratic structures over short time horizons. Consolidating peace may require domestic political leaders to work out bargains with ex-rebel commanders that look very different from the statebuilding blueprints drawn up by foreign actors. A more restrained international approach to postconflict military reconstruction has its own pitfalls, but this book provides a framework for understanding why it may be necessary.

CHAPTER 1

A Theory of Commander Embeddedness

> Conflict seldom ceases with victory.
> —Margaret Levi, "The Predatory Theory of Rule"

Many nonstate armed groups that challenge incumbent governments do so with the aim of taking over the military or, failing that, merging into existing state security forces. When rebel armies integrate into national militaries, the obedience of ex-rebel field commanders to central regime leaders is paramount to consolidating a stable polity. But the historical record shows striking variation on this score. Ex-rebel commanders sometimes become stalwart defenders of the new political order and transform themselves into reliable military officers. In other cases, commanders defy orders to demobilize their irregular militias and openly defy the authority of postwar regime leaders. These patterns of ex-rebel commander cooperation and resistance have far-reaching consequences for regime survival, the effectiveness of coercive institutions, and the extension of central state authority after war's end. What explains this variation?

This chapter offers a theoretical account of rebel-military integration in a weak state. Once a political-military coalition emerges that is sufficiently strong to end civil war, regime leaders in the capital wish to demobilize irregular armed militia and create a security apparatus that is governable. For this to occur, field commanders from integrating rebel groups are pressured to cooperate with donor-backed statebuilding schemes. However, ex-rebel commanders have mixed motivations regarding postwar statebuilding. While commanders wish to win the regime's favor and secure positions inside the security apparatus, they also want to preserve autonomy for fear that regime leaders may be unreliable partners in the future.

Ex-rebel commanders' willingness to resist postwar statebuilding depends on the degree to which ex-rebel commanders remain locally embedded in former rebel-controlled communities. These communities are typically located in peripheral areas of limited statehood where the majority of commanders' armed supporters live. Commanders' postwar embeddedness itself depends on the integrating rebel group's past governance practices. If the armed group provided goods on an inclusive basis, shared power with local elites, permitted civilian participation, and limited civilian abuses (what I term *collaborative rule*), field commanders are more likely to retain mobilization power and enjoy legitimacy as guarantors of local order—that is, they remain embedded. Embedded commanders are in turn more likely to resist postwar statebuilding, both because they possess greater coercive leverage vis-à-vis regime leaders and because embedded commanders are prone to develop grievances against regime leaders when statebuilding policies begin to threaten their parochial interests. Conflict between embedded commanders and the central state may or may not escalate to violence, depending on the concessions offered by regime leaders. Field commanders from zones of predatory rebel rule, by contrast, have difficulty sustaining mobilization power and local legitimacy in formerly occupied communities. Nonembedded commanders are less likely to orchestrate resistance because they lack coercive leverage vis-à-vis the central regime and because postwar statebuilding is less likely to trigger grievances. Table 1.1 summarizes the argument.

My theory differs in two major ways from previous accounts of civil war termination and security-sector reconstruction. First, unlike existing frameworks of state recovery through warlord coalitions, my theory does not assume interchangeability among field commanders.[1] Local mobilization

Table 1.1. A theory of commander embeddedness

Step 1: Practices of rebel rule	
Predatory rule	*Collaborative rule*
Noninclusive goods provision	Inclusive goods provision
Limited power sharing with local elite	Power sharing with local elite
Limited civilian participation	Civilian participation
Weak restraints on civilian abuse	Restraints on civilian abuse
Step 2: Postwar commander-community ties	
Nonembedded commanders	*Embedded commanders*
Decay of mobilization power	Sustained mobilization power
Decay of local legitimacy	Sustained local legitimacy
Step 3: Commander resistance to centralized statebuilding	
Nonembedded commanders	*Embedded commanders*
Low capacity and motive for resistance	High capacity and motive for resistance
Mutinies, coups, rebellions less likely	Mutinies, coups, rebellions more likely

power and legitimacy are crucial political resources during war-to-peace transitions, but they are held in varying amounts by different commanders. Military reconstruction and statebuilding after civil war do not play out on a tabula rasa. Rather, civil war processes and postwar recovery are closely intertwined. Second, unlike theories in the "liberal peacebuilding" tradition that stress the importance of third-party intervention or military professionalization, I argue that patterns of military obedience or resistance in war-torn states are primarily products of domestic bargaining.[2] Rebel-military integration simply does not follow formal blueprints drawn up in foreign countries. Obedient and legible militaries emerge when local field commanders believe that cooperating with the central regime is their surest path to security, whether or not foreign interveners are present.

Setting Up the Theory

I theorize a process of rebel-military integration in a weak state that experiences organized violence involving a government and territorially based rebel challengers who aim to increase their share of state power.[3] Politics in the weak state are not well institutionalized, and political authority does not derive from legal-rational norms and rules.[4] Rather, politics are characterized by fluid alliances among elites and competition over the distribution of power and wealth by specialists in violence who sit atop patron-client networks.[5] State security forces are partisan combatants as well as a prize that rebels are fighting to control. After a period of violent struggle, rebels either defeat the incumbent and take over state institutions or force the incumbent to share state power by incorporating rebel group members into the military and creating a new governing coalition. Formal state structures remain weak, and the fragile peace is underwritten by informal bargains among regime elites and field commanders who control the means of organized violence.

I assume that postwar regime leaders wish to cement their control over national security institutions and extend the state's monopoly over the use of coercion. To consolidate authority, regime leaders seek to reform the security sphere by dismantling irregular armed networks built up during war, by creating a legible military chain of command that is controlled by the state's chief executive, and by (re)extending the presence of the state's coercive institutions across the entirety of the country's national territory. A well-defined military command structure reduces opportunities for clandestine activity in the armed forces, makes the military easier to monitor, and provides the regime with a more efficient coercive apparatus that can be mobilized to confront enemies and deter new challengers.[6] In other words, regime leaders wish to engage in statebuilding. To implement these statebuilding plans, regime leaders require cooperation from the field commanders of the armed group(s) that successfully fought their way to power. These commanders are the actors who can order ex-rebel fighters outside the new military hierarchy to disarm and demobilize. The consent of these commanders is necessary for peace. To secure the continued support of commanders, regime leaders can promise high-ranking commissions, insertion into the armed forces for commanders' fighting units, generous demobilization packages for subordinates who are unfit to serve, and legal protection from prosecutions for human rights violations.

Ex-rebel commanders, however, juggle a complex array of interests during war-to-peace transitions. On the one hand, commanders want to stay on good terms with regime leaders because they covet official titles and salaried positions in the state apparatus. Formal military commissions allow these commanders to access state patronage, shield their activities from legal scrutiny, and advance the careers of subordinates in their own client networks.[7] Moreover, ex-rebel commanders may share the desire of regime leaders to build a centralized and cohesive military organization. A coherent military hierarchy reduces uncertainty about performance expectations and professional advancement and enhances the battlefield effectiveness of the national armed forces.[8] It also provides commanders with greater visibility over other elements within the security apparatus, reducing the likelihood that any individual commander will become marginalized in the event that another military faction attempts to seize power in the future.[9] Commanders may also simply wish to be respected as legitimate military professionals.

On the other hand, ex-rebel commanders have reasons to resist postwar statebuilding. Most importantly, commanders wish to preserve coercive leverage if they fear that regime leaders are unreliable. Such fears of betrayal are common. The state's exit from anarchy has just occurred, and credible commitments are difficult to make.[10] The postconflict military may comprise an amalgam of different factions competing for top military position, heightening individual commanders' sense of insecurity. Regime leaders may cut side deals with multiple factions to end the fighting and co-opt future resistance.[11] Such side deals leave less room for the integration of ex-rebel commanders. Moreover, for integrating rebel groups that install new regime leaders from their own movement, the balance of power between new regime leaders and field commanders may change dramatically once regime leaders take up government offices and control access to state patronage.[12] After being installed into power, these leaders can co-opt opponents with promises of cabinet positions, funnel development aid to particular areas in order to secure votes, or manipulate the state's financial controls to enrich allies and starve opponents.[13] These tools allow postconflict regime leaders to reshuffle and trim the ruling coalition over time.[14] Finally, in modern civil wars, postconflict regime leaders have incentives to signal their credentials as liberal democratic actors and establish recognition within the international arena.¹⁵ One strategy for regime leaders to appease foreign audiences—and especially Western governments—is to purge a handful of hard-line military elements or permit legal investigations into commanders accused of human rights violations.¹⁶ In short, ex-rebel commanders inside postwar militaries have good reason to fear for their future. This fear makes them reluctant to detach themselves from the wartime networks that constitute their private source of coercive power.

In addition to these defensive considerations, ex-rebel commanders may have other parochial interests at odds with centralized statebuilding. First, commanders might wish to preserve control over illicit commercial ventures and extralegal protection rackets created during war that continue to generate significant income for commanders in the postwar period. The return of law enforcement and administrative government structures within former rebel territory is likely to endanger these revenue-generating schemes. The postwar government cannot commit credibly ex ante to allowing commanders to retain control over their local economic assets, because governments can always renege on the deal later, once state institutions are redeployed.¹⁷ Second, ex-rebel commanders may wish to reserve bargaining power vis-à-vis the central regime to renegotiate the terms of military integration itself—for example, by demanding larger payouts, promotions, or the creation of prestigious and well-equipped units dominated by ex-rebels. Finally, field commanders who are ideologically committed to a particular revolutionary agenda may wish to preserve private military power so that they can coerce or replace regime leaders who deviate from their preferred policies.¹⁸

The bottom line is that for ex-rebel commanders who integrate into state militaries, the type of statebuilding that regime leaders and foreign donors want carries both benefits and significant risks. Given this uncertainty, ex-rebel commanders must decide whether to cooperate with regime leaders or to hold out and resist demands to dismantle their wartime armed networks.¹⁹ Cooperation implies that commanders will detach themselves from their armed subordinates and order these individuals to either integrate into the new military—where they may be retrained and assigned to different units—or demobilize and disarm. Cooperation also means obeying orders from regime leaders to mobilize military force against political opponents or other ex-rebel comrades who may resist the demobilization process. If a significant share of ex-rebel commanders cooperate, the postconflict regime can create an obedient military and deploy it as a reliable instrument of coercion. Irregular armed networks wither away or become politically inconsequential. Displays of military disobedience are rare. The Zimbabwe African National Union (since 1980) and the Rwandan Patriotic Army (since 1994) illustrate this trajectory of ex-rebel commander loyalty and centralized statebuilding.

If enough ex-rebel commanders resist the demands of regime leaders, however, the security sector is likely to remain fragmented and the risks of instability are heightened. In this scenario, instead of dismantling wartime command structures or importing those structures into a new military bureaucracy, ex-rebel commanders try to preserve parallel armed networks outside of the postconflict military hierarchy. These parallel networks may consist of former rebel fighters who remain attached to ex-combatant organizations or members of nonmilitary groups—such as village defense, vigilante, or traditional hunting associations—that can be repurposed in service of commanders' interests.[20] Preserving such off-the-books armed units allows ex-rebel commanders to sustain coercive leverage and hedge against the risk of exclusion by regime leaders.[21] Rebel demobilization is superficial, as ex-rebel military officers retain latent coercive power. Orders to disarm rogue militias are quietly ignored. Security-sector reform schemes that call for the downsizing of military units bloated with unqualified or undisciplined soldiers are placed in filing cabinets and left to collect dust. Commanders reserve the autonomous capacity to disrupt the fragile peace by instigating armed protests or mutinies or threatening the property of regime leaders.[22] Such brinkmanship tactics force the regime to distribute continuous bribes and payouts as the price of power. Instead of becoming centralized and legible, the security apparatus remains fragmented, hard to monitor, and plagued by parallel chains of command. Rebel-military integration in Libya (2011–) and South Sudan (2013–) resemble this path of ex-rebel commander resistance and failed statebuilding.

The core puzzle should now be clear. Why, when facing a precarious military integration process, do some ex-rebel commanders resist central regime leaders and obstruct centralized statebuilding while others do not?

How Wartime Governance Shapes Commander Resistance

This book argues that patterns of insurgent governance during civil wars shape the likelihood that ex-rebel commanders later engage in resistance after military integration. When the governance practices of armed groups create strong and enduring ties between field commanders and rebel-ruled communities, locally embedded commanders possess greater capacity to resist centralized statebuilding and are prone to develop stronger antiregime grievances. This combination of opportunity and motive heightens the chances of military disobedience and antiregime mobilization. When rebel rule creates weak commander-community ties, postwar resistance is less probable. My purpose is not to deny that other variables also influence rebel-military integration and the behaviors of field commanders; it is, rather, to stress a causal chain between wartime governance, commander embeddedness, and postwar civil-military relations that has received insufficient attention.

In this section, I flesh out this argument in three steps. First, I distinguish between two main variants of rebel rule: collaborative and predatory. Second, I discuss how these variants of rebel rule shape field commanders' local embeddedness following military integration. Third, I explain how embeddedness affects the likelihood of commander resistance to centralized statebuilding. Having established each link of the theory, I consider the issue of selection effects in the following section and whether there are confounding factors that explain both rebel governance type and postwar ex-rebel resistance.

STEP 1: PRACTICES OF REBEL RULE

Prior to ever reaching state power, armed groups must address a critical wartime task: the governance of civilians. A rebel group's relationship with civilians affects many vital organizational functions, including the ability to recruit new members, generate revenue through taxation, procure food, build grassroots political support, and project an image of strength to domestic and foreign audiences.[23] Civilians are also a source of essential information, such as the locations of enemy targets and the identities of government collaborators.[24] Rebels thus require some degree of civilian cooperation and obedience to achieve their strategic goals during civil war.

Different strategies exist for rebels to obtain civilian obedience. The simplest strategy is to compel obedience with threats of force and rule through coercion. Eventually, however, rebels confront what every autocrat knows: pure coercion is a costly and inefficient method of control.[25] Armed groups therefore frequently turn to some package of nonviolent governance practices in hopes of garnering voluntary civilian compliance. While the scope and form of these practices vary widely, the purpose of rebel governance can be understood in similar terms to constitutional governance by nation-states: to create enough trust between rulers and ruled such that civilians choose to invest in productive activities and to sustain enough popular legitimacy so that most residents do not actively resist the authority of the ruler.[26]

Building on the work of Ana Arjona, Zachariah Mampilly, Megan Stewart, and Jeremy Weinstein, I distinguish variants of rebel rule based on whether rebels: (1) offer inclusive goods and services to civilians, (2) share power with local elites in occupied communities, (3) create mechanisms for civilians to participate in public affairs, and (4) limit violent abuses against civilians.[27] I organize these practices of rebel rule in terms of a simple conceptual spectrum (table 1.2). At one end of the spectrum is *predatory rule*.[28] Under predatory rule, goods provision by rebels is minimal or restricted to active combatants.[29] Rebels rule through martial law, share little to no power with local elites in the community, and offer limited opportunity for civilian participation. Instead of building trust by restraining abuses, rebel occupiers rely on coercive violence to ensure obedience and force out or marginalize community leaders who oppose their authority.

At the opposite end of the spectrum is the most responsive and accountable form of governance, which I term *collaborative rule*.[30] At this pole, rebels invest in basic services and goods provisions for the general population (as opposed to restricting goods provision only to their own combatants or active supporters) in exchange for compliance with insurgent demands for resource extraction and recruitment. Power-sharing deals with local elites are struck, affording existing community leaders some role in local decision-making and the distribution of resources.[31] Rebel rulers provide opportunities for citizen input and voice through mechanisms of rebel-civilian dialogue.[32] Violence against civilians is restrained, and local rebel governors make deliberate efforts to discipline troops and prevent abuses.

Why theorize rebel rule in this way? First, this operationalization follows the existing literature in identifying goods provision, elite power sharing, civilian participation, and restraints on abuse as key elements of the underlying social contract between rebel rulers and civilians.[33] Second, while rebel governance arrangements are complex, there is reason to expect these four practices will tend to covary at the local level as rebels and civilians engage in repeated interactions and develop stable norms and expectations.[34] For example, rebels who garner legitimacy by providing goods and sharing power with local elites may encounter less hostility from occupied civilians and thus have less need to resort to coercion. Third, each practice of rebel rule in table 1.2 is empirically tractable. Thus, my operationalization allows theoretical propositions about the legacies of rebel rule to be rigorously scrutinized.

STEP 2: POSTWAR COMMANDER-COMMUNITY TIES

Rebel field commanders play essential roles on the front lines of territorial occupations by armed groups, but not all field commanders become locally embedded in occupied communities.[35] I argue that whether armed groups adopt predatory or collaborative rule affects not only the quality of

Table 1.2. Variation in wartime rebel rule

Predatory rule	*Governance practice*	*Collaborative rule*
Low	Inclusive goods provision	High
Low	Power sharing with local elite	High
Low	Civilian participation	High
Low	Restraints on civilian abuse	High

civilian welfare during war but also the kinds of social-political resources that field commanders develop and carry into postconflict transitions. Specifically, wartime governance practices shape ex-rebel commanders' mobilization power in former rebel-controlled territory and commanders' local legitimacy as a guarantor of order and security.

Conceptualizing Embeddedness: Mobilization Power and Legitimacy. I define local embeddedness as the extent to which field commanders in rebel-ruled communities acquire enduring mobilization power and legitimacy.[36] Mobilization power refers to the ability to efficiently assemble and control supporters for purposes of collective action.[37] Field commanders of territorial armed groups acquire mobilization power both directly and indirectly during civil wars. Directly, commanders can recruit armed networks of fighters within their local zones of control. These fighters include official units that appear on the written documents of the rebel group and that are recognized during formal peace negotiations as well as unofficial militias, self-defense groups, or other armed individuals who are in the orbit of the field commander but do not appear on the pages of disarmament and demobilization (DDR) programs. Both types of armed networks provide the basis for *postwar* mobilization potential. They establish an "organizational infrastructure" for commanders to continue tapping into as members of these armed networks develop social ties and bonds of trust with one another and with field commanders through repeated interactions, thereby reducing the transaction costs and monitoring problems of postwar remobilization of these same fighting units.[38]

Field commanders can also acquire mobilization power indirectly by subcontracting collective action from local elites in rebel-governed areas. Local elites are influential citizens who command loyalty from other members of their community by virtue of their control over access to critical resources (e.g., land, job opportunities) and/or because they hold positions of customary or social authority.[39] These local elites—who may be traditional chiefs, party bosses, or commercial business owners—function as a kind of "social membrane" between their communities and external actors and are therefore essential to the ability of field commanders to identify, contact, and successfully recruit supporters.[40] For example, local elites can distribute resources to clients on behalf of the commander, facilitate introductions between commanders and other community members, and broadcast public signals of their own good relations with the commander that lend the commander greater legitimacy and prestige. Local elites are likely to be particularly important conduits for accessing social networks in rural areas, where commanders cannot rely on the relative anonymity of chaotic urban environments to directly contact and recruit youth.[41] Ex-rebel commanders' mobilization power in former rebel territory thus reflects both commanders' direct linkages to armed networks in the community and their linkages to local elites who can help to indirectly subcontract collective action.

Legitimacy refers to the set of collective beliefs and expectations that are widely shared among residents regarding the appropriate role and authority of a given individual in the affairs of the community, particularly concerning matters of security, dispute resolution, and the creation of social order. Field commanders with a high degree of legitimacy are viewed as rightful protectors and guardians of the community. They are seen as having the appropriate authority to intervene in the resolution of local conflicts, whether or not these commanders hold legally recognized positions in domestic policing. Legitimacy and mobilization power are likely to be strongly correlated; political actors with the perceived capacity to effectively manage violence may garner higher levels of popular legitimacy, and vice versa.[42]

Rebel Rule Shapes Commander Embeddedness. The nature of rebel rule within a community shapes both dimensions of commander embeddedness during and after civil war. The first mechanism through which this happens is the acquisition of grassroots social support. In contexts of weak formal accountability, citizens can award "moral standing, esteem or respect" to local political actors as rewards for providing above-average goods and services.[43] Sarah Zukerman Daly, for example, argues that the extent to which armed groups remain connected to communities after war varies according to "the duration of the group's presence, the nature of its rule, and whether it brought positive changes to the neighborhoods, sparking a sort of 'retrospective voting' (an evaluation of the group based on its past performance)."[44] Perceptions of effective and responsive governance on the part of the commander and his/her subordinates can yield enduring social support for rebel group members among civilian populations. Occupying rebels are seen as making efforts to provide goods in an inclusive and accountable manner. Civilians who benefit from goods and services resulting from the actions of rebel occupiers are inclined to reward commanders with moral recognition.[45]

Grassroots social support, in turn, is likely to increase ex-rebel commanders' mobilization power by expanding the number of individuals within the community who would be willing to mobilize in service of the commander even after the commander leaves the zone. Social support for ex-rebels lowers the stigma and increases the prestige for community members who associate with the commander and ex-combatant networks generally.[46] Social support also translates naturally into perceived legitimacy for ex-rebel commanders as guarantors of local order in former rebel-controlled zones, even after commanders assume military duties elsewhere. Order provision—specifically, the enforcement of predictable rules of behavior and

CHAPTER 1

protection against arbitrary banditry—tends to be in high demand after civil wars. Police forces may be under-resourced, poorly trained, or perceived as corrupt. They may have been destroyed or disbanded during the conflict. Former rebel-ruled areas will likely have especially weak ties to regular police forces, either because these areas are located in peripheral regions or because citizens lose trust in regular police forces through exposure to rebel rule itself.[47] Popular ex-rebel commanders with proven track records of order provision are an attractive alternative to the police and may continue to be recognized as a legitimate authority, especially in the security sphere.[48]

In addition to grassroots social support, collaborative rebel rule can also enhance commander embeddedness through a second mechanism: the formation of alliances with local elites in former rebel-ruled areas. When local elites are brought into systems of collaborative governance alongside insurgent commanders under a wartime occupation, they develop a degree of dependency on the patronage resources and services that commanders help them to provide to their clients. Local elites may wish to see this arrangement persist in the postwar period, especially if alternative sources of patronage and services are unreliable.[49] In exchange for the preservation of an alliance with the commander, local elites can continue to hold the door open for commanders to exercise influence and sustain contacts within the community. For example, local elites can invite commanders to ceremonial events, solicit commanders' assistance to resolve problems of criminality, or facilitate introductions between commanders and other community members. Enduring relationships with local elites thus help ex-rebel commanders to simultaneously sustain mobilization power through an expanded ability to efficiently recruit from local social networks and further reinforce their legitimacy by winning the endorsement of respected community leaders.

Predatory rule is likely to have the opposite consequences for ex-rebel commanders' mobilization power and legitimacy in former rebel-controlled zones. Grassroots social support for the armed group will be weaker. When goods provision is not extended beyond core supporters, civilians in the rebel-ruled community may later feel resentment about the neglect that the armed group showed their community. Civilians exposed to coercion or abuse may also develop negative mental associations between individuals associated with the armed movement, on the one hand, and the well-being of their community, on the other.[50] Weak social support in turn undercuts commanders' ability to remain connected to local social networks. The unpopularity of the armed group creates a social stigma for individuals in the community who continue to associate with the former commander in the peacetime period.[51] Local youth and ex-combatants once in the employ of field commanders will likely seek out new sources of patronage.

Weak social support also diminishes the ability of ex-rebel commanders to sustain legitimacy as guarantors of local order in the postconflict period.

During civil war, even despotic local rulers may command a grudging respect for their ability to keep the worst excesses of anarchy at bay. After war's end, these field commanders can expect no such gratitude. Without an exceptional rationale for their involvement in local affairs, commanders who integrate into the military will find themselves with no legal basis for involvement in domestic security issues. Residents in former rebel-ruled areas are unlikely to welcome such intrusions. Residents are more likely to turn to alternative governance actors—including redeployed state police forces—than to continue to rely on ex-rebels with noxious reputations.

Predatory rule is also likely to yield more brittle alliances between field commanders and local elites. Rather than trying to preserve a patron-client link with the commander after the transition to peace, local elites who were expelled or sidelined from governance roles during the rebel occupation may instead seek to reestablish their own patronage networks and "box out" ex-rebel commanders' continued presence. The absence of strong ties to local elites further diminishes ex-rebel commanders' access to local information and social contacts and limits their ability to subcontract mobilization power or leverage the alliances of local elites to sustain legitimacy.[52]

This discussion leads to this book's first hypothesis, which links wartime rebel rule to postwar commander embeddedness:

H1: Rebel Rule and Postwar Commander Embeddedness. Collaborative (predatory) wartime rebel rule should increase (decrease) ex-rebel commander's postwar mobilization power and legitimacy in former rebel-controlled communities.

STEP 3: COMMANDER RESISTANCE TO CENTRALIZED STATEBUILDING

Rebel field commanders enter the military integration process with varied levels of embeddedness in former rebel-occupied communities. This variation derives in large part from wartime practices of rebel rule. In the final step of my theory, I explain how commanders' local embeddedness shapes their propensity to either cooperate with postwar regime leaders or resist centralized statebuilding and discuss the role of strategic interaction with the regime.

In zones of collaborative rebel rule, ex-rebel commanders enter the war-to-peace transition with a calculus that makes resistance more likely, for two reasons. First, unlike their nonembedded counterparts, embedded commanders possess significant bargaining leverage vis-à-vis the postwar regime. Enduring social support and local elite alliances in rebel-ruled areas allow these commanders to efficiently access and mobilize local networks of armed supporters, even after commanders integrate into the new military hierarchy and assume official duties elsewhere. Embedded commanders retain autonomous capacity for violent mobilization throughout the military integration process. Moreover, as popularly legitimate guarantors of social order, these commanders can present themselves as indispensable partners for national stability, property rights protection, and economic recovery.[53] Embedded commanders thus bargain from a position of strength, aware that regime leaders must think twice before punishing noncompliance. As Margaret Levi argues, state agents "are most likely to win concessions when they have enough military strength to threaten withdrawal of services on which the ruler depends."[54]

Second, embedded commanders are more likely to develop grievances against the government as postwar statebuilding progresses. With strong ties to former rebel-controlled areas, embedded commanders will feel that their status and security are directly threatened by postwar leaders' plans for combatant demobilization, security-sector reform, and the redeployment of regular law enforcement institutions to former rebel-held zones. The return of central state administrative structures and police forces to these areas may curtail the ability of ex-rebel commanders to sustain revenue from illicit commercial enterprises and protection scheme monopolies. Given the prevailing uncertainty during war-to-peace transitions, postwar statebuilding programs—while attractive to foreign donors—are easily perceived by embedded commanders as a hostile effort to undercut their political and economic power base at a sensitive moment.

The combination of opportunity and motive to resist postwar statebuilding thus accrues most strongly among locally embedded commanders from areas of collaborative rebel rule. Such resistance is likely to occur in subtle ways at first. Examples include slow-walking combatant demobilization programs, scuttling efforts to redeploy commanders away from their wartime zones, and undermining the authority of redeployed police forces by maintaining informal protection systems in former rebel-held areas. Such tactics allow commanders to preserve irregular armed networks outside of the regular military and ignore demands to downsize or demobilize bloated ex-rebel units. Particularly in the early stages of transition, embedded commanders may wager that regime leaders and international interveners will feel obliged to overlook such acts of disobedience as the price of taming violence and maintaining order in difficult-to-reach territories.

As the postwar political order crystallizes, embedded ex-rebel commanders may either continue low-level forms of resistance or escalate resistance to open protests and mutinies in the hopes of locking in larger concessions from the state. The degree of resistance is difficult to anticipate ex ante and depends on strategic interaction with the regime over time.

If regime leaders accept embedded commanders' demands as the price of stability, the rebel-military integration process ends with a form of mutual deterrence and tacit accommodation. Commander resistance is widespread but contained. Indeed, commander resistance may not even be visible to the international community or from within the capital city. Regime leaders remain in power but are blackmailed by their own military. Ex-rebel demobilization and statebuilding in peripheral areas are mostly superficial. Regime leaders are reticent to "rock the boat" by sanctioning or purging disobedient commanders for fear of triggering a destabilizing backlash that scares off foreign investment or erodes domestic support for the new governing coalition. To ensure survival, regime leaders in this scenario have strong incentives to engage in coup-proofing. They may create private militias or special security units that answer directly to the state executive, bypassing military chains of command controlled by unreliable ex-rebel officers. Such coup-proofing tactics make antiregime mobilization harder to coordinate and reduce the likelihood that an attempted coup deposes the regime.[55] These tactics, however, risk diminishing the combat performance of the armed forces and creating ballooning security budgets that strain the fiscal capacity of the state.

Alternatively, regime leaders may interpret initial acts of resistance by an embedded commander as a portent of future disloyalty by a threatening rival and take direct countermeasures against the commander.[56] Such countermeasures exist on a spectrum of potential severity. At a modest level, regime leaders can move against ex-rebel commanders by subtly undermining their local influence in former rebel zones. This could involve relocating or "shuffling" commanders away from their wartime areas; it could also entail the deployment of party cadres to former rebel zones to strengthen ties between citizens and local cells of the ruling party, thus edging out the influence of former rebel commanders.[57] Regime leaders can take more aggressive measures to increase the surveillance and policing of illicit resource extraction and protection schemes to disrupt ex-rebel commanders' links to local commercial networks. At the most severe level, regime leaders can try to purge commanders from the governing coalition entirely. Yet leaders take such countermeasures against locally embedded commanders at considerable risk. Hostile regime actions are certain to reenforce commanders' exclusionary fears and further intensify antiregime grievances. Once locked in a spiral of distrust and civil-military conflict, commanders have incentives to preempt the countermeasures of regime leaders by launching coups or allying with regime leaders' rivals.[58] Disrupting commander-community ties may also create disparities in the local balance of power that drive more aggressive remilitarization.[59] Outcomes in this scenario become highly volatile, and there is significant risk of renewed large-scale violence.

When rebels govern through predatory rule, by contrast, field commanders enter the military integration process weakly embedded in former rebel-ruled communities. These commanders have relatively little mobilization power outside of formal military structures and enjoy scant local legitimacy. Nonembedded commanders are more likely to cooperate with postwar statebuilding. These commanders have relatively little autonomous capacity to coerce central regime leaders or protect themselves from sanctioning.[60] Once rebel-military integration begins, any attempt to organize collective resistance to the regime would require nonembedded commanders to order regular military units to mobilize against the government. Such antigovernment mobilization within the security apparatus is difficult to initiate because regime leaders will monitor the postwar military closely and soldiers fear losing their new jobs and privileges if things turn out badly. Without the ability to easily identify and tap into networks of armed supporters outside of the regular military hierarchy, nonembedded commanders pose relatively little threat to capital-based elites. At the same time, nonembedded commanders cannot credibly present themselves as a locally legitimate bulwark of order in peripheral territories. With inferior abilities to co-opt or suppress local populations on behalf of the regime, nonembedded commanders are more expendable. These conditions limit commanders' bargaining leverage vis-à-vis the central regime and make them vulnerable to punishment. Failure to comply with demands for militia demobilization and security-sector reform may result in the commander being demoted, imprisoned, or worse.

Nonembedded commanders from zones of predatory rule are also less likely to develop grievances against regime leaders due to postwar statebuilding policies. With weak ties to former rebel-controlled communities, these commanders have relatively little to lose from the demobilization of wartime networks and the return of state administrative structures in areas of former rebel control. Lacking social support or legitimacy in these zones, nonembedded field commanders instead hope to secure choice positions in the capital to better their political and economic prospects. For their part, regime leaders can safely reward nonembedded commanders for cooperative behavior with high-ranking offices, confident that these commanders will be unlikely to later exploit their positions to threaten the regime. If nonembedded commanders see their initial acts of cooperation reciprocated by regime leaders, commanders' defensive fears of exclusion abate over time. Commanders judge that continued loyalty and cooperation with centralized statebuilding offer the surest path to security.

The bottom line for my theory is that field commanders who governed in areas of collaborative rebel rule navigate the rebel-military integration process from a fundamentally different starting point than commanders from areas of predatory rule. Locally embedded commanders are endowed with superior coercive leverage and are prone to developing grievances as postwar statebuilding begins to threaten their parochial interests. Thus, embedded commanders are more likely on average to choose resistance compared to nonembedded commanders. Making matters worse, regime leaders may take aggressive countermeasures against embedded commanders whom they fear. Once initiated, spirals of civil-military conflict have uncertain stopping points and risk escalation to coups or renewed violence.

This discussion leads to the book's second major hypothesis:

> **H2: Rebel Rule and Postwar Commander Resistance.** Collaborative (predatory) wartime rebel rule should increase (decrease) the likelihood of ex-rebel commander resistance to postwar statebuilding after military integration and should increase (decrease) the likelihood that antigovernment mutinies, coups, and rebellions occur.

These predictions are far from deterministic. Rebel-military integration is a complex process, and postwar orders are always open to renegotiation. Other factors can intervene to yield different outcomes. For example, situations of mutual deterrence between embedded commanders and regime leaders can be disturbed over time by exogenous events that affect commanders' relative capabilities or perceived threats. This could include the rise of new local elites in former rebel-ruled communities who lack connections to ex-rebel commanders, the election of new political leaders in the capital, or investigations launched by domestic or international legal bodies to hold commanders responsible for war crimes. Erratic or unpredictable regime leaders could also trigger preemptive resistance from ex-rebel commanders, even those with relatively weak local ties. Alternatively, field commanders within rebel movements that experience intense threats during war may develop especially strong trust in their political leaders due to past experiences of collective action and sacrifice—as in cases like the RPF in Rwanda or the Tigray People's Liberation Front (TPLF) in Ethiopia—thus easing commitment problems and lowering commanders' defensive motivations for resistance.[61] While acknowledging such complexities, my theory nonetheless expects that commanders from zones of collaborative rule will be more likely to engage in antiregime resistance than those from areas of predatory rule, all else being equal.

Anticipating Selection Concerns: Why Does Rebel Rule Vary?

My argument to this point raises a natural question: Why do armed groups employ different practices of wartime governance in the first place? While the origins of wartime institution-building remain an active area of research, there is general agreement among scholars that several factors influence the selection of rebel governance type. These include: (1) the quality of prewar institutions, (2) the degree to which rebels depend on civilian cooperation for resources, (3) the intensity of armed competition, (4) ethnic and partisan identity cleavages, and (5) ideology. In this section, I briefly consider each variable as a potential threat to the validity of my theory.

First, existing social structures and institutions in rebel-occupied communities can influence the quality of wartime governance. In particular, when rebel-occupied communities possess strong local elites or dense kinship ties, rebels may be more inclined to respect civilian interests in order to avoid the high costs of antirebel resistance.[62] Drawing on field research in several Ivorian towns controlled by the FN, Sebastian van Baalen argues that "local elites that have strong clientelist networks can . . . mobilize both greater support for, and civil resistance against, the rebels. This mobilization capacity determines local elites' bargaining power in negotiations over local governance, allowing some local elites to demand greater governance responsiveness than others."[63] In addition to shaping rebels' strategic incentives for responsiveness, the presence of effective local institutions opens the possibility for occupying rebels to co-opt those institutions to expand their capacity to provide goods and control civilians.[64]

Local elite strength would be a concerning confounder for my argument if the presence of such elites independently threatened postwar statebuilding and regime stability. Yet in weak state contexts defined by neopatrimonial governance, it is not clear that strong local elites per se increase the likelihood of antistate collective action.[65] As Catherine Boone reminds us, national leaders in African states have long struck patronage-based deals with traditional leaders, powerful family heads, and business elites to consolidate their rule and repress local rivals.[66] In Côte d'Ivoire, the Ouattara government's postwar political patronage networks ("tontine") have largely replicated this formula among northern Malinke and Senoufo elites.[67] What matters in the context of rebel-military integration is whether the field commanders of integrating armed groups leverage the presence of local elites to become locally embedded in occupied territories during civil war and, in turn, whether field commanders sustain coercive leverage vis-à-vis the central regime after war's end. In chapter 5, I trace qualitatively how rebel commanders utilized their ties to local elites in northern Côte d'Ivoire to build autonomous bases of power in wartime that later led those commanders to resist centralized statebuilding—even in areas where local elites had long partnered with the central state.

A second factor that may influence the selection of rebel governance institutions is the degree to which rebels depend on occupied civilians for resources. Analogous to the logic of the "resource curse" in rentier states, rebel organizations that are endowed with lucrative natural resources or external financing may be less inclined to make concessions to civilians.[68] Resource-rich insurgents may also find more opportunistically motivated recruits filling their ranks, leading to predatory behavior.[69] Resource endowments are also an unlikely confounder for my theory, however. The logic of rentierism predicts that field commanders in resource-rich territories should be *more* likely to resist postwar statebuilding to sustain private monopoly control over economic rents. My argument, by contrast, anticipates that if natural resources lead to predatory rule, then commanders in these zones are likely to have a weaker incentive for postwar resistance because they will be unable to sustain local influence within their wartime fiefdoms.

Third, rebel governance type might be shaped by conditions on the battlefield. Exposure to armed competition creates uncertainty about rebels' ability to maintain a permanent presence in occupied territories. Rebels under high threat may therefore adopt a short "shadow of the future" and govern occupied communities without regard for long-run civilian welfare.[70] Intense counterinsurgency pressure may also discourage local residents from collaborating with insurgents out of fear of reprisals.[71] And threats from counterinsurgent forces make it riskier for rebels to invest in governance practices that are easily visible to the adversary, such as holding public meetings, running schools or health facilities, or building infrastructure. However, even if armed competition does affect the quality of governance in rebel-ruled communities, there is little reason ex ante to expect that local patterns of battlefield competition—which reflect many contingent circumstances in civil wars—will also covary consistently with postwar ex-rebel commander resistance *other* than through the logic of commander embeddedness specified by my theory. One exception is that intense wartime threats may cause the senior leadership circle of rebel groups to become more cohesive as members share collective experiences of sacrifice.[72] Yet such group-level dynamics still cannot easily explain subnational patterns of ex-rebel resistance.

Fourth, the distribution of ethnic and partisan identities among occupied populations could affect the type of rebel rule that emerges. Coethnicity with occupying armed groups may bias civilians' assessments of rebels in a favorable direction, encouraging trust-building and rapport. As Laia Balcells argues in the case of conventional civil wars with stable front lines, occupying rebels also have less incentive to coerce local populations to eliminate rear-guard threats when civilians support the group along the conflict's master cleavage.[73] By contrast, where ethnic or political cleavages favor the government, rebel rulers may be unable or unwilling to establish effective institutions.

The subnational research design of this book allows me to account for identity-based cleavages directly. Surprisingly, I find little evidence that prewar ethnic or partisan identities are predictive of the form of rebel rule that emerged in northern Côte d'Ivoire between 2002 and 2011. If anything, FN rebels appear to have made greater effort to build collaborative rule in non-coethnic communities. This pattern may reflect two dynamics. First, while rebel groups can count on (initial) popularity in areas dominated by copartisans, civilian support in other areas is contingent upon rebel governance performance. Second, rebel groups have incentives to use coercion against coethnic or copartisan populations to ensure active cooperation and to eliminate potential leadership rivals.[74] Ethnic and political cleavages are therefore unlikely to be a reliable guide to the practices of governance that emerge in rebel-occupied territories.

Finally, rebels' selection of governance practices can be influenced by militants' ideological orientation. Groups with revolutionary worldviews that call for wholesale transformation of the existing social order, such as Marxist and Islamist groups, may seek to replace or heavily reform local institutions and force those institutions to conform to their ideological preferences.[75] Again, however, it is difficult to account for subnational variation in patterns of rebel rule with respect to group-level variables like ideology. In the Ivorian case, significant variation in rebel governance practices existed from one locality to the next, despite the uniform (nonrevolutionary) ideology of the FN. Moreover, while the content of insurgents' ideological doctrines may influence the aims of rebel occupiers, there is no guarantee that those aims are compatible with the interests of local populations. Revolutionary rebels in Syria and Sri Lanka, for example, struggled to build legitimacy among occupied populations because their ideological demands clashed with local civilian preferences.[76] Revolutionary ideology may lead to either collaborative or predatory forms of rule.

Ultimately, the governance practices of armed groups are complex, vary for many reasons, and are hard to predict in advance at the local level. Other factors beyond those that have just been discussed—including the idiosyncratic traits of rebel leaders—will no doubt be relevant for explaining individual cases. Some variables that shape wartime governance quality—such as the presence of strong prewar local elites—can be difficult to measure ex post. Yet in general, I do not find that any single factor causes clear endogeneity issues for my argument (and these concerns are treated at some length in the empirical chapters that follow). Taking wartime patterns of rebel-civilian relations as an analytical starting point, this book addresses the following question: Given the emergence of collaborative rebel rule, what are the implications for commanders' choices in the postwar context? It would be interesting to investigate and rank the full suite of factors that contribute to armed groups' governance practices, but that is a project that lies beyond the scope of this book.

This chapter has sketched a theory to explain variation in ex-rebel commander resistance to the central state following postconflict military integration. Regime leaders require the cooperation of ex-rebel field commanders to demobilize irregular militia and construct a legible security apparatus. Postwar state structures are weakly institutionalized, and ex-rebel commanders fear exclusion once regime leaders begin to consolidate their power. Ex-rebel commanders' incentives to resist statebuilding are influenced by commanders' embeddedness in former rebel zones. Embedded commanders from areas of collaborative rebel rule are likely to sustain autonomous mobilization power and local legitimacy as guarantors of order, while nonembedded commanders from areas of predatory rule are not (H1). During rebel-military integration, these embedded commanders have greater coercive leverage and are more likely to develop antiregime grievances in the face of centralized statebuilding. Collaborative rebel rule thus engenders postwar commander resistance (H2). Strategic interaction between commanders and regime leaders over time determines whether initial commander resistance leads to accommodation and mutual deterrence or escalates in a conflict spiral to violence and renewed rebellion.

To illustrate and test these hypotheses, the rest of the book draws on comparative evidence collected over the course of six years of research. The next two chapters focus on H1, presenting qualitative and quantitative evidence from northern Côte d'Ivoire that illustrates how varied practices of rebel rule during the Ivorian civil war endowed some field commanders but not others with local ties to rebel-ruled communities that outlived the end of the war. Chapter 4 examines the impacts of these commander-community ties for commanders' resistance to the central state after rebel-military integration. Consistent with H2, ex-rebel commanders from areas of collaborative rule were best positioned to leverage their mobilization power to organize military mutinies and antigovernment protests by irregular armed networks. Chapter 5 traces the causal processes of the argument in detail in four rebel-ruled towns in northern Côte d'Ivoire. Chapter 6 goes beyond Côte d'Ivoire and evaluates the relationship between wartime rebel rule and commander resistance in sixty cases of rebel-military integration since 1946.

II. CÔTE D'IVOIRE

CHAPTER 2

Rebel Rule in the Ivorian Civil War (2002–2011)

In the spring of 2011, rebel soldiers loyal to Alassane Ouattara marched on Côte d'Ivoire's capital city of Abidjan. For the first time in nine years, insurgent troops—recently known as the Forces Nouvelles (FN) and now fighting under the banner of the Forces Républicaines de Côte d'Ivoire (FRCI)—had broken through the cease-fire zone that separated the government-held south from the rebel-ruled north. After several weeks of fighting in March and early April, the remaining loyalist forces of President Laurent Gbagbo collapsed. Facing defeat but still refusing to accept his recent electoral loss and relinquish power, Gbagbo urged his family members and close advisers to flee the country. On the morning of April 11, FRCI soldiers entered Gbagbo's residence and arrested the former president in his bedroom.[1]

Gbagbo's downfall marked the climax of a tumultuous decade in Côte d'Ivoire, a country once lauded as the "miracle" of West Africa.[2] In the fall of 2002, rebel forces comprised of an alliance of northern army officers and former university student activists seized control of nearly 60 percent of the country. Over the next eight and a half years, the FN insurgency built a powerful political-military coalition and ran a parallel governance system across more than two hundred northern subprefectures, an area about twice the size of Austria.[3] Though the FN possessed little ideological vision ex ante beyond removing Gbagbo from power, by the end of the conflict, rebel rulers had fashioned a remarkably diverse array of local governance arrangements in their zones of control. These institutions provided the basis for rebel recruitment, financing, and political support that enabled the FN to survive as an organization and, eventually, to install their leaders into positions of power in the state. At the same time, varied patterns of rebel rule laid the groundwork for strikingly different trajectories of commander-community relations and postwar statebuilding after the FN's official demobilization in 2011.

How did history take this turn of events? This chapter explores the first step in my argument, examining the process by which varied patterns of rebel rule emerged in Côte d'Ivoire. The chapter begins by providing the reader with a general introduction to the Ivorian civil war and the origins of the FN. It then analyzes the wartime governance arrangements that arose under the FN from late 2002 onward. Here the chapter addresses an important question: How did a rebel group that lacked a programmatic ideology build a sovereign counterstate?[4] I suggest that two features of the wartime context in northern Côte d'Ivoire proved fortuitous for rebel institution building: (1) the presence of external peacekeeping forces that protected rebels from counterinsurgency pressure, and (2) an established local elite willing to strike bargains with rebel rulers. Within this environment, a wide variety of wartime governance practices emerged endogenously as FN rebels interacted with civilians and navigated the practical realities of raising revenue, attracting recruits, and sustaining a minimum of popular support.

To explore these practices of rebel governance in Côte d'Ivoire systematically, the chapter introduces an original dataset of rebel-ruled localities. Drawing on a survey of key community informants, the chapter maps out spatial variation in FN presence and wartime governance in northern Côte d'Ivoire at a granular level. Consistent with theoretical expectations, practices of collaborative rule under the FN tended to cluster together strongly at the locality level, reflecting a process of institutionalization of rebel-civilian relations over time. I also show that local variation in patterns of collaborative and predatory rebel rule during the Ivorian conflict cannot be easily explained by factors that might later confound my argument, such as local demography, socioeconomic conditions, or kinship ties between FN commanders and occupied communities. With these empirical foundations in place, subsequent chapters trace the consequences of these varied practices of rebel rule for commanders' local embeddedness and resistance to postwar statebuilding.

Background to Rebellion in Côte d'Ivoire

What caused the Ivorian civil war?[5] Past accounts have identified many supposed root causes of the conflict. These include, among others, the national power vacuum following the death of President Félix Houphouët-Boigny in 1993, subsequent opportunistic behavior by Houphouët-Boigny's successors, interference by meddling foreign powers (particularly France and Burkina Faso), tensions between indigenous (*autochtones*) and migrant communities (*allogènes*) over access to land, structural adjustment and austerity policies in the 1990s that exacerbated economic inequality, and a cultural "malaise" in the late postcolonial period in West Africa.[6] It is not hard to find anecdotal evidence to support most of these theories.

More than any other single factor, however, the proximate cause of the Ivorian civil war stemmed from the problem of ethnopolitical exclusion.

After Côte d'Ivoire attained independence from France in 1960, Houphouët-Boigny and the Parti Démocratique de Côte d'Ivoire (PDCI) ruled the country as a single-party but multiethnic coalition.[7] Houphouët-Boigny's reign was prosperous, and the president fashioned together a stable patrimonial regime from the country's disparate language groups and regional elites in the rural hinterlands.[8] In this sense, Houphouët-Boigny's method of rule loosely resembled earlier French strategies of control in francophone West Africa, wherein colonial officials deputized local chiefs from diverse cultural communities to act as auxiliaries of the state.[9] By the late 1980s, however, this informal ethnic power-sharing system began to unravel. A series of interlinked crises triggered by rising government debt and austerity, intercommunal land tensions in the cocoa-rich western regions, and widespread dissatisfaction with the PDCI's single-party regime pushed ethnic and identity cleavages to the foreground of Ivorian politics.[10] When the aging Houphouët-Boigny died in 1993, former PDCI cabinet members vied to gain the upper hand in the ensuing succession struggle by appealing to their own coethnic bases at the expense of a more inclusive national vision.[11]

Presidential elections in 1995 marked a turning point in the violent politicization of Côte d'Ivoire's identity cleavages, which increasingly fell along a northern/Muslim ("Dioula") versus southern/Christian axis.[12] Competing factions from the old PDCI solidified around the sitting President Henry Konan Bedié, an ethnic Akan who consolidated support in the central and southeastern regions of the country, and the former Prime Minister Alassane Ouattara, who drew strong support among the northern Malinke and Voltaic/Senoufo ethnic groups. In a move that escalated north-south tensions, Bedié introduced a new electoral code that effectively blocked Ouattara from competing in the election.[13] Bedié also introduced the concept of *ivoirité* during a speech to PDCI supporters, arguing that the unity of the nation demanded that "we continue to assert our cultural distinctiveness, and to foster Ivoirian uniqueness."[14] *Ivoirité* soon became shorthand for an ethnic-cultural conceptualization of Ivorian citizenship, drawing a sharp distinction between *autochtones* ("native" Ivorians of southern and central origins) and *allogènes* (foreign migrants and persons of northern heritage, typically Muslims).[15]

Ethnic polarization in the 1990s soon carried over into the ranks of the armed forces, raising the specter of a military coup for the first time in Côte d'Ivoire's history. Army officers, especially those with northern and western ethnic backgrounds, felt threatened by President Bedié's perceived pro-Akan favoritism in military recruitment and officer promotion.[16] Fearing for their professional futures and angered by Bedié's efforts to exclude Ouattara once again from running in the next presidential election, mutinous pro-Ouattara soldiers took to the streets in Abidjan on December 23, 1999.[17] On December 25, the former chief of staff of the army, General Robert Gueï, announced that a new military junta controlled the country. Gueï himself assumed the title of president. Among the coup leaders were future FN commanders Ibrahim Coulibaly ("IB"), a charismatic staff sergeant who once served as a bodyguard for Ouattara, and Tuo Fozié, the head of the Republican Guard. Nearly all the key leaders of the junta had personal ties to Alassane Ouattara, and all were from northern or western regions.[18] The 1999 "Christmas coup" established a template for the rapid seizure of power by northern military forces that FN leaders would attempt to repeat less than three years later.

The junta behind Gueï's putsch soon disintegrated amid tensions between Gueï and his coconspirators. Several northern soldiers and student activists were tortured for information in an effort to root out enemies of the new president.[19] Led by Coulibaly, Fozié, and Chérif Ousmane—the commander of a special operations unit formed under Gueï—a group of defecting officers fled to Burkina Faso, taking with them approximately seven hundred Ivorian soldiers.[20] While in Burkina Faso, the exiled soldiers were sheltered by President Blaise Campaoré. They were also introduced to an ambitious young politician, Guillaume Kigbafori Soro, the former leader of the Ivorian national student union.[21] Soro would later become the political chief of the FN and a key protagonist of the Ivorian crisis.

In Abidjan, meanwhile, new elections in October 2000 handed power to Gbagbo and the Front Populaire Ivoirien (FPI). The FPI was a populist-nationalist party, long critical of the PDCI's single-party rule, with strong support among the Kru ethnic groups in the southwest. To shore up his political base, Gbagbo traded on the rhetoric of ivoirité even more aggressively than Bedié. The FPI painted northern politicians as stooges of French neocolonialism and tapped into nativist grievances about northern labor migration into Kru homeland regions. Gbagbo was not interested in seeing the exiled northern soldiers in Burkina Faso return to Côte d'Ivoire, nor in rectifying grievances about anti-northern discrimination in the military. Instead, Gbagbo cultivated his own support base within the police and gendarmerie forces. He also sponsored the creation of a vast network of pro-FPI youth militias, known as the "Patriotic Galaxy."[22] Aiming to reestablish their foothold in the army, Coulibaly's group of exiled soldiers in Burkina Faso returned to the country through a system of clandestine cells.[23] In the summer of 2002, fearing that another northern coup attempt was in the works, Gbagbo ordered the demobilization of several army units with suspected ties to Coulibaly's network.

Convinced that the window of opportunity to remove Gbagbo was closing, the northern mutineers struck on September 19, 2002. In an orchestrated attack that echoed the events of the 1999 coup, army units launched operations to seize critical infrastructure and telecommunications facilities in the capital. This time, however, the anti-Gbagbo rebels were quickly repulsed to the north by loyalist troops of the Forces Armées Nationales de Côte d'Ivoire (FANCI). The rebelling soldiers regrouped and seized control of the northern cities of Bouaké and Korhogo, branding themselves as the Mouvement Patriotique de Côte d'Ivoire (MPCI). MPCI troops rapidly swept west and south in October, capturing territory and growing in size as more soldiers—especially those of northern origins—defected from their positions to join the mutineers.[24] Within two months, rebel forces controlled nearly 60 percent of the national territory with an army of over five thousand.[25] After merging with two smaller anti-Gbagbo militias—the Movement for Justice and Peace (Mouvement pour la Justice et la Paix, or MJP) and the Ivorian Popular Movement of the Great West (Mouvement Populaire Ivoirien du Grand Ouest, or MPIGO)—the MPCI rebranded itself as the FN in late December 2002.[26] The politicization of Côte d'Ivoire's ethnic cleavages that had begun in the waning years of Houphouët-Boigny's rule had turned into an open civil war.

The Gbabgo regime was shocked and embarrassed by the rebels' rapid takeover in the north, and the president vowed to reclaim the lost territory by force. Pitched battles ensued in several regions. The most intense conventional fighting occurred during battles for the central city of Bouaké in October 2002 and those to control the resource-rich western region near Man until April 2003.[27] Counterinsurgency efforts in this early phase included conventional military ground operations, air strikes against rebel positions, and attempts by intelligence agents to infiltrate the FN using spies from northern ethnic backgrounds.[28] Gbagbo also stepped up the mobilization of armed youth militias, recruited three thousand additional ethnic southerners into the army, and hired mercenaries from Liberia, South Africa, Angola, and Eastern Europe to fight alongside the FANCI to try to crush the rebel armies.[29]

High-intensity warfare did not last long. By mid-2003, the conflict settled into an uneasy territorial stalemate with limited active combat, and the war did not fully reescalate until the 2010–2011 election crisis. Why? One reason was that the Gbagbo regime was ill-equipped to prosecute a sustained counterinsurgency campaign in northern Côte d'Ivoire. Gnangadjomon Koné notes that the FANCI army was not an experienced fighting force—Côte d'Ivoire having never fought a war—and the mercenaries and irregular militias sponsored by Gbagbo's government had limited offensive utility against an organized and entrenched adversary in hostile territory.[30]

The most important reason for the conflict's prolonged stalemate, however, was the presence of a French interposition force (Operation Licorne) deployed at an early stage of the war. The French government of Jacques Chirac had expressed initial reluctance to intervene in Côte d'Ivoire's internal affairs, but the realization that MPCI/FN rebels could overwhelm Gbabgo's government and destabilize the former French colony prompted a policy change. In early October 2002, French forces stationed in Gabon mobilized to protect French nationals and to honor France's defense agreement with the Ivorian government.[31] Licorne troops blocked the advancing rebel columns south of Vavoua and Bouaké and established a cease-fire zone that stretched across the middle belt of the country.[32] Though the French intervention was intended to thwart the rebel offensive, it also protected the MPCI/FN from government counterattack.[33] The Gbagbo government was dismayed by the perceived pro-rebel bias of the intervention forces and blamed French meddling for the inability of loyalist forces to recapture the north.[34] In May 2003, the United Nations took control of peacekeeping operations, launching the United Nations Mission in Côte d'Ivoire (MINUCI).[35] Operating from a series of outposts in larger towns and cities, UN and French peacekeeping forces administered the cease-fire zone and established security patrols in potential conflict hot spots.[36] The peacekeeping intervention was so effective at cauterizing violence that by late 2003, some FN soldiers began to drop out of the rebel army because of "boredom at the inactivity in the northern zone."[37]

A signal feature of Côte d'Ivoire's civil war, therefore, was its relatively low amount of combat.[38] To be sure, there were well-documented episodes of horrific violence, particularly in the west.[39] Yet relative to the size of the country and the number of combatants under arms, the conflict generated few casualties or reversals in territorial control. Over a span of nine years between 2002 and 2011, the number of conflict-related deaths in Côte d'Ivoire likely totaled less than 3,500, with an upper bound closer to 4,400.[40] While these crude body counts do not capture the totality of trauma inflicted by organized violence, they do underscore the relatively weak level of military pressure faced by the FN. This aspect of the Ivorian civil war is theoretically relevant for my argument because it helps to explain how a rebel group that lacked a programmatic ideology could nevertheless build a quite sophisticated system of civilian governance within its territory. Protected from intense armed competition, FN rebels adopted relatively long time horizons in their zones of control, while external peacekeeping forces protected the FN's visible targets. The security blanket provided by external interveners enabled the FN to operate a parallel governance system that, as we shall see, had far-reaching consequences for rebel commanders' local ties.

From late 2002 onward, a de facto partition in Côte d'Ivoire prevailed: FN rebels ruled in the north, while the Gbagbo government maintained secure control of the south. Stymied in their push to capture Abidjan, the FN soon shifted its strategic priorities away from the battlefield. FN leaders looked to win allies abroad, to press the Gbagbo government for power-sharing concessions, and above all to build up a popular support base inside the country that could sustain their political-military movement for the long run. On-again, off-again peace talks produced a slate of five negotiated settlements between 2003 and 2008, but none of these peace deals succeeded in reunifying the country. The war would only truly end after the resumption of large-scale violence in 2011, the arrest of Gbagbo himself, and the

FN's integration into the national armed forces. These events are discussed in future chapters.

Viewed at an analytical distance, the onset of rebellion in Côte d'Ivoire appears both familiar and distinctive in the context of postcolonial Africa. As with other civil wars in Rwanda, Zimbabwe, and Uganda, the impetus for violent antistate mobilization in Côte d'Ivoire centered around the issue of ethnic exclusion.[41] Rebel leaders hailing from the north took up arms to reverse their declining access to state power and "put an end to Ivorianness," a noxious conceptualization of national identity that defined ethnic northerners as being outside the authentic national community.[42] The incumbent ruler (Gbagbo) failed to contain the outbreak of violence because he did not trust his northern rivals not to exploit a toehold in the military to usurp power again, a bargaining failure that echoes Philip Roessler's "coup–civil war trap" model.[43] Importantly, accounts that characterize the Ivorian conflict as reducible to the ambitions of self-interested "warlords"— a popular caricature of civil wars in West Africa—ought to be handled with skepticism.[44] The argument that the FN was merely an opportunistic loot-seeking rebellion devoid of genuine political grievances and that subsequent postwar frictions between ex-rebel commanders and the Ivorian state are therefore overdetermined appears closer to an ex post facto judgment than a compelling reading of history.[45]

But the Ivorian civil war *was* unusual in one sense: FN rebels enjoyed relative security in a large zone of territorial control for nearly nine years, shielded from counterinsurgency pressure by a robust international peacekeeping force. As described in the next section, this uninterrupted period of territorial control—in combination with the local social structures of northern Côte d'Ivoire—created space for the emergence of a wide range of rebel governance practices.

Variation in Insurgent Governance in Côte d'Ivoire

Nonstate armed groups are driven by the desire not only to gain and preserve territorial control but also to maximize the byproducts of that control, including economic revenues, membership recruitment, and political support.[46] For the FN, acquiring the benefits of territorial control required an organizational infrastructure capable of addressing the basic needs of civilians while also sustaining the livelihoods of rebel soldiers without constantly resorting to extortion. By improving governance in the north, FN leaders hoped to revive economic activity in the rebel zone, solidify their tax revenue base, and increase popular support and recruitment.[47]

At the risk of overgeneralization, insurgent governance in northern Côte d'Ivoire from 2002 to 2011 can be described as progressing through two distinct stages: an initial period of social disorder following the collapse of the regular state administration, and a subsequent period of uneven recovery and local institutionalization that saw new governance arrangements take shape as rebels and occupied civilians converged on a shared set of expected behaviors.[48] The duration and specifics of each stage varied considerably from locality to locality. Here I simply offer a qualitative sketch to give a sense of the key dynamics of each phase and the types of governance arrangements that developed. The next section fleshes out this picture with more systematic quantitative evidence.

The initial stage of disorder began in the fall of 2002, immediately following the failed putsch in Abidjan and rebel retreat to the north. Within a span of three months, a rebel army of hardly five thousand soldiers seized control of more than sixty thousand square miles of land inhabited by at least five million people. Civil servants, along with the Ivorian prefectoral corps and police, withdrew from the north on the orders of the Gbagbo government. The result was an immediate crisis of service provision and food security and a breakdown of law and order.[49] Hundreds of thousands of civilians became internally displaced. Amid a wave of widespread looting and property damage, economic activity ground to a halt in cities like Bouaké. Many civilians caught behind rebel lines found themselves with diminished income or none at all. "The arrival of the insurgency disrupted patterns of daily life," writes Kathrin Heitz-Tokpa; "the familiar social world was shattered."[50]

Leadership change at the top of the FN soon ushered in a new phase of administrative organization in the north—at least on paper. By early 2003, the initial nucleus of military conspirators around Coulibaly had become overshadowed by a set of northern civilian elites who saw the FN rebellion as a vehicle to achieve their own political ambitions.[51] The leader of this political elite was Guillaume Soro, an ambitious young cadre of Alassane Ouattara's Rassemblement des Républicains (RDR) party. Soro gained national prominence and political connections in the 1990s as the head of the Fédération Estudiantine et Scholaire de Côte d'Ivoire (FESCI), a powerful student union that advocated for multiparty democracy and protested the hegemony of the old PDCI. As the imperative for military action against pro-Gbagbo forces was subsumed by diplomacy and political organizing, Soro expanded the secretariat of the FN and recruited his associates into top leadership positions.[52] Eager to shore up the FN's local support, Soro also created a system of *délégué civiles*, political commissars who represented the secretariat within each rebel-occupied zone.[53] By 2004, the FN had reorganized itself into three distinct bodies: the military wing, the Forces Armées des Forces Nouvelles (FAFN), which established a series of military commands across the north; the political branch (*cabinet civile*), headed by Soro and his representatives in Bouaké; and a financial wing, known as *la Centrale*, headed by a former economics professor, André Ouattara, and represented in each zone by tax agents (*régisseurs*).[54] This rebel bureaucracy—intended to showcase the FN's competence as a government-in-waiting and legitimate alternative to the Gbagbo regime—formulated policies over taxation, education, customs collection, and traffic regulation throughout FN territory.[55]

While the FN regime was in theory run out of Bouaké, in reality the frontline FAFN military commanders who actually controlled the north enjoyed broad discretion in the implementation of governance practices and the methods used to obtain civilian obedience. These commanders exercised authority within ten zone commands (led by a *com'zone*) roughly corresponding to Côte d'Ivoire's preexisting administrative regions. Each zone command was further divided into sectors that typically conformed to the boundaries of subprefectures.[56] In many cases, zone and sector commanders modeled their authority—and even their appearance and titles—on that of previous state officials, particularly the prefectoral corps. Below sector commanders, smaller platoon-sized units headed by a *chef de poste* were stationed in outlying villages and road intersections and ranged in size from a handful of soldiers to several dozen.[57] Almost all of the zone and sector commanders in the FN were former FANCI officers or enlisted men, and almost all of these commanders were ethnic "northerners"—that is, from northern Mande or Voltaic communities.[58] These field commanders wielded so much clout within the FN organization that Heitz-Tokpa—one of the foremost experts on the group—characterized the FN regime as an "authoritarian military administration."[59]

With limited oversight or guidance from the FN headquarters in Bouaké, this decentralized and ad hoc rebel regime produced a kaleidoscope of governance arrangements that varied a great deal across geographic space. Drawing on the theoretical framework outlined in chapter 1, I highlight four wartime governance practices that shaped rebel-civilian relations in northern Côte d'Ivoire.

GOODS PROVISION

For a nonstate armed group, efforts to supply basic goods to the civilian population are crucial to establishing social control and acquiring legitimacy. Rebel goods range from fully inclusive services (e.g., security, education, or health care that is available to any resident) to exclusive (goods are only made available to rebel group members) or may be nonexistent.

In the immediate aftermath of the FN's arrival in northern Côte d'Ivoire, public goods provision collapsed almost entirely. The state administration—including the courts, the police, municipal governments, the prefectoral corps, schools, health clinics, and basic infrastructure upkeep—ceased to function. This void created popular pressure on the FN to ensure continuity in basic goods provision. The top priority of FN commanders and their lieutenants was typically to establish patrols to ensure security and reduce arbitrary banditry and to coordinate the distribution of humanitarian relief supplies by international organizations like the UN and Médecins Sans Frontières (MSF). In the western zone of Man, for example, Heitz-Tokpa notes that under the command of Losseni Fofana, the com'zone of Man, the FN restored the functioning of local prisons, police stations, and the gendarmerie (now operated by FAFN soldiers).[60] In the peripheral northeastern zone of Bouna, the FN enjoyed initial support due to their ability to maintain relative political order and safety.[61] In several regions like Korhogo, FN commanders collaborated with local *dozo* hunting associations to establish security patrols that upheld a relatively effective crime deterrent.[62] Lower-ranking civil servants who remained in the FN zone, such as tax agents and clerks of the mayoral office, were also recruited to work for the local FN administration. These agents allowed the FN to collect taxes more efficiently, issue birth and death certificates, and commission infrastructure repairs.

Beyond security and policing, FN provision of other types of goods—such as education and health care—was sporadic. While some civilians I interviewed recalled the FN occupation as a time of continuity with the service provision previously supplied by the state (and in some cases even an improvement), others felt that rebels failed to provide even a bare minimum of public goods in their communities. Research by other scholars paints a similarly heterogenous picture. Sebastian van Baalen, for example, observed that while the FN engaged in "extensive" service provision that included police patrols, cleaning streets, and investing in public schools in the northwestern town of Odienné, in other areas like Vavoua, goods provision was "limited" and rebels largely ignored the service needs of the population, leading to "an emergency in education and health care."[63] Overall, goods provision under the FN ranged from thoroughgoing and inclusive in some areas to negligible in others.

POWER SHARING WITH LOCAL ELITES

The second key practice of rebel rule identified in chapter 1 is the degree of power sharing with local elites. Local elites in the towns and rural communities of northern Côte d'Ivoire are usually those with status derived from their connections to traditional chieftaincies, local state or party structures, powerful family lineages, or some combination of these.[64] As elsewhere in Africa, the status of traditional leaders in Côte d'Ivoire both predated and was shaped by colonial and postcolonial statebuilding.[65] Though the *chefferie* system in Côte d'Ivoire was arguably less integrated into the French colonial state than under the British system in neighboring Ghana, many family patriarchs in Akan, Malinke, and Senoufo communities retained (and sometimes expanded) their authority in the colonial era.[66] The Houphouët-Boigny regime continued the policy of accommodating the northern chiefs, offering state recognition of indigenous land claims in exchange for political support for the ruling PDCI.[67] These political bargains upheld the social authority of traditional local elites across northern Côte d'Ivoire and reenforced their roles as important brokers of patronage resources.

The FN's rapid conquest of such a large amount of territory in the fall of 2002, along with the rebels' lack of governance experience, made the FN ill-equipped to rule effectively without assistance from local elites in the north. Like French colonial agents and Ivorian state prefects before them, FN field commanders attempted to co-opt northern local elites as a necessary expedient to collect information, mobilize populations, and legitimize their authority. The hierarchical social structure of many northern Ivorian communities, dominated by a strong set of family patriarchs, created both opportunities and constraints for rebel rule. On the one hand, these local elites—many of whom shared the FN's disdain for the Gbagbo regime and the ideology of ivoirité—provided a ready set of partners for the rebel regime. By allying themselves with local elites, FN commanders could quickly provide a modicum of social order and handle urgent practicalities such as distributing aid supplies and arranging security patrols.[68] To establish political control, therefore, local commanders typically approached the population "from above" by reaching out to established community leaders and negotiating informal arrangements that granted local elites safety and a degree of autonomy in exchange for their endorsement of the rebel cause. Building ties with leaders at the top of the local social hierarchy allowed commanders to interface with a range of other community members, including civil society groups who could help the FN to reestablish basic services such as schools and health clinics.[69] Rebel commanders could similarly use partnerships with local elites to adjudicate disputes and administer justice within a framework that was accepted as more legitimate by the occupied population.

Yet power sharing with local elites under FN rule was not ubiquitous. In a handful of areas, traditional authorities balked at the authority of FN commanders—who were often much younger—and ended up threatened, killed, or driven out of their positions.[70] Elsewhere, entrenched local elites managed to retain their positions while withholding cooperation with the FN. In rare cases, local elites mobilized active resistance to rebel rule, though this occurred infrequently (a common refrain in interviews with traditional leaders in the north was that there was "no choice" but to accommodate the FN during the war). Finally, some localities simply lacked strong and respected local elites at the onset of the rebel occupation, forcing FN rebels to ignore or work around these individuals.[71] The general result in such cases was that rebel commanders had restricted access to local social networks and tended to rely more on coercion to control civilians. Notably, local elite reactions to the FN were *not* necessarily determined by ethnic or kinship relations. Local FN commanders rarely shared familial connections to their areas of operation, and the FN established power-sharing arrangements with local elites in many communities that were dominated by non-northern groups.[72] Chapter 5 illustrates such a case in the western Yacuba town of Sangouiné.

CIVILIAN PARTICIPATION

Rebel rule in Côte d'Ivoire permitted a modicum of civilian participation, albeit within strict limits and—as with goods provision and local power sharing—significant regional variation. In some areas, local commanders conducted regular meetings with community leaders and citizens to communicate information to residents and to resolve land and property disputes, akin to the public meetings held by traditional leaders and government prefects. Moussa Fofana's important study of the FN highlights the creation of various "community associations" by the FN designed to bridge divides between rebels and the population and bolster the FN's ground-level support.[73] These associations included the Union des Femmes pour la Démocratie en Côte d'Ivoire (UFDCI), La Jeunesse Forces Nouvelles (JFN), and the *senats*. The latter institution was a forum for political discussion modeled on the agoras ("street parliaments") common in southern Côte d'Ivoire, where youth and students assemble to discuss political issues. The senats in the FN zone served as a kind of clearinghouse for a wide range of issues of concern to the population, including health, sanitation, and the distribution of humanitarian relief.[74] In other towns, like Odienné, the FN established local "councils" to coordinate input from civilians and NGOs.[75]

Yet civilian participation under the FN was always confined within limited boundaries. There was no mechanism of electoral democracy within the rebel administration. The FN's power-sharing deals with traditional elites gave the rebel administration a conservative character that typically avoided threatening established social hierarchies. The community associations created by the FN were hardly spontaneous or egalitarian. Rather, they were structured and organized in a top-down fashion by FN agents or existing community leaders.[76] Frequently, these associations operated as forums for pro-rebel propaganda and the dissemination of information favorable to the FN and the RDR. In some areas, even pro forma mechanisms of civilian participation were absent. In Vavoua, for example, van Baalen observed that rebel governors "ignored civilian sentiments and created no mechanisms for soliciting civilians."[77]

RESTRAINTS ON CIVILIAN ABUSE

The final practice of rebel rule identified in chapter 1 is the degree to which armed groups constrain abuses of civilians. In this respect, conditions also varied sharply across FN territory. It is true that many Ivorian civilians suffered violence and humiliation at the hands of vengeful, intoxicated, or undisciplined FN troops. Evidence from a survey of civilians in former FN-controlled territory in Côte d'Ivoire that I commissioned in 2018 indicated that 55 percent of civilians experienced some form of physical abuse or property theft during the conflict. In Man and Vavoua, van Baalen reports that many residents were reluctant to approach the FN "for fear of reprisals" and tended to see the rebel taxation system as "blatant extortion" that existed in the shadow of physical threat.[78] In some areas where I conducted interviews and focus groups with community members, such as the village of Kpata in the Tonkpi region, civilians interacted with FN rebels mainly during irregular patrols that—in the eyes of my interlocutors—more closely resembled bandit raids than policing.[79]

At the same time, other localities witnessed significant efforts on the part of FN commanders to limit abuses. In Odienné, for example, the zone commander Ousmane Coulibaly took actions to discipline the rank and file and limit predations against the local population.[80] Local elites and ordinary Ivorians alike sometimes used the public meetings organized by the FN to request such discipline or the removal of rebel soldiers accused of abusive behavior from the community. In the western zones, for example, Liberian mercenary fighters were a common target of complaint from civilians. Under popular pressure, the FN leadership decided to withdraw the bulk of these fighters from Ivorian territory by the end of 2003.[81] Throughout my research in northern Côte d'Ivoire, the ability of civilians to lobby for the relocation of abusive rebels away from their community was often highlighted as an important signal of FN commanders' perceived "reasonableness" and concern for local interests.

Overall, wartime governance arrangements in northern Côte d'Ivoire defy broad-brush classifications that are valid across geographic space. FN rule began in a context of chaos and disorder in the fall of 2002, when a mutinous group of soldiers found themselves suddenly responsible for the welfare of millions of civilians. Over time, more organized and predictable governance systems emerged as rebel commanders acclimatized to their positions, negotiated local power-sharing arrangements, and adopted governance practices to serve their own needs while managing bottom-up demands from civilians. Top-down pressure from FN political leaders in Bouaké, who wanted the movement to project an image of a "statelike" administration, encouraged rebel institution building but did not determine its structure. The result was a patchwork of governance practices that varied dramatically in terms of goods provision, power sharing with local elites, civilian participation, and restraints on abuse. To document these patterns of rebel rule in a more systematic fashion and to investigate whether varied governance practices are attributable to particular local conditions, I now turn to quantitative evidence from an original dataset of rebel-ruled localities.

Quantitative Evidence on Patterns of Rebel Rule

This section documents patterns of wartime rebel rule in Côte d'Ivoire using an original dataset of FN-controlled localities. The dataset combines a novel survey of local community informants that I designed and implemented in 2017, three waves of the Enquête niveau de vie des ménages (ENV) household socioeconomic surveys from the Ivorian National Institute of Statistics (INS) between 2002 and 2014, electoral data, and a large-scale citizen survey that I carried out in partnership with two colleagues and the United States Agency for International Development (USAID) in 2018.[82] This integrated dataset represents the first effort to systematically document spatial variation in rebel group presence and wartime governance practices in Côte d'Ivoire and to document commander-community ties at the subnational level after civil war.[83] In the next section, I concentrate on findings from the community informant survey, which provides rich data on practices of wartime rebel rule. I also evaluate whether localities that experienced collaborative forms of rebel rule differed systematically from those that experienced predatory rule in ways that might also affect commanders' postwar ties and capacity for resistance vis-à-vis the central regime. The evidence suggests a high degree of similarity between areas of collaborative and predatory rule in many respects.

SAMPLE AND DATA COLLECTION

Between July and November 2017, I carried out a community informant survey in ninety-three localities in northern Côte d'Ivoire, including eighty-eight subprefectures and five urban *quartiers* in the larger cities of Bouaké and Korhogo. Since many key practices of FN governance were centralized in the hands of sector commanders, subprefectures are the most disaggregated administrative unit suitable for my analysis. While the FN controlled 219 subprefectures between January 2003 and April 2011, the time-intensive nature of data collection required me to construct a stratified sample.[84] Readers interested in the details of the sampling design can consult the appendix. The rationale of my approach was to achieve a sample of localities that was representative in terms of important social and political covariates. Comparing subprefectures in which I collected data in the community informant survey to those where I did not, I can verify that there is no statistically significant difference in terms of population size, the vote share for President Ouattara's RDR party in the 2010 elections, the average level of household poverty, the level of household exposure to conflict-related injury or economic losses, or ethnic composition.

The survey itself targeted key informants within each locality. These were normally traditional authorities (e.g., the *chef de village* or *chef de canton*), leaders of youth or women's associations, or civil society leaders who possessed deep knowledge about local history and the relevant political actors within the community.[85] After obtaining permission from the Ivorian Ministry of Interior in Abidjan, I first visited the seat of the prefecture in the regional capital, accompanied by an Ivorian research assistant, in order to explain the purpose of the research project. The *préfet* or another official then contacted the subprefectures we planned to visit to notify authorities of our presence in the area.[86] Given the sensitive nature of some survey questions, it was imperative to obtain these official forms of approval—often at multiple levels of administration—before conducting interviews. In each locality, the survey enumerator (myself or a research assistant) interviewed one or, in many cases, multiple informants to fill out the questionnaire. The survey mostly consisted of closed-ended factual questions but also included open-ended responses that gave informants the opportunity to elaborate on answers or raise additional subjects. Given the public nature of many informants' roles within their community, interviews often took the form of focus groups, with multiple community members participating and helping to respond to survey questions.

Interviewing a small, intentionally selected set of key informants posed both advantages and drawbacks. As repositories of unwritten local knowledge, these informants could respond to questions relating to the entire subprefecture (or quartier) and about the interactions between rebel commanders and community authorities. Many of these questions would be difficult to pose to a random sample of ordinary citizens. Interviewing a select set of informants was also more logistically feasible than attempting to survey dozens of citizens in each subprefecture, which expanded the number of localities I could reach. On the other hand, trying to learn about an entire community's history through the keyhole of only a handful of individuals poses risks of bias. For one, my informants tended to be older males, whose knowledge of local history is sure to have blind spots. Informants might also consciously or unconsciously present events in a skewed manner, either to place themselves or their allies in a favorable light or to conform to a narrative that they think will help attract resources to the community. To minimize these risks of bias, the questionnaire was designed to capture information considered "common knowledge" among politically informed persons in the community rather than subjective assessments or opinions. To this end, the questionnaire was refined through multiple rounds of piloting and extensive feedback from Ivorian scholars and an experienced local survey firm.[87]

CHAPTER 2

DESCRIPTIVE FINDINGS: PATTERNS OF REBEL RULE AT THE SUBPREFECTURE LEVEL

The community informant survey measured a series of wartime governance practices in FN territory between 2002 and 2011. Consistent with the anecdotal qualitative evidence previously discussed, the quantitative findings reveal significant variation in terms of wartime rebel goods provision, power sharing with local elites, the existence of mechanisms for civilian participation and dialogue, and the restraints on civilian abuse.

FN involvement in local goods provision in northern Côte d'Ivoire varied widely by domain (table 2.1). Policing and security services were nearly universal: informants reported that FN rebels were involved in policing against criminality (including issuing sentences through informal courts) in 90 percent of sampled localities and in protecting the community from external attacks in 82 percent. In contrast, FN rebels were involved in regulating issues of land governance and property disputes in only 54 percent of localities. Less frequently, informants reported that rebels provided direct assistance to the education sector (e.g., donations and salaries for schools and teachers), health care services (including the recruitment of doctors and donations for clinics), and local infrastructure repairs to roads and bridges and supplied loans for businesses and traders. Importantly, informants were asked whether different types of good were provided to *all* community members by the FN and not merely to the rebels' active supporters or a particular ethnic group or tribe.

To capture rebel power sharing with local elites, informants were asked whether any local community leaders actively cooperated with rebels to

Table 2.1. Practices of rebel rule in FN territory (2002–2011)

Inclusive goods provision	
Policing / criminal justice	90%
Protect from external threats	82%
Dispute resolution (e.g., land)	54%
Education	23%
Health care	15%
Infrastructure	10%
Loans	4%
Power sharing with local elite	
Leaders cooperated	79%
Leaders excluded	19%
Civilian participation	
Organized meetings	60%
Restraints on civilian abuse	
Civilians physically victimized by rebels	75%
Civilian property pillaged by rebels	62%
Tensions due to violent actions	78%

provide goods and services during the FN occupation, whether local elites mediated disputes between rebels and civilians, or whether local elites helped to mobilize the population through the FN's political structures or helped to identify military recruits (*Leaders Cooperated*). Overall, informants in 79 percent of surveyed localities reported that at least one of these forms of local elite cooperation occurred (conversely, in 19 percent of localities, informants reported that either no elite collaboration occurred or local elites actively opposed FN rebels [*Leaders Excluded*]). When asked which local elites participated, informants typically indicated that traditional leaders (*la chefferie*) almost always served as the primary interlocutors with the FN and were sometimes assisted by other prominent individuals, such as the leaders of women's and youth organizations, business owners, and former civil servants.

To measure civilian participation, the survey posed questions to informants about the existence of forums for rebel-civilian dialogue. An especially important mechanism for rebel-civilian dialogue under the FN was the practice of organizing public meetings chaired by the local commander or his/her representative. These meetings were significant because they provided a platform for face-to-face interactions and trust building and a venue for citizens to raise issues and grievances in spaces where such concerns would be heard by a senior member of the FN administration.[88] In a majority of localities (60 percent), informants indicated that FN rebels organized such meetings regularly (i.e., on a weekly or monthly basis).

Finally, the community informant survey underscored striking variation in wartime violence and abuse of civilians under the FN occupation. Of all forms of violence reported by informants, aggression by rebels against unarmed civilians was the most common (75 percent of localities), followed by government-rebel combat (25 percent) and intracommunal violence (15 percent). Informants in a majority of localities also reported that their community experienced pillage and looting at the hands of rebel forces, and a majority of informants indicated that significant tensions arose between community members and the FN either "occasionally" or "frequently" due to the violent actions of rebel soldiers.

Figure 2.1 visualizes the spatial distribution of rebel rule practices in wartime northern Côte d'Ivoire. I created a single aggregate index, *Collaborative rule*, that adds a point if the locality experienced at least two forms of inclusive rebel goods provision, if power sharing with local elites existed, and if there were regular organized meetings. A point was subtracted from the index if any form of rebel abuse of civilians was reported. This generated a scale ranging from −1 to +2. Though crude, this index captures the conceptualization of rebel rule as a spectrum ranging from highly predatory to highly collaborative. The map in figure 2.1 indicates that both predatory and collaborative rule occurred in all geographic regions reached by the survey sample.

CHAPTER 2

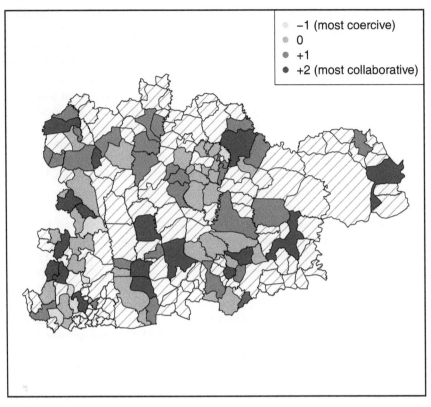

Fig. 2.1. Spatial patterns of rebel rule in northern Côte d'Ivoire, 2002–2011
Note: Subprefecture boundaries shown on map. Diagonally shaded areas not included in sample.

Overall, evidence from the community informant survey confirms the existence of significant variation in local practices of rebel rule in northern Côte d'Ivoire. Areas of collaborative rule saw inclusive public goods provision across a range of services, collaboration with local elites, a degree of civilian participation, and restraints on rebel abuses of civilians. Areas of predatory rule saw fewer, if any, of these governance practices.

What Explains Rebel Rule in Côte d'Ivoire?

A core claim of this book is that wartime practices of rebel rule shape postwar politics by determining whether commander-community ties endure or decline after war's end and, in turn, whether ex-rebel commanders who integrate into state militaries possess the capacity and motive to resist central regime leaders. But to know if rebel rule really matters for these postwar outcomes, it is important to consider whether the quality of wartime governance in Côte d'Ivoire was itself endogenous to other characteristics of rebel-controlled localities. We need to know whether rebel rule varied systematically as a function of conditions that could also explain commanders' postwar local ties and incentives for resistance. In particular, we might suspect that when rebels govern in areas that are initially sympathetic to an insurgency, they will choose to invest in civilian welfare out of an affinity for the local population (and less politically sympathetic communities may be treated more harshly). Such "rebel-friendly" areas may also be more likely to sustain strong ties to ex-rebel commanders in the postwar period, independently of rebels' actual wartime governance performance.

I conduct a series of pairwise tests to examine whether practices of wartime rebel rule correlated with any fixed or prewar characteristics of my sampled localities, drawing on data from the community informant survey and the 2002 ENV household survey. These tests and full variable descriptions appear in the appendix. To proxy for pro-rebel sympathies, I measure the percentage of households within each subprefecture that self-identify as belonging to a *nordiste* ethnic group (north Mande or Voltaic/Senoufo). Given the high political salience of ethnicity in Côte d'Ivoire since the mid-1990s, I consider nordiste ethnic share to be the best available measure of likely prewar political support for the FN at the time of rebel arrival.[89] I also coded whether the local FN commander was a native resident of the subprefecture or department to capture kinship ties.[90] To account for the availability of resources, I examine the population size of subprefectures, the presence of a paved road leading to the subprefecture capital, and the presence of a diamond- or gold-mining site. Armed competition is proxied with the distance of the subprefecture to the cease-fire zone border and whether armed combat between rebel and government forces occurred in the locality in the fall of 2002. Finally, I account for the strength of local "social capital" within each subprefecture using questions on the 2002 ENV survey that pertained to households' prosocial behaviors and trust in other community members.

I find that areas of collaborative and predatory rebel rule in northern Côte d'Ivoire appear to have differed little in terms of most of these characteristics. Using the *Collaborative rule* scale to create bins, I categorize localities with scores of −1 or 0 as areas of predatory rule and localities with scores of 1 or 2 as areas of collaborative rule. Using two sample t-tests, I observe no statistically significant differences in sample means between the bins for measures of nordiste ethnicity, the presence of a mining site, distance to the cease-fire line, prewar social capital, paved roads, or government-rebel combat. I do find that localities with larger populations were somewhat more likely to experience collaborative rule, as were areas where local FN field commanders hailed from the region ($p < 0.05$). This is not surprising; more developed population centers in the north likely provided larger governance dividends for the FN in terms of potential recruitment and tax revenues, and commanders with kinship ties to their areas of control may have felt stronger social pressures to respond to local civilian needs. Yet even these covariates provide an underwhelming amount of predictive power. Localities at every level of the *Collaborative rule* index can be found across each quartile of population size, indicating that development levels did not predetermine rebel rule practices. And while localities where field commanders had existing kinship ties were more likely to experience collaborative rule, only a small proportion of localities in the sample (11 percent) had such a "native" field commander. Most FN commanders were assigned from elsewhere, a fact that reflects a deliberate—if only partly effective—strategy by FN political leaders to try to limit the local embeddedness of their field commanders.

These patterns of rebel rule in Côte d'Ivoire may appear surprising, particularly given scholarly claims about the role of armed competition and natural resources in determining wartime governance. What explains this apparent discrepancy? A partial answer has already been hinted at. The fact that the FN zone was cleanly separated from government military forces by French and UN peacekeeping troops meant that almost *all* FN territory was relatively secure from government counterattack for most of the war. Thus, even in frontline zones where government-rebel combat was more intense in the opening phases of the conflict, FN rebels could eventually adopt longer time horizons and invest in institution building. There were a few exceptions to this pattern, such as the rebel capital of Bouaké, where government counterattack did remain a consistent threat. The case of Bouaké is discussed in depth in chapter 5.

As for the resource curse argument, it is worth noting that natural resources never constituted the primary source of FN funding. The FN successfully captured several resource-rich regions in central and western Côte d'Ivoire and generated revenue from gold, coffee, and timber exports.[91] Yet these revenues were never large enough to sustain the expenses of the FN's combined military and political operations. Supplementary revenues derived from the local population, particularly taxes levied at road checkpoints and high-volume trading markets, were critical sources of financing for middle- and lower-ranking commanders and soldiers.[92] Indeed, the key mechanism of the "rentierism" argument—that easily lootable resources reduce the need for taxation of civilians—is not supported by the evidence; a simple linear regression reveals no significant correlation between the presence of a mining site and FN taxation. The FN were neither fiscally independent of the population they governed nor completely reliant on it.

One factor that likely *did* shape the quality of governance under the FN was the existence of a strong local elite willing to collaborate with rebel rulers.[93] Given the scarcity of prewar indicators of subnational social structure in Côte d'Ivoire, this variable is admittedly difficult to capture in quantitative datasets. Yet, as discussed in chapter 1, even if strong prewar elites increased the probability that collaborative rule emerged under the FN, this need not detract from the independent significance of those governance arrangements. Traditional authorities and family heads in northern and western Côte d'Ivoire have long acted as intermediaries between local populations and central state authorities. These elites have tended to ally themselves with government elites from the south in exchange for state recognition of their customary prerogatives, both historically and under the Ouattara regime.[94] Thus, the presence of strong local elites is not likely, by itself, to drive postwar resistance to the central regime. What matters is whether the collaborative governance practices enabled by strong local elites caused FN zone and sector commanders to become locally embedded.

Put together, several features of the FN's wartime environment—low armed competition, local elites of varied strength and willingness to collaborate, partial resource dependency on civilians, and the decentralized nature of the rebel regime itself—created space for wide-ranging variation in local governance practices. Moving forward, I treat this variation as a useful analytical starting point for understanding subsequent trajectories of commander embeddedness after the war-to-peace transition in 2011. I do so fully aware that I cannot rule out the possibility that other unobserved characteristics of communities in northern Côte d'Ivoire affected rebels' governance behaviors. Nor do the tests discussed thus far imply that patterns of rebel rule could not have been affected by the choices of FN leaders to deploy certain commanders and units to particular areas. Nonetheless, the fact that local patterns of rebel governance in Côte d'Ivoire are not easily explained by geographic, demographic, or socioeconomic conditions makes it more likely that—after adjusting for development levels—any observed links between wartime rebel rule, postwar commander-community ties, and ex-rebel commander resistance can be plausibly interpreted in terms of the explanatory logic of my theory.

This chapter has established the historical and empirical foundations for the rest of this book's analysis of the impacts of rebel rule on ex-rebel commanders' local embeddedness and resistance to the postwar state in Côte d'Ivoire. Armed rebellion in Côte d'Ivoire emerged in the early 2000s as a response to widespread perceptions of exclusion among ethnic northerners and the inability of the Gbagbo regime to credibly commit to sharing power with northerners who possessed a foothold in the armed forces. Weak counterinsurgency pressure created an environment in which FN rebels could build a quasi-state-like system of civilian governance. With a high degree of organizational decentralization and confronted with local elites of mixed strength and willingness to collaborate with rebel occupiers, FN rule generated social order to varying degrees across localities. These differences in rebel rule practices were at best weakly correlated with the prewar socioeconomic and geographic characteristics of communities. Whether a community in northern Côte d'Ivoire experienced collaborative or predatory rule under the FN was simply difficult to predict in advance. In the next chapter, I turn to the postwar transition and examine how these wartime governance practices shaped the local ties and political resources that FN field commanders carried with them as they integrated into the state.

CHAPTER 3

Commander Embeddedness in Postwar Côte d'Ivoire (2011–2017)

In Sangouiné, not far from the Liberian border, everybody knows Kassero. The commandant is building a new hotel at the west end of town. Villagers say they are proud of the hotel; they hope it will help put Sangouiné on the map. Even though Kassero is a *nordiste*—a Senoufo from Korhogo—the village chief still calls him a *fils du village*. If there is a death in an important family, Kassero is likely to help pay for the funeral. If there is a problem between residents and the *coupeurs de route* or members of the local gendarmes outpost, Kassero is called to advise on the situation. When Kassero visits, he greets the village chief and his *notables* as a gesture of respect. "When you do good for people, for the community," one resident explained, "the people will hold you in their heart, they will not cross their arms for you."[1] This certainly seems true. Kassero built his hotel on a plot of land that was given to him by the mayor himself. Several of his fellow comrades from the Forces Armées des Forces Nouvelles (FAFN) rebel army have also stuck around in the town. On a day I visited the hotel construction site in 2017, I met several ex-FN members at work unloading trucks and pouring concrete in the blazing afternoon sun. Though Kassero himself—now an army captain in the Forces Républicaines de Côte d'Ivoire (FRCI)—no longer lives in the region and has not called himself *commandant de secteur* in Sangouiné in over seven years, it is difficult to imagine life in the town without him.

Less than thirty kilometers west, along the pothole-filled road to Danané, is the town of Mahapleu. Mahapleu is slightly larger than Sangouiné, but on first impression, a visitor could easily mistake one for the other. Like Sangouiné, Mahapleu is a predominantly Yacouba-speaking community with small pockets of Malinke, Senoufo, and Guineans. Unlike in its neighbor to the east, however, in Mahapleu, the former FN commander—an army captain named Ondo—is rarely seen today. Ondo once ruled Mahapleu as his personal fiefdom. Like Kassero, Ondo was an ethnic nordiste and

CHAPTER 3

a stranger to the community at the beginning of the war. Yet after Ondo integrated into the FRCI after 2011, his ties to Mahapleu all but vanished. Nobody can recall the last time Ondo came to greet the village chief. Residents balk at the idea that Ondo would be invited to weddings or funerals. Village leaders turn to the local *préfet*, not the former FN sector commander, to address security problems. As one resident of Mahapleu remarked: "He [Ondo] did nothing for us here. He has no more power. If he came, the population would not welcome him."[2]

The anecdotes of Sangouiné and Mahapleu—two villages that are discussed in greater depth in chapter 5—illustrate concretely how ex-rebel commanders vary in the extent to which they remain embedded in rebel-controlled communities after integrating into the postconflict state. In Sangouiné, FN rule was characterized by goods provision, power sharing with local elites, institutionalized practices of rebel-civilian dialogue, and restraints on civilian abuses. As a result, Kassero maintained significant social support in the community, his links to latent mobilization networks remained rooted in place after his promotion into the FRCI, and he retained status as a legitimate "fixer" for local security issues. In places like Mahapleu, by contrast, where FN rebels failed to deliver basic services or develop mechanisms to restrain civilian abuses, commander-community ties withered away after rebel-military integration. After Ondo took an FRCI post in the nearby town of Dabakala, his connections to both community leaders and local FN sympathizers in Mahapleu became little more than a memory.

This chapter traces a key step in this book's argument: the link between wartime insurgent governance and field commanders' postwar embeddedness in rebel-ruled communities. Leveraging the quantitative data on rebel rule introduced in the previous chapter and novel measures of postwar commander-community ties, I present a locality-level statistical analysis to show that ex-rebel commanders who presided over areas of collaborative rebel rule were better positioned to sustain mobilization power and local legitimacy after the demobilization of the FN rebel organization in 2011. These commanders preserved control over the means of violence in Côte d'Ivoire's rural hinterlands. By contrast, in areas where FN rule was more predatory during the civil war, ex-rebel commanders were less likely to maintain ties to mobilization-ready networks after relocating away from their areas of wartime control. Consistent with H1, I show that field commanders in Côte d'Ivoire did not operate from a tabula rasa as postwar peacebuilding began after 2011. Rather, field commanders' chances of remaining locally embedded in rebel-ruled communities were shaped by earlier practices of wartime governance.

The chapter proceeds as follows. First, I discuss the context of rebel-military integration at the end of the Ivorian civil war. Second, I describe and conceptualize two elements of FN commanders' local embeddedness in the postwar period: mobilization power and legitimacy. Third, I present quantitative evidence at the locality level that shows a strong link between wartime insurgent governance practices and postwar commander embeddedness. Finally, I consider evidence for the causal mechanisms of my theory using both locality and individual survey data.

At War's End: Gbagbo's Defeat and the Rebel-Military Transition

After years of stalemate and stalled peace talks, an election crisis in the fall of 2010 triggered the end of the Ivorian civil war.[3] In the second round of the presidential ballot on November 28, Alassane Ouattara and the Rassemblement des Républicains (RDR) party—backed by the FN—carried the election with nearly 2.5 million votes to Laurent Gbagbo's 2.1 million.[4] Gbagbo and his stalwart Front Populaire Ivoirien (FPI) supporters, however, refused to cede power, alleging "blatant irregularities" at polling stations in departments occupied by FN forces.[5] Under the direction of a chair appointed by Gbagbo, the Constitutional Council upheld the Gbagbo camp's appeal, discarded the contested votes, and pronounced Gbagbo the winner.[6] On December 4, while Ouattara took the presidential oath of office from his party headquarters at the Golf Hotel in Abidjan, Gbagbo staged his own swearing-in ceremony at the Presidential Residence.

The proclamation of two different presidents shattered Côte d'Ivoire's uneasy stalemate. Pro-Gbagbo militias stepped up violent harassment of Ouattara supporters at rallies and in the nordiste-dominated suburbs of Abidjan.[7] In the Far West, rebel troops launched a new offensive to break through the buffer zone and carried out reprisal killings against members of the pro-Gbagbo Guéré and Wê ethnic groups.[8] Rebel units infiltrated the northern suburbs of Abidjan to carry out urban guerrilla warfare against the government.[9] On March 17, 2011, Alassane Ouattara announced the creation of the FRCI under his command. The FRCI was a rebranding of the FN rebel army already fighting for Ouattara, together with a handful of defecting Forces Armées Nationales de Côte d'Ivoire (FANCI) elements.[10] On March 28, FRCI units swept south toward the capital using a pincer movement to envelope the remaining pro-Gbagbo forces. Resistance to the advancing rebel columns crumbled, and hard-core government loyalists retreated to defend Abidjan. With support from UN and French peacekeeping forces—now openly siding with Ouattara—FRCI soldiers encircled and captured Gbagbo at the Presidential Residence on April 11.[11] On May 4, the Constitutional Council affirmed Ouattara as president. The FN chief Guillaume Soro was installed as prime minister and minister of defense. After nine years, the Ivorian civil war was over.

To many observers at the time, the Ouattara-Soro coalition government seemed poised to rebuild the country's institutions from a position of strength. The new regime's enemies were defeated or in exile, and the FN-turned-FRCI was the only capable fighting force left standing.[12] Government leaders made explicit comparisons to postgenocide Rwanda, stating that rebel-military integration in Côte d'Ivoire was an opportunity to replicate the success of Paul Kagame's government by promoting rapid postwar economic growth backed up by a strong military.[13] Top commanders in the FRCI pledged their loyalty to the new government. The new army chief, Soumaïla Bakayoko, the former FAFN *chef d'état majeure*, was viewed as a staunch Ouattara supporter.[14] Other senior FAFN commanders—including Tuo Fozié, Issiaka Ouattara ("Wattao"), and Chérif Ousmane—assumed control of the most sensitive security positions, including the elite Special Forces and Republican Guard. In a signal of the FN's support for the new government, Soro announced at a meeting in August 2011 that the FN would not continue as an independent organization, but rather its political leaders would merge into Ouattara's existing RDR party.[15] Internationally, the new Ivorian government also enjoyed strong backing. France and the United States welcomed the removal of Gbagbo as a chance to return Côte d'Ivoire to the control of a Western-friendly government.[16] Western donors extended aid to restore economic infrastructure and unfreeze lines of credit to the government and invested resources to modernize, equip, and train the new national army.[17]

Yet these outward signals of stability masked a slew of serious challenges. Ouattara's political coalition was beset by internal divisions.[18] While quick to declare the war over, civilian leaders in Abidjan had little direct control over the security situation in much of the country. Towns and rural areas alike teemed with young men with guns, most of whom were primarily loyal to their local commanders—who continued to provide resources, food, and shelter for subordinates—or to community-based self-defense groups that proliferated since 2002. This mélange of fighters included approximately 75,000 ex-combatants in the northern, central, and western regions who identified themselves as belonging to the FN/FRCI or pro-rebel militias. Thousands more former FANCI and village defense militia members with varying loyalties were scattered around the country.[19]

Facing a fragmented security sphere, government elites in Abidjan were dependent on the continued support of ex-FN commanders to restore central state authority beyond a handful of urban enclaves. Former FN zone and sector commanders, however, also perceived themselves to be in a precarious position. While Outtara indicated his support for the insertion of more former FN rebels into the Ivorian military in the summer of 2011, the timeline and specifics of rebel-military integration remained murky. FN soldiers at all ranks reasoned that they had made the biggest contribution to the military victory against the Gbagbo regime and therefore deserved to make up the lion's share of the country's new army.[20] But the FRCI, now under the authority of the Defense Ministry, lacked the capacity to absorb all of these combatants at once. To make matters worse, Ouattara had decreed in May 2011 that former FANCI members who had remained loyal to Gbagbo would also be eligible for military insertion, a step that Ouattara believed necessary to legitimize his regime and avoid future war.[21] Rumors circulated within ex-FN gossip networks that the few available military positions were unfairly going to the much-hated Gbagboïste officer corps.[22] On June 24, the Defense Ministry promised that it intended to integrate up to eleven thousand former FN rebels into the FRCI but then cautioned that this was only a long-term goal.[23] As the months ticked by into the summer in 2011, the Defense Ministry offered few specifics about when the integration of ex-rebel fighters would happen. Eager to reunify the state administration across the nation's territory and with no concrete plan yet in place to integrate remaining ex-FN forces, in July 2011, the Ouattara government called for the immediate demobilization of all militia and ex-rebel forces not already integrated into the FRCI.[24]

Ex-FN commanders were thus left in the uncomfortable position of being asked to dismantle their wartime armed networks without credible commitments from the regime about their future roles or the status of their subordinates. Adding even more uncertainty, the Ouattara regime faced pressure to open criminal investigations of wartime atrocities by FN/FRCI forces. In November 2011, Gbagbo was indicted by the International Criminal Court (ICC) for alleged war crimes during the 2010/2011 crisis and was transferred to The Hague. Wishing to present himself as an even-handed liberal democrat rather than as a military conqueror, Ouattara faced "a phalanx of criticism from international human rights organizations, donor states, and domestic civil society to avoid one sided justice."[25] To reduce the perception of impunity within the FRCI, Ouattara stood beside an ICC investigator in June 2011 and pledged that *"all* those responsible for crimes will be punished [emphasis added]."[26] This statement led ex-FN commanders to fear that the government might permit ICC investigations into former rebel officers linked to atrocities and human rights abuses.[27] Commanders with spotty human rights records had the most cause for worry.[28]

Côte d'Ivoire's postwar transition thus closely resembles the framework of rebel-military integration amid weak state institutions outlined in chapter 1. Regime stability and centralized statebuilding depend on precarious informal bargains between capital-based leaders and specialists in violence from the integrating armed group. Ex-rebel commanders in Côte d'Ivoire saw themselves—correctly—as one faction among many in a competition to claim the spoils of war and feared that regime leaders might exclude their former military allies at some point in the future.[29] But many ex-FN commanders had a powerful card to play: the ability to manage violence on behalf of capital-based leaders, particularly in peripheral spaces and social milieus in which postwar state institutions had limited penetration. The next section discusses these enduring commander-community ties in greater depth.

Postwar Commander Embeddedness in Côte d'Ivoire

The quality of ex-FN commanders' local ties to rebel-ruled communities in the north shaped the bargaining position of commanders during the rebel-military integration process. First, commanders gained leverage from their autonomous mobilization power—that is, their capacity to control and mobilize armed fighters outside of the formal security apparatus. While the Ouattara regime had ordered nonintegrated FN fighters to demobilize in the summer of 2011, thousands of ex-combatants remained connected to their wartime units outside of the official military structure. Some of these fighters took control of urban zones in Abidjan and tapped into new lucrative opportunities for racketeering and extortion in the capital. The bulk of ex-rebel combatants, however, remained rooted in their former wartime zones of operation in the north, where they exploited any economic opportunities that could be found, legal or otherwise.[30] Armed men and youth in combat fatigues calling themselves ex-FAFN continued to operate checkpoints to extract tolls and bribes; others became guards or enforcers for commercial businesses that controlled illicit markets in gold, coffee, and timber. Still others became outright brigands (coupeurs de route) who terrorized roads through violent robberies. Put together, these irregular armed networks formed a universe of fighters larger than the FRCI itself. Ex-FN commanders with a demonstrated capacity to exert control over these networks could present themselves as valuable allies of the central regime—and dangerous enemies.

Second, beyond their capacity to control fighters, many ex-FN commanders retained local legitimacy as informal guarantors of social order in hard-to-govern areas of the country. Though the regular police, gendarmerie, and prefectoral corps returned to northern Côte d'Ivoire after Gbagbo's defeat in 2011, these institutions remained distrusted by many civilians and local elites in former rebel-held territory.[31] In many areas, civilians looked instead to former FN zone and sector commanders to continue providing critical services—most importantly, protection against banditry. Ex-rebel commanders with support from local traditional leaders and strong ties to local armed networks could act as informal security "consultants," for example by ensuring that the extortionary activities of area ex-combatants did not exceed certain thresholds or by mediating disputes between ex-FN fighters and local civilians. By performing such duties, ex-FN commanders acted as valuable subcontractors of order for the central government in Abidjan.

The northern town of Katiola—which I visited in 2017—offers an illustration of these dimensions of postwar commander embeddedness. During the war, the local FN zone commander Herve Touré (alias "Vetcho") cultivated a reputation as an effective wartime governor and crime fighter, bolstering his grassroots social support. "Things changed when Vetcho arrived," one resident recalled. "He could see the needs of people here and explain to them the political goals that they [the rebels] were fighting for. Most of all he restored security, a sense of safety."[32] Vetcho's reputation for effective governance planted the seed for his enduring influence in Katiola after he was promoted to the Agence Nationale de Stratégie et d'Intelligence in Abidjan in 2011. Vetcho leveraged his enduring grassroots social support and alliances with local elites to maintain contact with militia members. Working through an alliance with the local Tagbana chieftaincy, Vetcho continued to visit Katiola in a private capacity to meet with area leaders, attend social ceremonies, and extend his patronage resources—including jobs, pocket money, and bags of rice and sugar—to local youth and ex-combatants.[33] "Vetcho still comes all the time," the deputy mayor said. "He still has a lot of influence. He comes to all the major cultural events, and he gives support to the population."[34] Another resident made clear that Vetcho's local ties extended to influence over combatant networks: "Many former FN are still in contact with Vetcho. . . . DDR was pretty pitiful, so he [Vetcho] and his *proches* take care of many ex-combatants here."[35] These types of social visits and informal interactions provided ex-FN officers like Vetcho with ample opportunity to regenerate wartime ties, keep tabs on local fighters, and identify new potential supporters. Katiola also illustrates the importance of commander-community ties for the preservation of commanders' status as legitimate guarantors of social order. When the road axis linking Katiola to Bouaké became a target of local coupeurs de route after 2011, Vetcho was called upon frequently to intervene.[36] "He remained very approachable," said one traditional leader. "Everyone could call him if there were problems."[37]

Commanders like Vetcho—strongly embedded in their wartime zones of control—enjoyed relative immunity from threats of legal prosecution in the early postwar years. The Ouattara-Soro government could not afford to rock the boat by upsetting these rebels-turned-officers with such deep support bases. Yet not all ex-rebel commanders were so embedded. Some FN commanders, once promoted to positions in the south, found it hard to monitor former combatant networks in their wartime zones of control. In places like Mahapleu and many neighborhoods of Bouaké, former combatants lost contact with their old wartime commanders and drifted away from ex-FN networks as the postconflict transition progressed. Indeed, a central goal of security-sector reform—including the national disarmament, demobilization, and reintegration program administered between 2012 and 2015—was to break the links between ex-FN combatants and their former commanders and to restore regular policing institutions across former rebel-ruled territory in the north. As one UN security adviser put it, the central question for the Ouattara government was "how to reduce their [ex-FN commanders'] influence without threatening the security of the state.... You can't just cut the branches."[38]

Why did some ex-FN commanders remain closely embedded in their former zones of control, with mobilization capacity and legitimacy as guarantors of order, while others did not? To explain this variation in commander embeddedness after the initiation of the rebel-military integration process and explain why some commanders remained powerful enough to eventually resist the central regime openly, we must look to the wartime legacies of rebel rule.

Rebel Rule and Postwar Commander Embeddedness

This section examines the impact of wartime governance practices on FN commanders' maintenance of mobilization capacity and local legitimacy after the 2011 transition. If this book's argument is right, we should expect commanders from zones of collaborative rebel rule—such as Sangouiné and Katiola—to retain strong social and political ties to communities in their former zones of control, granting them access to high-quality information about local social networks and the identities of potential supporters. In localities that experienced predatory rebel rule—such as Mahapleu—we should expect commander-community ties to weaken after rebel-military integration.

OUTCOME VARIABLE: POSTWAR COMMANDER EMBEDDEDNESS

Measuring ex-rebel commander embeddedness within formerly occupied communities poses a significant challenge. Some linkages—such as commanders' ties to irregular armed fighters or illicit businesses—are clandestine and cannot always be observed even by knowledgeable and honest informants. My community informant survey therefore focused on readily observable indicators of ex-commanders' social, political, and economic presence between the official demobilization of the FN organization in 2011 and the time of the survey in 2017. While indirect, these indicators provide important information about ex-rebel commanders' abilities to contact, recruit, and control potential supporters within the locality as well as their status as legitimate guarantors of social order.

First, I measured whether former FN commanders continued to make regular visits to the community in a private capacity in the first six years of the postwar transition (*Commander visits*). The purpose of these visits ranged from attending ceremonial events (such as marriages, funerals, and religious celebrations), to visiting the homes of customary authorities, to bringing donations to local development projects such as schools, health clinics, or mosques. In the context of Ivorian social and political life, these kinds of face-to-face visits and gift-giving practices are an essential indicator of one's local political capital, depth of mobilization power, and quality of alliances. In over half (54 percent) of the localities in the sample, the ex-FN commander who governed the community during the civil war continued to make such visits in the post-2011 period.

Second, among localities that received such private visits from ex-rebel commanders, I measured whether commanders were known to provide material support in the form of spending money, food, or jobs to former combatants, armed supporters, or youth in the community (*Material support*). Though such meager resources may not be sufficient to meet the basic needs of all the supporters in an ex-rebel commander's network, these resource flows play an important role in sustaining the dependency and loyalty of former combatants to their ex-military leaders amid challenging postwar economic circumstances and therefore preserving the mobilization power of commanders.[39] Ex-FN commanders provided these forms of postwar material support in approximately one-quarter (27 percent) of surveyed localities.

To measure ex-rebel commanders' legitimacy in the community, I first assessed whether local elites continued to call on the former FN commander to help resolve problems of criminality and public order after the 2011 transition (*Provides order*). For instance, in some areas, traditional authorities considered the FN commander as an "adviser" who could be relied on to address disciplinary issues with local ex-combatants or seek compensation for victims in the case of theft at the hands of former rebel members. Informants in over a third of localities (39 percent) indicated that ex-FN occupied such an informal role. Second, I measured whether the former FN commander held a formal position of authority in the community, such as that of legislative deputy, mayor, deputy mayor, prefect, or other bureaucratic post (*Political position*). A majority of sampled localities (58 percent) saw ex-FN commanders occupy such positions.

For the main analyses presented here, I combine the indicators in table 3.1 into a single summary index, *Postwar commander influence*. This index ranges from 0 to 4 and receives one point each for *Commander visits*, *Material support*, *Provides order*, and *Political position*.

EXPLANATORY VARIABLES

To test the argument that collaborative (predatory) rebel rule predicts strong (weak) postwar commander-community ties, I assess several indicators of collaborative wartime rule. First, I analyze *Collaborative rule*, the in-

Table 3.1. Postwar commander influence in Côte d'Ivoire (2011–2017)

Mobilization power	
Commander visits community	54%
Material support to ex-combatants/youth	27%
Local legitimacy	
Provides order	39%
Political position	58%

dex of rebel rule described in chapter 2. As an alternative measure, I also construct an index of civilian services, *Rebel goods provision*, which ranges from 0 to 6 and scores a point for each of the following goods provided by the FN: protection from external attack, local dispute resolution and justice, health care, education, infrastructure, and private loans. Finally, I analyze the variable *Organized meetings*, a binary indicator of whether FN rebels organized regular meetings with civilians.

To address alternative theoretical accounts of postwar commander-community ties, I also measure a host of additional variables. First, I measure rebels' wartime coercion against civilians. Several accounts of politics and insurgency in weak states argue that armed groups and warlords establish authority through means of coercion and violent intimidation.[40] Whereas my theory expects such abusive practices to reduce the willingness of civilians to sustain ties with commanders, the inverse could be true: commanders might be better understood as violence entrepreneurs whose power hinges on a demonstrated capacity to apply deadly force. Local civilians may be psychologically intimidated or resign themselves to accepting ex-commanders as the only actors capable of restoring security. Commanders' reputations for violence could also deter other local elites from challenging their positions. To account for this possibility, I use several indicators from the survey related to wartime violence, summarized in the ordinal variable *Coercion*.[41]

A related set of arguments depict territorial rebel groups like the FN as extraction-maximizing organizations that prey upon occupied populations for their own self-enrichment.[42] Seen from this perspective, rebel commanders' incentives to establish long-term control in a locality ought to be driven largely by the availability of natural resources that can be exploited for personal profits. Such revenues may also expand commanders' patronage power, further entrenching them in the local political economy. If so, localities with abundant lootable resources (especially mineral resources) should be more likely to attract sustained attention from ex-rebel commanders who seek to continue capturing economic rents in peacetime. To test this rent-seeking hypothesis, I control for *Mining site*, indicating whether there is gold or diamond mining in the subprefecture.

Kinship-based ties may also be important elements of rebels' grassroots infrastructure. Familial ties can facilitate trust, information sharing, and the expectation of continued interactions.[43] Ex-rebel commanders who share kinship or familial bonds with formerly occupied populations may be embedded in strong social and tribal networks and therefore will be more likely to sustain strong postwar ties compared to commanders who governed outside of their home areas. I therefore control for whether the commander was a native resident of the department (*Commander native*).[44]

Preexisting political cleavages among occupied populations could also affect the strength of commander-community ties after war. Partisan identification with occupying armed groups may bias civilians' assessments of commanders in a favorable direction, encouraging trust building and rapport. By contrast, where prewar cleavages favor the government, rebel commanders may be unable to establish political capital and sustain mobilization power in peacetime. To account for prewar cleavages, I constructed a dummy variable for whether the primary ethnic group within the locality is Malinke or Voltaic/Senoufo (*Ethnicity northern*). These ethnic groups were generally viewed as the political support base for the FN, and almost all FN commanders were themselves of northern origin.

Initial analyses discussed in chapter 2 revealed that practices of rebel rule in Côte d'Ivoire were correlated with local development levels. I therefore account for the accessibility of localities and the size of potential recruitment networks by controlling for logged population size and whether the locality is accessible by a paved road. To account for the strategic importance of the territory, I include binary indicators for whether armed combat between organized military forces occurred in the locality and whether the FN recruited fighters during the civil war. Finally, all analyses include department-level fixed effects to account for potential spatial dependence among neighboring localities.

A FIRST CUT AT THE EVIDENCE: THE CORRELATES OF POSTWAR COMMANDER INFLUENCE

My argument anticipates that wartime governance practices during civil wars will shape whether ex-rebel commanders maintain strong local linkages after integrating into national armies. If this theory is correct, ex-rebel commanders' local ties should be strongest in areas where insurgents responded to citizen interests by providing goods and services and institutionalizing mechanisms of rebel-civilian dialogue. On first inspection of a simple scatterplot, there indeed appears to be a clear link between *Collaborative rule* and *Postwar commander influence*. Figure 3.1 shows that rebel-ruled localities in Côte d'Ivoire that experienced collaborative rebel rule between 2002 and 2011 also tended to have stronger postwar ties with FN

CHAPTER 3

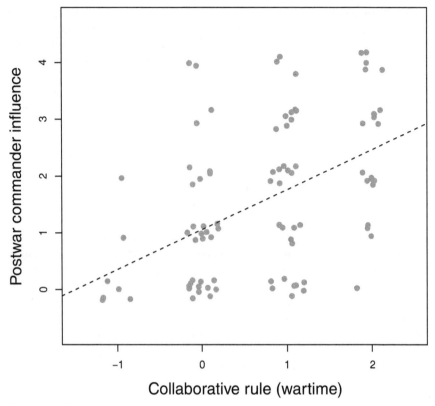

Fig. 3.1. Wartime rebel rule and postwar commander influence in sampled subprefectures

field commanders. While this correlation must be interpreted cautiously, it provides encouraging support for a key step in this book's argument.

Does this link stand up to more rigorous statistical scrutiny? Results from a battery of linear regression analyses confirm that FN investment in collaborative wartime governance increases the likelihood of strong postwar commander-community ties, even when a host of potential confounding variables are controlled for. For ease of presentation, I eschew lengthy regression tables in favor of the confidence interval plot displayed in figure 3.2. The plot shows that a one-unit increase in the variable *Collaborative rule* is associated with an average increase in *Postwar commander influence* of 0.66. The chances that this relationship is a random statistical fluke are less than one in a thousand ($p < 0.001$). These findings thus bear out H1: where practices of collaborative rebel rule existed, field commanders are much better positioned to preserve mobilization power and legitimacy after integrating into the postwar military.

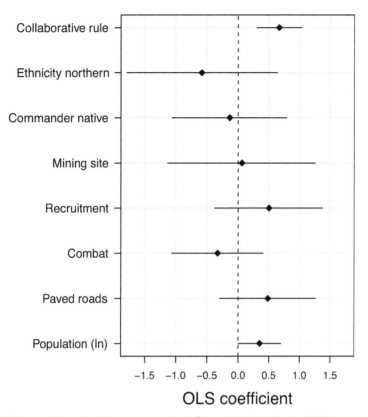

Fig. 3.2. The correlates of postwar commander influence in Côte d'Ivoire (OLS)
Note: Lines show 95 percent confidence intervals.

Alternative explanations perform relatively poorly. There is no apparent association between *Mining site* and *Postwar commander influence*. The coefficients for *Commander native* and *Ethnicity northern* are also negative and statistically insignificant, suggesting that neither personal kinship ties nor prewar social cleavages and ethnicity outweigh the impact of rebels' wartime governance practices. Commanders in localities that experienced *Combat* appear less likely to sustain postwar mobilization power or status, though these links fall short of statistical significance. In fact, outside of rebels' wartime governance practices, only *Population (ln)* appears as a positive predictor of postwar commander influence.

ROBUSTNESS CHECKS

I conducted a battery of supplementary analyses to scrutinize the robustness of the link between wartime rebel rule and postwar commander-community ties. Full results are available in the appendix. First, I employed alternative measures of wartime rule. Both *Rebel goods provision* and *Organized meetings* are positive and significant predictors of *Postwar commander influence* at the 95 percent confidence level (table A.4). *Coercion* is negatively associated with *Postwar commander influence*, though the coefficient is not statistically significant. Second, to verify that the results are robust to other potential omitted variables and alternative data sources, I introduced a series of additional controls. Using the baseline linear regression model in figure 3.2, I added controls for alternative measures of ethnic demography, measures of household poverty from the 2008 ENV survey, and distance from the cease-fire boundary. To ensure the findings are not sensitive to covariates measured on the same survey instrument as the outcome variable, I used independently collected data from a 2018 US Agency for International Development (USAID) commissioned survey of Ivorian citizens to control for department-level rates of rebel taxation and local support for the FN. Across all models, the key findings are upheld (table A.4). The inclusion of additional controls from alternative data sources does not substantially change the relationship between collaborative rule and postwar commander influence in former rebel-ruled localities.

Third, I break down the dependent variable, *Postwar commander influence*, and analyze each measure of commanders' postwar mobilization capacity and legitimacy separately. To do so, I constructed the binary indicator *Mobilization power*, which takes a value of 1 if *Commander visits* or *Material support* are present and 0 otherwise. I constructed a similar indicator for *Local legitimacy* based on the measures *Provides order* and *Political position*. I find that the estimated effects of collaborative rule on both outcomes are directionally similar (table A.5), though the coefficients in the models estimating *Mobilization power* are larger and more precisely estimated than the coefficients in the models estimating *Local legitimacy*.

Finally, I return to the issue of endogeneity. It is important to recall that, as noted in chapter 2, collaborative wartime governance under the FN was not predicted by factors such as favorable ethnic demography. Thus, while one might assume that collaborative governance only occurs in areas where preexisting political sentiments were already favorable to rebel commanders, this appears not to be the case in Côte d'Ivoire. If anything, FN rebels appeared to invest in collaborative rule in *non*-coethnic areas with equal or even greater frequency (perhaps because local support for the FN in these areas was more contingent on rebels' governance performance). Nonetheless, one might remain concerned about other unobserved factors that could explain initial selection of rebel governance type. To address potential bias stemming from unobservables, I conduct two additional checks. First, I use two-stage Heckman probit models to estimate the effects of the binary variable *Organized meetings* (table A.6). This analysis explicitly accounts for the initial selection probability of wartime governance type in a first-stage selection equation and then uses the transformed predicted values to estimate *Postwar commander influence* in the second stage.[45] In the selection equations, I include variables that are plausibly linked to postwar commander influence only through their impact on the FN's wartime governance, including government-rebel armed combat and distance to the cease-fire zone.[46] Second, I use propensity score matching to compare subsets of highly similar subprefectures that vary in terms of their scores on *Collaborative rule*, relying on the preprocessing step to account for potential bias from a large number of observables (table A.7). I use coarsened exact matching to cull the data to highly comparable localities with similar propensity for treatment that are fully balanced on *Paved road*, *Combat*, *Ethnicity northern*, *Commander native*, and *Mining site* (figure A.1). I also run nearest neighbor and genetic matching models that include covariates for population size, infrastructure, and recruitment. The substantive findings remain unchanged in all checks; measures of collaborative wartime rebel rule consistently have a positive and statistically significant association with measures of postwar commander influence.

Of course, these tests cannot account for all possible sources of bias. Notably, due to data constraints, the statistical tests in this chapter do not directly account for the strength of prewar local elites. As with all research conducted in postconflict contexts, the findings reported here should be interpreted with healthy caution. Nonetheless, practices of rebel rule in Côte d'Ivoire do appear to exert an important effect on postwar commander embeddedness, even after accounting for many sources of potential confounding.

Probing the Mechanism of Social Support

The analyses presented to this point corroborate H1 insofar as they demonstrate that wartime insurgent governance and postwar commander-community ties covary at the locality level in the direction expected by this book's theory. What about the intervening causal mechanisms? My theory posits that wartime governance affects commander embeddedness in part through the mechanism of social support: civilians who experience collaborative rebel rule should tend to view rebels and commanders in a more positive light and accord them heightened legitimacy in the community, while civilians in areas of predatory rule should exhibit more negative sentiments toward ex-rebel members. While the mechanisms of my argument are investigated further in the case studies presented in chapter 5, I conclude this chapter by considering two pieces of quantitative evidence at the locality and individual level.

First, it might be argued that the link between wartime governance and postwar commander-community ties is explained not by the mechanism of social support but rather by unobserved commander-specific attributes, such as commanders' personal ambition. Ambition could account for both wartime governance practices *and* commanders' willingness to expend effort to sustain local postwar ties. To assess this mechanism at the locality level, I code all observations in terms of commander rank (zone or sector commander), which may loosely proxy for the ambition of individual commanders. I find there is no significant association between commanders' rank and postwar commander-community ties (table A.4). Moreover, even after removing all subprefectures that were governed by an FN zone commander (com'zones)—the most powerful and well-connected FN field commanders, whose ambition might confound my argument—I find that *Collaborative rule* retains a positive and statistically significant association with *Postwar commander influence*. While the potential impact of unobserved commander attributes cannot be ruled out, these findings reinforce the idea that commander-community relationships in peacetime are likely to be shaped by the agency of civilian populations to reward or punish past governance performance.

Second, I examine the link between wartime rebel rule and social support for ex-rebel commanders directly, using survey data from a representative sample of nine hundred civilians in FN-controlled territory. The survey was designed and administered in 2018 by myself along with Jeremy Speight and Giulia Piccolino, in partnership with USAID Côte d'Ivoire and the Center for Research and Training for Integrated Development.[47] This survey covered ninety enumeration sites in former rebel zones (including different sites than those covered by the community informant survey) and included a battery of questions related to citizens' attitudes about governance and politics and to respondents' past wartime experiences and interactions with armed groups. I analyze several outcomes to gauge the local status of ex-FN field commanders in each survey site. Specifically, I assess respondents' perceptions about whether ex-rebel actors remained influential in their communities in terms of policing and order provision and their subjective attitudes about the local roles of ex-rebel commanders. I construct the variable *Ex-Rebels Influential Today* as a dichotomous variable that takes a value of 1 if respondents reported that they "agree" or "strongly agree" that former armed groups and their commanders remain influential in the policing and security sphere. The variable *Ex-Rebels Positive Today* takes a value of 1 if respondents agree that former armed groups and their commanders still play a positive role in the community.

As an indicator of wartime rebel governance quality, I construct the variable *Wartime Services Quality*. This ordinal variable receives a point for each of the following services that respondents indicated was present in their community during the 2002–2011 period under FN rule: order and crime prevention, health care, and education. To adjust for other socioeconomic characteristics of respondents, I include additional covariates for age, sex, religion, ethnicity, urban/rural, poverty, and education. Figure 3.3 displays the effect of increasing *Wartime Services Quality* on both outcomes using a binomial logistic regression model controlling for an array of covariates (see table A.8 for full results).

Consistent with the logic of my theory, there is a strong link between the quality of rebel rule and postwar civilian perceptions of ex-rebels. I find that *Wartime Services Quality* is a positive predictor of *Armed Groups Positive Today* at the 95 percent significance level. *Wartime Services Quality* is also positively associated with *Armed Groups Influential Today*, though the coefficient is not as precisely estimated. Notably, figure 3.3 also indicates that while effective governance improves postwar perceptions of ex-rebels, the base-

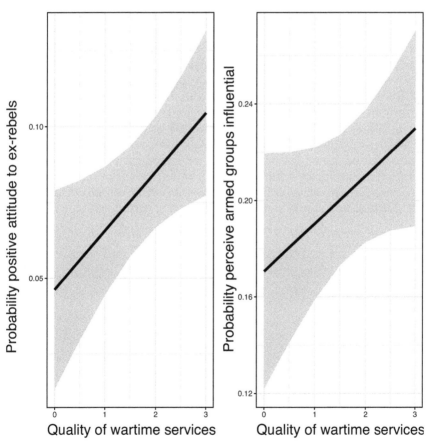

Fig. 3.3. Rebel rule and postwar civilian perceptions of ex-rebels
Note: Bars show 95 percent confidence intervals.

CHAPTER 3

line for positive attitudes toward ex-rebels is low. This is unsurprising, given that expressed attitudes about ex-rebels (or other armed actors) in Côte d'Ivoire are likely pegged to overall feelings about the civil war and electoral crisis, which are almost universally viewed as negative events. There may also be a degree of social desirability bias in these measures; expressing positive attitudes toward armed actors in Côte d'Ivoire can be considered impolite or politically incorrect. To the extent it exists, this kind of measurement bias likely makes it harder to detect the association between rebel rule and postwar attitudes toward ex-rebels. Overall, these findings provide provisional support for the causal chain stipulated by my theory: collaborative rebel rule leads to sustained commander-community ties in the postwar period *because* former rebels and commanders retain stronger grassroots social support in their areas of wartime control.

This chapter shows that understanding the local embeddedness of ex-rebel field commanders after war-to-peace transitions demands an appreciation of wartime dynamics and the agency of local communities to sustain or terminate linkages to commanders in response to their past governance performance. While all observational data gathered in a postconflict environment should be interpreted cautiously, the weight of the evidence across varied sources and measures accords with the logic set out by this book's theory. In localities where rebel occupiers demonstrated concern for the well-being of populations and established reputations as valuable community allies, commanders were able to reach back into these communities to exercise influence and sustain support networks, even after the rebel-military integration process removed commanders from their wartime zones. The next chapter examines the implications of ex-rebel commanders' local ties for their resistance to the central regime during postwar state consolidation.

CHAPTER 4

Ex-Rebel Commanders and the Ivorian State

One of the foremost challenges of political order and regime survival in war-shattered states is the (re)construction of a state security apparatus that is obedient to the ruler. In the aftermath of rebel-military integration, security force loyalty is a particularly fraught challenge. Some ex-rebel commanders may become loyal agents of the regime, while others resist centralized statebuilding. This book argues that armed groups' wartime governance influences the willingness of commanders to organize such resistance by determining whether local commander-community ties endure or decay after civil war. Chapters 2 and 3 illustrated the first step in this argument by examining varied patterns of rebel rule and postwar commander embeddedness in Côte d'Ivoire. The chapters demonstrated that whereas field commanders in zones of collaborative rule became locally embedded in communities controlled by the Forces Nouvelles (FN), commanders from zones of predatory rule saw their local ties decay after the Alassane Ouattara government disbanded the FN in 2011. Embedded commanders entered the war-to-peace transition with more resilient bases of regional support, greater mobilization power, and enduring local legitimacy as guarantors of order in areas of limited statehood.

This chapter turns to the consequences of ex-rebel commanders' local embeddedness after these specialists in violence transition from being insurgents to military officers. Specifically, I analyze how the legacies of rebel rule in Côte d'Ivoire affected relations between former FN field commanders and the Ouattara regime during the postwar phase of peacebuilding and security-sector reform. My theory anticipates that ex-rebel commanders who operated in areas of collaborative rebel rule should be the most likely to resist central regime authority. Endowed with local support, access to information, and ties to mobilization-ready networks of young men in the rural hinterlands, these commanders can efficiently summon and control armed networks both inside and outside of the regular military chain of command. Equipped with this leverage, these embedded commanders have the autonomy to openly challenge regime leaders and bargain coercively for a greater share of postwar state rents. Moreover, since the parochial interests of embedded commanders are directly threatened by centralized statebuilding, these commanders are likely to be driven by stronger antiregime grievances. By contrast, ex-rebel commanders from areas of predatory rebel rule should be less likely to defy regime leaders after integrating into the military. These nonembedded commanders have less coercive leverage vis-à-vis the postwar regime and are less threatened by postwar statebuilding. If this book's argument is correct, patterns of wartime governance should provide significant insight into patterns of postwar military obedience and resistance following rebel-military integration.

To study subnational variation in ex-rebel commander resistance, I leverage new data on military mutinies and demobilized rebel protests in postwar Côte d'Ivoire (2011–2020). These are the main dependent variables of the chapter. Mutinies and protests by military forces are of increasing interest to scholars of civil-military relations and intrastate conflict. These "lesser forms of insubordination" are employed as a tactic of coercive bargaining by military actors seeking to extract financial or policy concessions from the state.[1] Military mutinies also tend to be associated with increased risks of subsequent military coups.[2] In Côte d'Ivoire, mutinies and protests by former FN forces against the Ouattara government were the most visible manifestation of civil-military conflict after the end of the Ivorian civil war in 2011 and sustained concerns about regime collapse and the renewal of large-scale organized violence.[3]

By merging my community-level data on wartime rebel rule in Côte d'Ivoire with geolocated data on postwar mutinies and demobilized rebel protests by former FN forces, this chapter reveals several important trends. First, it shows that military mutinies and armed protests by ex-FN soldiers have occurred widely across northern Côte d'Ivoire since the end of the civil war—even though the FN army was responsible for bringing the Ouattara government to power. Second, I find that both mutinies and protests by demobilized ex-FN soldiers have occurred with greater frequency in localities that experienced collaborative rebel rule during the civil war, the same places where commanders maintained strong local ties after integrating into the Forces Républicaines de Côte d'Ivoire (FRCI) regular army. By contrast, mutinies and demobilized rebel protests were less common in areas that witnessed predatory rebel rule. This relationship appears at both the subprefecture and com'zone level and is robust to a variety of statistical tests. Contrary to the conventional view that effective rebel governance fosters postwar institution building, this chapter underscores that collaborative rebel rule can later incentivize embedded ex-rebel commanders to organize resistance to regime leaders and fragment postwar state authority.

To supplement this novel analysis of military mutinies and demobilized rebel protests, the chapter also briefly explores the impacts of ex-rebel commanders' local ties in a second domain—police-citizen relations in former rebel-governed territory. I probe an important implication of this book's theory: where ex-rebel commanders are locally embedded and have strong ties to rebel-ruled communities, these embedded commanders "crowd out" the law enforcement functions of the postwar state. I explore this hypothesis by leveraging several sources of survey data on police-citizen relations in former FN-held territory. I show that in localities with past experiences of collaborative rebel rule, Ivorians have less confidence in redeployed state police forces, and civilians are more likely to turn to ex-rebels for security and justice. These effects are detectable seven years after Côte d'Ivoire's territorial reunification, providing further evidence that postwar statebuilding in Côte d'Ivoire was deeply marked by the legacies of insurgent governance.

Military Mutinies and Demobilized Rebel Protests in Postwar Côte d'Ivoire

To analyze resistance by ex-rebel commanders to the central state following rebel-military integration, I collected data on two types of events in postwar Côte d'Ivoire: military mutinies and demobilized rebel protests. These measures, while imperfect, enable me to examine patterns of postwar commander-regime relations in a systematic fashion. In the following sections, I discuss the substantive significance of mutinies and demobilized rebel protests in the Ivorian context, explain my empirical approach and data-collection procedures, and summarize the results.

CONCEPTUALIZING MUTINIES AND DEMOBILIZED REBEL PROTESTS

One of the defining characteristics of a state with consolidated authority is the ability of political rulers to reliably command obedience from the military elite and other specialists in violence. Acts of resistance by military commanders that challenge the ruler's authority—even if such acts fall short of a full-fledged coup—are symptoms of a breakdown in civil-military cooperation that can undermine political order and decrease the regime's ability to deter other challengers.[4] I conceptualize ex-rebel commander resistance as actions by commanders that defy the authority of central state rulers, in particular the organization of mutinies and protests by ex-combatants who are at least partially under commanders' control. By leveraging their mobilization power to put armed men and women into the streets, to seize control of buildings or property, or to use violence against other branches of the armed forces, commanders resist and undermine the authority of the incumbent ruler and weaken the cohesion of the postwar security apparatus—even if they do not overthrow the government.

Military mutinies and demobilized rebel protests have been a central tactic of coercive bargaining between former FN forces and the Ouattara government since the end of the Ivorian civil war in April 2011. Rebel-military integration involved a high degree of uncertainty for ex-FN field commanders. These commanders saw themselves as one faction among many in the winning civil war coalition and feared that the government might purge them or hand them over to the International Criminal Court (ICC) at some point in the future. At the same time, the return of central state institutions across the north threatened the grip of ex-FN commanders over their bases of support, revenue-generating schemes, and local protection rackets. In this context, military mutinies and protests among ex-combatants have served as a means for ex-rebel commanders to demonstrate their coercive capacity and push back against government policies that threaten their interests and bargain for a larger share of postwar rents. According to one ex-rebel officer, street protests by former FN soldiers are intended to remind the government that "we [the FN] put you [Ouattara] in power, and we can take you out again."[5] Between 2011 and 2020, more than sixty significant mutinies and armed protests by ex-FN soldiers occurred around the country (data collection and coding are discussed later in the chapter). The largest spikes in mutiny activity occurred in January and May 2017, when ex-rebel soldiers inside the FRCI mobilized to take control of dozens of police and army camps.[6]

Among rank-and-file ex-rebel soldiers, mutinies and armed protests serve as a means of threatening and embarrassing the government to press for concessions they feel they are owed. For ex-FN members who integrated into the FRCI, grievances circle around the government's failure to deliver bonus payouts and back pay to fighters who participated in the 2010/2011 campaign to defeat Gbagbo's regime. These frustrations first boiled over into street protests by FRCI soldiers as early as December 2011 and simmered under the surface in the Ivorian military ever since.[7] Ex-FN combatants *outside* the FRCI have also been important participants in antigovernment protests since 2011. The grievances of these demobilized fighters include frustration over their ineligibility for military insertion, inadequate compensation packages provided by the national disarmament, demobilization, and reintegration (DDR) program, and the generally poor living conditions and social alienation among war veterans in postwar Côte d'Ivoire.[8] The military integration process was formally completed by 2012, and the national Authority for Disarmament, Demobilization, and Reintegration (ADDR) claimed to have processed over sixty thousand individuals between 2012 and 2015. Yet in reality, the government in Abidjan possessed relatively little information—and even less control—over the sprawling networks of demobilized combatants (popularly known as *démos*) that remained spread around the country, especially in former rebel-ruled areas in the north.⁹ From the perspective of many démos, the official DDR process was superficial and brief, provided few long-term employable skills, and was disconnected from efforts to achieve social reintegration in combatants' home communities.¹⁰ As a result, many démos struggled to pull away from their wartime social networks and remained in the orbit of former comrades and commanders who could offer periodic employment, housing, and a sense of acceptance and belonging.¹¹ While the grievances and claims of the démos are varied, violent street protests by these ex-rebel fighters have amplified government fears of the coercive power available to ex-rebel commanders in postwar Côte d'Ivoire.¹²

Given the complex assortment of motives among mutiny and protest participants in Côte d'Ivoire, these events can be taken only as indirect evidence of ex-FN commander resistance. Though I conducted many interviews with former FN soldiers and security-sector experts in order to understand the organization and chains of communication behind ex-rebel mutinies and protests—many of which occurred during my field research in Côte d'Ivoire in 2017—reconstructing the origins of specific mutiny and protest events is a murky business. Some respondents claimed that the impetus for the mutinies and protests originated with the lower ranks and that senior ex-rebel commanders were kept in the dark. Others allowed that ex-FN commanders in the FRCI were typically aware of the planning for these events but did not involve themselves directly, while still others maintained that powerful ex-FN leaders pulled strings to coordinate mutiny and protest activities within their old wartime networks.¹³ Several security-sector specialists I interviewed drew a direct link between the fraying relations between Ouattara and Soro and the eruption of mutinies and ex-rebel protests in 2017.¹⁴ One interviewee remarked: "Between the government and the [former FN] com'zones, loyalty is very doubtful. Nobody knows who will go with who. It is a question of money and relations of force."¹⁵

What can be said with confidence is that many former FN commanders in Côte d'Ivoire after 2011 were in a position to monitor networks of ex-rebel fighters both inside the regular army and outside of it and coordinate and control those fighters by virtue of their positions at the head of resilient patron-client networks. These commanders also had reason to want to demonstrate their coercive potential to protect their parochial interests in an uncertain postwar environment. Former FN commanders possessed the power—at least to a significant extent—to turn military mutinies and demobilized rebel protests "on and off" within particular areas. As one interviewee remarked about the role of several prominent ex-FN commanders during the 2017 mutinies: "They [the com'zones] could probably have stopped this pretty quickly if they had wanted to. But they aren't interested in saving Ouattara's skin."[16] By observing the incidence of these mutinies and protests, we gain a rough—though admittedly imperfect—means to study ex-rebel commanders' resistance to the state after rebel-military integration.

DATA COLLECTION AND MEASUREMENT

To measure mutinies and protests by ex-rebel actors, I coordinated a team of research assistants to gather information on two types of events between May 2011 and December 2020: mutinies by uniformed FRCI soldiers (*Mutiny*) and protests or demonstrations that were held by ex-combatants affiliated with the FN but that did not involve soldiers inside the FRCI (*Demobilized rebel protest*). By accounting for both types of events, I seek to track the mobilization of ex-rebel networks both inside and outside the official military chain of command.

Data sources included the Armed Conflict Location Event Dataset (ACLED) as well as region- and Côte d'Ivoire–specific media sources of varied political leanings, including *Africa Research Bulletin*, *Fraternité Matin*, *Le Patriote*, and *Nord-Sud*. Using clear coding guidelines, research assistants generated a list of "candidate events" that were then scrutinized in a second round of research by the author. Mutiny events were included in the final list only if there was clear evidence that the participating soldiers were active members of the FRCI, and demobilized rebel events were coded as such only if there was clear evidence that participants were former Forces Armées des Forces Nouvelles (FAFN) members. Several candidate events were removed from the list because either the identities of the mutiny/protest participants were ambiguous or the event represented an episode of interforce fighting (for example, between factions of FRCI soldiers) and not collective mobilization by ex-rebel forces against the state. In total, we coded sixty-one separate episodes of collective resistance by ex-FN actors, including forty-seven military mutiny events and fourteen demobilized rebel protests. These events occurred across twenty-three separate subprefectures in five different years.

It is worth noting that my analysis explicitly disaggregates mutiny and ex-rebel protest events in terms of geographic location, counting incidents in separate localities as separate events. This departs from the approach of scholars like Rebecca Schiel, Jonathan Powell, and Christopher Faulkner, who aggregate temporally proximate military mutinies within a country as a single "wave" event.[17] For my purposes, geographic disaggregation is essential because it permits me to investigate subnational variation in the mobilization of ex-rebel military networks, holding other factors constant. I explore whether armed ex-rebel networks in a specific locality were mobilized in the context of coercive bargaining between ex-FN commanders and the central state and how this variation is connected to patterns of wartime rebel rule and commanders' local embeddedness.

ANALYSIS

This section tests the hypothesis (H2) that ex-rebel commanders from areas of collaborative rebel rule are more likely to resist central regime leaders after rebel-military integration compared to commanders who governed in areas of predatory rebel rule. Recall that my theory of commander embeddedness, laid out in chapter 1, posits that wartime governance institutions that are viewed as responsive to civilian interests allow local field commanders to acquire enduring social support among rebel-ruled populations. Strong social support, in turn, increases ex-rebel commanders' postwar mobilization power by expanding the number of individuals within the community who would be willing to mobilize in service of the commander even after the commander leaves the zone. Moreover, collaborative rule allows commanders to maintain informal alliances with local elites in rebel-ruled areas, who in turn facilitate commanders' postwar access to social networks (including networks of ex-combatants living in the community). Collaborative rule helps commanders to bolster their influence, sustain contacts and information, and efficiently revitalize local ex-rebel networks even after leaving the zone once military integration occurs.

To measure wartime rule by the FN, I draw on my community informant survey, which gathered data in ninety-three subprefectures and *quartiers* across northern Côte d'Ivoire where the FN governed for nine years between 2002 and 2011. This survey provided detailed information about the socioeconomic characteristics of rebel-ruled localities, the nature of the FN's governance practices, and the postwar ties between FN field commanders and local communities. Merging this evidence with postwar mutiny and demobilized rebel protest data, I estimate the likelihood of mutiny and demobilized rebel protest events in northern Côte d'Ivoire between 2011 and 2020, using the subprefecture year as the unit of analysis. This panel approach allows me to account for time fixed effects in my analysis and address bias from unobserved factors that are constant across units but evolve over time, such as the national political mood. It also allows me to account for past mutiny and demobilized rebel protest events within localities, which may predict future similar events.[18]

I first analyze the association between mutinies, protests, and the variable *Collaborative rule*, the index introduced in chapter 2 that measures the quality of rebel governance within a subprefecture (ranging from −1 to +2) based on inclusive goods provision by FN rebels, power sharing with local elites, institutions for civilian participation, and restraints on civilian abuse. Importantly, I showed previously that *Collaborative rule* is not itself well predicted by several variables that might be concerning confounders to my argument, such as rebels' coethnicity with civilians, natural resource availability, or prewar social capital. When we evaluate the data as a simple cross section, we see that rates of military mutinies and demobilized protests are notably higher in localities with collaborative wartime governance. For example, in subprefectures with *Collaborative rule* scores of +1 or +2, the average number of military mutinies and demobilized rebel protests is 0.96 and 0.13, respectively, compared to just 0.10 and 0.025 in subprefectures with *Collaborative rule* scores of −1 or 0. Put differently, military mutinies were over nine times more frequent in areas of collaborative rebel rule, while demobilized rebel protests were about five times more frequent in areas of collaborative rebel rule.

To account for other characteristics of subprefectures that may also affect the likelihood of mutinies and demobilized rebel protests, I next estimate both types of events in a multivariate regression framework. Since the outcome variables are overdispersed, I employ negative binomial logit models.[19] I include several covariates at the subprefecture level. I use *Population (ln)* to account for the size and development levels of localities and *Recruitment* to adjust for the number of ex-rebel combatants who are likely to reside there. I control for *Paved roads* to account for the accessibility of localities and the monitoring capacity of the state. To capture the financial resources available to commanders, I control for *Mining site*, which measures whether gold or diamond mining was present in the subprefecture. *Ethnicity northern* is a dichotomous variable indicating whether the community is predominantly a *nordiste* community (north Mande or Voltaic/Senoufo), and *Commander native* accounts for whether the local FN commander who controlled the area during the war was a resident of the community beforehand. Finally, I control for *Prior mutiny* and *Prior demobilized rebel protest* to account for potential path dependence in mutiny and ex-rebel protest events, and I include year fixed effects to account for unobserved time-varying conditions.

The negative binomial models show a positive and statistically significant association between *Collaborative rule* and both *Mutiny* and *Demobilized rebel protest* ($p < 0.05$). Full results appear in appendix G, table A.9. Figure 4.1 shows the predicted number of mutiny events and demobilized rebel protests for different values of *Collaborative rule*, using the negative binomial estimator. For localities with scores below 1 (where rebel rule was most predatory), the chances of mutiny and protest events are virtually zero. As the *Collaborative rule* index increases to its maximum value, the predicted number of mutinies in a locality year reaches approximately 0.15, and the predicted number of protests increases to 0.025. Considering the overall rarity of mutiny events in any given locality year, these effects are substantively noteworthy. Among the other covariates, only *Population (ln)*

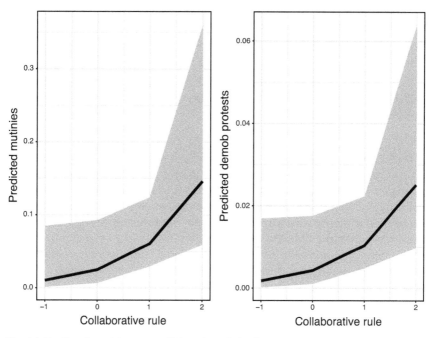

Fig. 4.1. Predicted mutinies over collaborative rebel rule
Note: Bars show 95 percent confidence intervals.

is also a significant and positive predictor of both mutinies and demobilized rebel protests.

As alternative tests of H2, I examine whether military mutinies and demobilized rebel protests are associated with other measures of insurgent governance and with measures of postwar commander-community ties. Rerunning the negative binomial regression model with the same set of control variables, I find positive and statistically significant associations between *Rebel goods provision* and *Organized meetings* and mutiny and protest events as well as between *Postwar commander influence* (a summary index of commanders' postwar local ties) and mutiny and protest outcomes (table A.9). Because both the mutiny and demobilized rebel protest outcomes have an abundance of zeros, I also rerun the analyses using zero-inflated negative binomial models. This estimation strategy separately models excess zeros and count values in the outcome as distinct phenomena. Because this approach is significantly more taxing on my data, I pare back the models by omitting controls and fixed effects.[20] The zero-inflated models show that higher values of both *Collaborative rule* and *Postwar commander influence* significantly reduce the likelihood of observing zero mutinies with a locality, though they do not clearly predict the subsequent count (table A.10).

Results for demobilized rebel protests are more mixed, but *Postwar commander influence* is a significant positive predictor of the protest count. Overall, the weight of the evidence suggests that where collaborative rebel rule led FN field commanders to become locally embedded during the civil war, ex-rebel armed networks were more likely to be mobilized against the state in the postwar period.

ALTERNATIVE EXPLANATIONS

It is worth considering whether patterns of military mutinies and demobilized rebel protests are influenced by the presence of military bases that provide natural "focal points" for soldiers and ex-combatants to organize collective action.[21] The locality in northern Côte d'Ivoire with the largest number of mutinies and protests—Bouaké—is unusual because it was the headquarters of the FN rebel administration, the site of several military installations, and home to several demobilized combatant associations.[22] However, mutinies and demobilized rebel protests also occurred in more outlying regions, such as Kabadougou, Tchologo, and Haut-Sassandra, which do not have significant military bases. Moreover, ex-rebel mutinies and protests occurred both at military bases and sites like police stations and prefectoral offices, which are present in almost all departments and subprefectures in Côte d'Ivoire. In other words, while many subprefectures were *possible* sites for the mobilization of ex-rebel military networks, only those places where ex-rebel commanders retained strong local ties were likely to witness these events. Removing Bouaké from the analysis, I find similar results.

Another potential concern is that mutinies and protests only occur in localities where FN rebel soldiers who integrated into the FRCI actually live. In communities where the FN did not recruit during the war or where its fighters did not integrate into the FRCI after 2011, field commanders may not have local armed networks available to mobilize. To address this issue, I use the community informant survey to code the variable *FRCI integration*, a binary indicator of whether local FN recruits in the locality were subsequently integrated into the national army. *FRCI integration* occurred in approximately 70 percent of the subprefectures in my sample. I subset to these localities and rerun the analyses to see if the results remain stable when only examining areas where local FN rebels integrated into the FRCI. I find that they do.

As an alternative way to address concerns about the comparability of potential sites of mutinies and demobilized rebel protests in former FN-controlled territory, I analyze variation in the incidence of mutinies and protests across each of the ten urban localities in the north that served as the seat for an FN zone commander (com'zone). As discussed in chapter 3, the com'zones were the primary leaders of the FN's political-military administration in northern Côte d'Ivoire, and local com'zones amassed a great deal of power within their fiefdoms. In the aftermath of the 2011 transition, many demobilized combatant associations remained headquartered in the former regional capitals of their FN zone. All of the cities that were sites of an FN com'zone headquarters also host police and gendarmerie installations. Thus, it is plausible that mutiny events or demobilized rebel protests *could* have occurred at any of these sites.

Of the ten localities that hosted an FN com'zone headquarters, four experienced military mutinies by ex-FN forces within the FRCI between 2011 and 2020, and three were sites of protests by demobilized rebels. By contrast, six former com'zone sites experienced neither mutiny events nor demobilized rebel protests. Do wartime patterns of rebel rule in these areas correlate with these postwar outcomes? Though the small sample size prevents me from conducting a multivariate analysis, I find bivariate patterns that are consistent with my theory (figure A.2 in appendix G). There is a positive association between *Collaborative rule* and incidents of military mutinies and demobilized rebel protests in the 2011–2020 period. In former com'zone seats where FN rebels governed in a more collaborative manner, and therefore where commander-community ties persisted into the postwar period, ex-rebels both inside and outside the FRCI were more likely to be mobilized in acts of collective resistance to the central state. In com'zones that saw more predatory rule, such acts of postwar resistance were less frequent.

A final consideration is whether coordination among similarly located commanders undermines the assumption of independence. Perhaps some ex-rebel commanders challenged the state because they belonged to a military clique or faction that included other commanders already doing so. While such network politics inside the FRCI are very hard to observe, there are reasons to believe that ex-FN commanders tended to operate independently of each other during periods of antiregime mobilization. In my interviews, former combatants and FRCI officers described their professional and social networks as tightly knit but narrow and largely separate from other ex-FN forces who operated in different zones and sectors during the war. Analysts of the Ivorian security sector since 2011 have also described the FRCI officer corps as a highly fragmented body that does not operate as a unified collective. The "com'zone galaxy," writes Leboeuf, "is very heterogenous."[23] To investigate potential spatial dependence in the data, I follow the procedure recommended by Nathaniel Beck, Kristian Gleditsch, and Kyle Beardsley and test for spatial autocorrelation in military mutinies and demobilized rebel protests.[24] Calculating the Moran's I statistic for each outcome, I fail to reject the null hypothesis of zero spatial dependency across subprefectures.[25] Thus, it appears that commanders in Côte d'Ivoire made decisions about collective resistance on a largely independent basis, taking into account their own local coercive leverage and capacity for autonomous mobilization.

Crowding Out the State: Embedded Commanders and Postwar Policing

In addition to explaining ex-rebel commanders' willingness to directly resist the state, my theory of commander embeddedness also carries implications for another domain of postwar statebuilding: local security and policing.[26] When commander-community ties remain strong in former rebel territory, civilians will expect embedded commanders to continue to serve as informal guarantors of security and justice. While ex-rebel commanders can help to preserve social order and protect basic property rights, their security roles may also circumvent the ability of the redeployed state to establish the efficacy and legitimacy of the regular police among civilian populations. This "crowding out" effect may occur either because police organizations are unable to penetrate governance domains already occupied by other actors or because civilians interpret informal service provision as compensation for state failure or neglect, leading to weaker citizen attachments to the state.[27] When commander-community ties wither away, by contrast, civilians should be more likely to turn to other postwar governance actors—including the police—who are available to offer protection from violence. To the extent there is evidence of such a pattern between commander embeddedness and police-citizen relations, this implies another pathway through which the local ties of commanders impact postwar politics and potentially hinder centralized statebuilding.

Policing arrangements in northern Côte d'Ivoire have a complex history in the postcolonial era.[28] Under Félix Houphouët-Boigny, the Ivorian state employed prefects to act as agents of central government power in the north, who in turn depended on the gendarmes to implement orders and manage security issues. This system unraveled in the 1990s, as local power brokers, vigilante groups, and security firms began to privatize the management of violence. The informalization of policing reached a zenith during the 2002–2011 period, when police and gendarmerie forces withdrew from the north and crime prevention fell to occupying rebel soldiers, local self-defense groups, and *dozoton* hunters working in partnerships with area FN rebel commanders.[29] When the Ouattara government took power in 2011, it made the normalization of police-citizen relations in the north a key policy priority. Between 2012 and 2019, public spending on policing increased by 64 percent.[30]

I explore the hypothesis that localities exposed to collaborative rebel rule during the 2002–2011 FN occupation will tend to have weaker police-citizen relations in the postwar period. To do so, I analyze evidence from the Political Transition and Inclusion Survey conducted in 2018 among nine hundred respondents in former FN territory (for design details about this survey, see chapter 3 and appendix C). Specifically, I consider whether respondents indicated that they would turn to the police if they were victims of a crime.[31] In the field of criminology, citizens' willingness to call police to report crime or ask for assistance has been found to correlate strongly with both underlying trust in police and the perceived legitimacy of police.[32] Respondents were given the following options as potential sources of assistance after experiencing crime: (1) "the police or gendarmerie forces"; (2) "a member of your family"; (3) "a traditional or religious leader in your community"; (4) "an ex-combatant or commander"; (5) an "NGO"; or (6) "other." I coded respondents' choice as a nominal variable, *Crime assistance choice*. I then estimated *Crime assistance choice* as a function of the variable *Wartime services quality*, an index of the quality of rebel governance ranging from 0 to 3 that captures the quality of security, health care, and education goods provision under the FN from 2002 to 2011. I include covariates for age, sex, religion, ethnicity, urban/rural, poverty, and education. While this survey data does not permit a strictly causal analysis (there may be other factors that influence both wartime rebel rule and postwar police-citizen relations), I am able to address important observable confounders.

Because the outcome *Crime assistance choice* is an unordered choice among several alternatives, I employ a multinomial logit (MNL) model, using the "police and gendarmerie forces" response as the reference level. The coefficients of this model represent the relative impact of each explanatory variable on the log-odds ratio of each outcome for *Crime assistance choice*, relative to the reference option. I selected the police and gendarmerie forces response as the reference category because it best illustrates the potential decision of respondents to turn to the redeployed police in comparison to other possible sources of assistance.

Consistent with expectations, the MNL model shows the salience of wartime rebel rule for the choice of whom civilians turn to in the postwar period when confronted with the hypothetical prospect of criminal victimization. Because the log-odds ratio of an MNL model is not intuitive to interpret, I generate a first differences predicted probability plot (figure 4.2). This plot shows how the probabilities of selecting different options for *Crime assistance choice* are affected by increasing *Wartime services quality* from its minimum to maximum level, holding other variables constant. Respondents who reported higher levels of *Wartime services quality* in their communities—indicating more collaborative rebel rule—were less likely to turn to "police and gendarmerie forces" after being the victim of a hypothetical crime. Substantively, as the variable *Wartime services quality* moves from its minimum to its maximum, the predicted probability that a respondent chooses to turn to the police or gendarmerie forces after being the victim of a crime falls by approximately nine percentage points. At the same time,

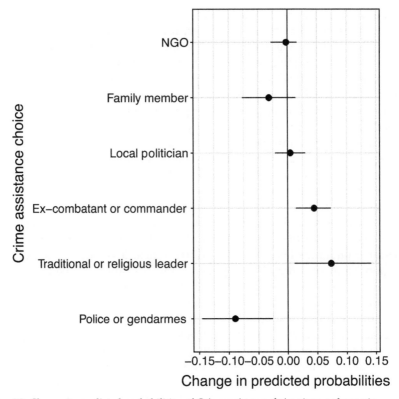

Fig. 4.2. Change in predicted probabilities of *Crime assistance choice* given a change in *Wartime services quality* from its minimum to maximum (multinomial logit)
Note: Lines show 95 percent confidence intervals.

the predicted probability that a respondent would turn to an ex-combatant or ex-rebel commander increases by approximately four percentage points, and the predicted probability that the respondent turns to a traditional or religious leader increases by seven percentage points. These changes are statistically significant at the 95 percent confidence level, controlling for a large set of covariates (full results in table A.11).

To further investigate the link between wartime rebel rule, commander-community ties, and postwar civilian relations with the police, I also construct and analyze a measure of police-citizen relations using the 2014 Enquête niveau de vie des ménages (ENV) survey conducted by the Ivorian National Institute of Statistics. This survey of over twelve thousand households collected information on household access to a variety of services, including the nearest police/gendarmerie commissariat. I construct the variables *Visit police* and *Visit prefecture* as binary measures of whether anybody in the household reported having previously visited the police commissariat or the government prefecture office (Ivorian prefects are responsible for overseeing local police and gendarmerie forces within their jurisdictions) to seek services in the last twelve months.[33] While the ENV enumeration areas overlap with sixty-seven subprefectures covered by my community informant survey, I restrict my analysis to those subprefectures where a police/gendarmes commissariat existed in 2014, yielding a sample of 2,724 households across forty-eight localities. In other words, I remove areas where civilians had no practical means of accessing the police. Importantly, this measure of police-citizen relations offers a means of empirically validating my theory's observable implications using independent data not collected by the author.

I estimate the relationship between *Visit police* and *Visit prefecture* (measured at the household level) and measures of rebel rule and commander-community ties (measured at the subprefecture level) from my community informant survey using logistic regression. I include many control variables at the individual and subprefecture level (table A.12). I also adjust for respondents' baseline knowledgeability and responsiveness by controlling for whether the respondent explained how they accessed the local market. Even after accounting for these potential confounders, there is a negative link between *Collaborative rule* and *Visit police* ($p < 0.05$) and between *Collaborative rule* and *Visit prefecture* ($p < 0.05$) and a positive association between *Coercion* and *Visit police* ($p < 0.05$). There is also a negative association between *Postwar commander influence* and both *Visit police* and *Visit prefecture*. Figure 4.3 shows that respondents in areas where ex-rebel commanders had strong local ties were approximately three percentage points less likely to report visiting a police commissariat and four percentage points less likely to visit a government prefecture office than citizens in areas with weak commander-community ties.[34] Placebo tests show that respondents' access to other types of services, such as education, health care, markets, and telephones, is *not* affected by the quality of commander-community ties, suggesting that ex-rebel commander embeddedness has consequences for citizen-state relations that are unique to the security sphere. These findings further corroborate the idea that strong postwar commander-community ties—which in turn derive from collaborative rebel rule during wartime—lead ex-rebel commanders to "crowd out" the postwar police forces even after formal rebel demobilization.

It is important to acknowledge that the regular police and ex-rebel commanders are not necessarily mutually exclusive sources of security and justice. In some of my field research sites—such as Korhogo—government officials indicated that partnerships between ex-rebel commanders and redeployed police forces allowed for more effective control of violent crime. Local orders in postwar states are complex, and the provision of security by

CHAPTER 4

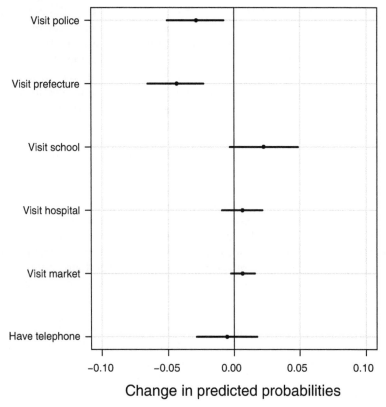

Fig. 4.3. Effects of increasing *Postwar commander influence* from minimum to maximum on Ivorian household access to services in 2014
Note: Lines show 95 percent confidence intervals.

strongmen or informal governance actors need not diminish the ability of state institutions to garner legitimacy. Specifying the conditions under which embedded ex-rebel commanders act as substitutes or complements to redeployed police forces in former rebel-governed territory and the ultimate consequences of these arrangements for justice and human security is an important subject for continued research. Nonetheless, the findings presented here raise intriguing insights about how local variation in ex-rebel commander embeddedness may influence citizen-state relations in the aftermath of civil wars while challenging the conventional wisdom that rebel institution building in civil wars translates into successful postwar statebuilding.

Together, chapters 3 and 4 provide detailed quantitative evidence in support of this book's theory of commander embeddedness after rebel-military integration. Chapter 3 examines the correlates of postwar commander influence within rebel-ruled communities to demonstrate that different wartime practices of insurgent governance translated into ex-rebel commanders' local mobilization power and legitimacy being either preserved or eroded after rebel demobilization and military integration. This chapter looks at relations between ex-rebel commanders and the Ivorian state, assessing the implications of commander embeddedness for ex-rebel resistance to postwar regime leaders and police-citizen relations in former rebel-ruled communities. Across varied data sources and levels of analysis, the chapters document a consistent relationship between collaborative rebel rule and commanders' subsequent trajectories of local embeddedness and resistance to central state authority.

The cross-sectional analyses presented in this chapter leave two important questions yet to be answered. First, why did ex-rebel resistance in Côte d'Ivoire escalate *when* it did? As with other types of conflict processes, it is hard to predict the timing of military resistance with precision.[35] The prevailing perception among ex-FN soldiers that the Ouattara government had failed to fully deliver on the promises made at the outset of rebel-military integration, combined with the enduring mobilization capacity of embedded ex-FN commanders, created a sort of powder keg that could have exploded at any point. It is also likely that the largest wave of mutinies and demobilized rebel protests in 2017 was partially instigated by the deteriorating political alliance between Ouattara and Soro. Spurned by the ruling Rassemblement des Républicains (RDR) party in his ambitions to succeed Ouattara as the RDR presidential candidate, Soro is suspected to have encouraged and even materially supported the mutineers, apparently hoping to exploit the grievances and mobilization power of ex-FN fighters to intimidate Ouattara into reversing the party's candidate-selection decision.[36] In the end, this effort failed. The ex-rebel mutineers were bought off with new payouts from the government, and Soro found himself ostracized from the ruling coalition.

Second, why did civil-military conflict not escalate further through a security-dilemma-driven spiral? Ex-FN military networks were repeatedly mobilized against the Ouattara government in former rebel zones in the north from 2011 to 2020, but few of these episodes—with the notable exception of the January 2017 mutinies—ultimately escalated to the point that they posed a credible threat to regime survival. While a full accounting of (de)escalation dynamics in specific resistance episodes is beyond the scope of this chapter, the absence of extreme escalation spirals between ex-FN commanders and the Ouattara government from 2011 to 2020 can be partly attributed to the strategic choices of the regime itself. On the one hand, the Ouattara regime was quick to accommodate the financial and professional demands of ex-FN military commanders to alleviate grievances when the risks of brinkmanship bargaining appeared too great. The January 2017 mutinies ended when the government agreed to pay out approximately $150 million USD to former FN soldiers and officers, and the May mutinies of the same year were resolved with additional promises of around $11,500 each to 8,400 former FN members.[37] Since the start of the rebel-military integration process, the government has granted nearly all senior and mid-ranking ex-FN commanders the opportunity to integrate into the FRCI, often at ranks well above their prewar station. And while some former FN civilian elites close to Soro have been purged or imprisoned, virtually no prominent ex-FN military commanders have been directly targeted with state repression.[38] The Ouattara government, in other words, carefully calibrated its strategic concessions to accommodate ex-rebel commanders' interests and prevent the escalation of civil-military conflict.

At the same time, the Ouattara government has also subtly manipulated the security apparatus through coup-proofing tactics to minimize the risk that individual episodes of resistance could snowball into large-scale collective action. Coup-proofing efforts began as early as June 2011, when Ouattara ordered the restructuring of the Groupement de Sécurité de la Présidence de la République de Côte d'Ivoire (GSPR). Previously a special unit assigned to the protection of visiting dignitaries, the GSPR was divided into two new units under the authority of the presidential office: Les Gardes du Corps, commanded by Lieutenant Colonel Ibrahima Gon Coulibaly ("Goz"), and the Unité d'Intervention, under Captain Dao Mourlaye. Gon Coulibaly recruited loyal members of the gendarmerie—some of them former Gbagbo supporters—into his unit, providing a counterweight to northern officers in the Republican Guard, which was controlled by the former FN zone commander of Bouaké, Chérif Ousmane.[39] The regime also created another unit under special presidential authority—the Forces Spéciales, led by Lieutenant Colonel Lancina Doumbia—as well as new military police and security brigades within the gendarmerie that operated autonomously from the regular army.[40] By building up units such as the Republican Guard, the Special Forces, and the GSPR, the Ouattara government quarantined the threat of antiregime mobilization by maintaining several parallel security forces all with direct links to the president.[41] Over time, this coup-proofing strategy has even allowed Outtara to make incremental steps toward shuffling out some ex-FN commanders without risking destabilization. In the aftermath of the 2017 wave of military mutinies, for example, several prominent ex-FN leaders in the FRCI, including the former FN military chief Soumaila Bakayoko, were relieved of their commands and replaced with non-FN officers viewed as more loyal to Ouattara.[42] In short, while the legacies of wartime rule help us understand why some ex-rebel commanders resisted centralized statebuilding while others did not, the dual strategy of accommodation and coup-proofing by regime leaders in Abidjan helps to explain why the escalation of ex-rebel resistance remained contained.

Ultimately, the findings in this chapter underscore vividly a core theoretical contention of this book concerning the legacies of wartime governance. Contrary to the view that effective rebel governance breeds more durable postwar peace, welfare-enhancing governance practices may not translate into effective postwar statebuilding. Rather than preparing armed groups to be effective institution builders, collaborative wartime governance can disrupt postwar stabilization by creating locally embedded military actors who are difficult for the central regime to control and who disrupt the normalization of postwar citizen-state relations in the security domain. At least in the Ivorian case, effective wartime governance bred fragmented state authority.

What the preceding chapters have not shown is extensive qualitative evidence about the proposed causal process linking each step in the argument. The next chapter addresses this omission by exploring paths of ex-rebel commander embeddedness and resistance in four case study areas of Côte d'Ivoire.

CHAPTER 5

Tracing Commander Embeddedness in Four Case Studies

When insurgents integrate into national militaries and the possibility of state consolidation or fragmentation hangs in the balance, ex-rebel commanders do not operate from a tabula rasa. Rather, commanders' willingness to resist regime leaders is conditioned by their local embeddedness in areas of former rebel control. I have argued that collaborative rebel rule engenders embeddedness among commanders, while predatory governance results in weaker postwar commander-community ties. Variation in ex-rebel commanders' local ties in turn shapes the capacity and motive of these rebels-turned-officers to resist centralized postwar statebuilding. Ironically, collaborative wartime rule raises the subsequent likelihood of civil-military conflict and security-sector fragmentation. The quantitative evidence presented in the preceding chapters confirms that the proposed variables of my theory correlate as expected in northern Côte d'Ivoire. However, a more detailed account is needed to explore whether the proposed causal mechanisms are also borne out by the evidence.

This chapter dives deeper into how commander embeddedness is created and sustained in practice and how it impacts postwar statebuilding after rebel-military integration. I present an in-depth study of four rebel-ruled localities in northern Côte d'Ivoire: Korhogo, Bouaké, Sangouiné, and Mahapleu. All four localities were conquered by the Forces Nouvelles (FN) at roughly the same time in late 2002 and were exclusively controlled by the rebel group until the demobilization of the FN in 2011. The rebel commanders in charge of each area subsequently integrated into the Ivorian army, the Forces Républicaines de Côte d'Ivoire (FRCI). Yet differences in the evolution of wartime institutions and commander-community ties meant that these commanders integrated into the national military with a different political calculus. In Korhogo and Sangouiné, where the FN occupation involved inclusive goods provision, power sharing with local elites, mechanisms for civilian participation, and restraints on civilian abuse, local rebel commanders became embedded and established an enduring power base that outlived the civil war. For more than half a decade after the formal demobilization of the FN, ex-rebel commanders in these areas remained fixtures in local politics, maintained strong ties to armed networks, and provided security and justice to civilians outside of formal channels. Endowed with private mobilization power and local legitimacy as guarantors of order, these commanders had strong incentives to resist the Ouattara government's statebuilding agenda. In both cases, ex-rebel networks were mobilized against the central regime. In Bouaké and Mahapleu, by contrast, occupying FN rebels employed more predatory governance. As a result, ex-rebel commanders lacked strong local ties after integrating into the army. With little to lose from the return of central state institutions to former rebel zones and without the ability to effectively control ex-rebel networks, these commanders chose not to openly resist the Ouattara regime. The nature of wartime rebel rule in each case thus explains commanders' subsequent trajectories of embeddedness and resistance (table 5.1).

To maximize the analytical value of qualitative case studies, this chapter utilizes a case-selection strategy that matches "most similar" pairs of subprefectures for in-depth research.[1] Matching methods permit the researcher to transparently choose cases for analysis wherein each pair varies on the explanatory variable (in this case, collaborative or predatory rebel rule) but is otherwise comparable in terms of relevant characteristics.[2] Using a matching algorithm to calibrate among subprefecture covariates such as population, development levels, and ethnic demography, I identified pairs of cases—Korhogo and Bouaké, and Sangouiné and Mahapleu—that serve as optimal counterfactuals. The matching procedure is described fully in appendix H. Each pair is similar in many ways but differ in the quality of wartime rebel rule. With important potential confounders addressed at the matching stage, we can make more reasonable conjectures at each step in the historical chain of events about what *would* have happened in each case if the explanatory variable had occurred differently.

Table 5.1. Paths of commander embeddedness in four matched cases

	Matched pair 1		Matched pair 2	
	Korhogo	Bouaké	Sangouiné	Mahapleu
Commander	Martin Kouakou Fofié	Chérif Ousmane ("Papa Guépard")	"Kassero"	"Ondo"
Rebel rule	collaborative	predatory	collaborative	predatory
Postwar commander embeddedness	strong	weak	strong	weak
Postwar resistance?	yes	no	yes	no

CHAPTER 5

This chapter has several goals. First, I seek to trace the links between wartime rebel rule, commander embeddedness, and resistance to the postwar state following rebel-military integration. The chapter brings the story of rebel rule and commander embeddedness in Côte d'Ivoire to life, drawing on qualitative data collected during my research in these towns conducting interviews with residents, community leaders, demobilized fighters, state and military officials, and former FN commanders. Second, I use the case studies to explore whether other factors, such as material resources or personal leadership, are driving the key outcomes of interest in my theory or if these factors affect the intervening mechanisms of my argument. In the case narratives that follow, I show how ex-rebel commanders' resistance to the postwar state is deeply intertwined with commanders' local embeddedness in former rebel-ruled communities.

Matched Pair 1: Korhogo and Bouaké

Korhogo and Bouaké were the largest and most important cities ruled by the FN during the Ivorian civil war. The cities constitute the heartland of Côte d'Ivoire's northern political bloc, with many prominent Rassemblement des Républicains (RDR) politicians hailing from these areas.[3] Korhogo and Bouaké both provided large recruitment pools for the FN's military wing, lucrative zones of taxable economic activity, and spaces for the FN to showcase their movement to international observers as a viable alternative to Laurent Gbagbo's regime in Abidjan. Based on these structural characteristics alone, one might have expected similar trajectories of wartime governance and commander embeddedness in both cases.

Yet for all their similarities, patterns of rebel rule in Korhogo and Bouaké differed significantly. In Korhogo, the civil war left a tremendous amount of power in the hands of a single military commander: Martin Kouakou Fofié. Fofié's rule brought an impressive degree of political order to the city, characterized by inclusive goods provision, strong alliances with local elites, mechanisms for civilian participation, and relatively robust restraints on civilian abuse. These practices helped to cement Fofié's private mobilization power and legitimacy in Korhogo after his integration into the FRCI and eventually brought the powerful com'zone into conflict with the Ouattara government. By contrast, predatory rule in Bouaké left the rebel commander who governed this city—Chérif Ousmane—with comparatively weak local postwar ties. The absence of commander embeddedness in Bouaké led Ousmane to align himself closely with the government in Abidjan after integrating into the FRCI, even as mobilization-ready networks of ex-FN fighters remained active in the former rebel capital.

REBEL RULE IN KORHOGO AND BOUAKÉ

Korhogo is situated in the heartland of the Senoufo people.[4] During the reign of President Félix Houphouët-Boigny, significant numbers of Senoufo men from Korhogo were recruited into the Ivorian army as part of the country's ethnic power-sharing balance.[5] Many of Ibrahim Coulibaly's military associates at the initial nucleus of the Ivorian rebellion hailed from the area.[6] Although it is hard to generalize about the effects of armed conflict even within a single city, I often heard it said that if anywhere in Côte d'Ivoire did well from the civil war, it was Korhogo. Motorcycles fill the city's streets at all hours, along with overloaded flatbed and box trucks carrying loads of cotton, peanuts, rice, and livestock. The bustling commercial activity and the rows of newly constructed houses in the city's outlying suburbs advertise recent inflows of wealth.

When the Mouvement Patriotique de Côte d'Ivoire (MPCI)/FN rebellion began in September 2002, Korhogo was among the first cities to fall into the hands of insurgent forces. Pro-rebel army units, reinforced by troops from Burkina Faso, entered the city and clashed briefly with pro-Gbagbo Forces Armées Nationales de Côte d'Ivoire (FANCI) soldiers. After several days of combat, loyalist forces fled the city along with most police and gendarmerie personnel. Teachers, hospital workers, and staff at the prefectoral offices soon followed.[7] As in much of northern Côte d'Ivoire, the rebel takeover in Korhogo triggered an initial shockwave of economic disruption, crime, and disorder. As one resident recalled: "We started to hear gunfire left and right, and we heard there was another attempted coup d'état. After two or three days, the real crisis started.... Our building was pillaged during that time. Life at the beginning was very difficult. We didn't have access to our institutions, the banks were closed ... we had to ask our parents for loans."[8]

The first rebel commander to govern the city, a mid-ranking army officer named Koné Messamba, took limited steps to restore social order. The commander organized a meeting at the prefectoral compound soon after his arrival. There, Messamba and his lieutenants outlined the political goals of the rebel movement. They emphasized that "northerners" had become second-class citizens in Côte d'Ivoire and underscored the need for unified resistance to remove the Gbagbo government.[9] Messamba also worked with humanitarian agencies to distribute food and medical relief supplies through churches and mosques in the city.[10] In January 2003, another army officer with close ties to Coulibaly, Zoumana Diarrassouba, was appointed as the Korhogo zone commander.[11] However, a growing feud between Coulibaly and FN Secretary General Guillaume Soro meant that Diarrassouba—along with other close associates of Coulibaly—soon fell out of favor with the FN leadership.[12] Leadership turnover and factional feuding plagued the FN administration in Korhogo for the first year of the war.

CHAPTER 5

In 2004, more stable governance arrangements in Korhogo began to take shape. Amid his purge of pro-Coulibaly officers from the FN ranks, Soro selected Fofié as the new commander of Korhogo (now designated "zone 10"). Cutting a striking image with a full beard, Fofié was an army officer from the eastern town of Bondoukou who had served as chief of security for the FN in Korhogo under Diarrassouba. Fofié's military career included an earlier posting to Korhogo in the 1990s, along with stints in Bouaké and Abidjan as an aide to General Robert Gueï.[13] Alongside Fofié and the Forces Armées des Forces Nouvelles (FAFN) military command, the FN also established a small civilian branch in Korhogo under the leadership of Kanigui Soro and Alphonse Soro.[14] This "civilian cabinet" officially exercised authority as the local political and administrative arm of the FN, though in practice members of this cabinet reported to Fofié.[15]

Under Fofié's stewardship, the FN occupation in Korhogo evolved into a paradigmatic example of collaborative rebel rule. A complex set of interlocking governance practices underpinned a robust social contract between rebels and civilians. The FN won initial support by establishing systems of goods provision and material aid to city residents. To crack down on criminality and restore a sense of safety, Fofié established regular policing patrols in the city and administered harsh punishments (up to and including summary executions) against alleged criminals. Fofié also contracted the security services of the traditional *dozoton* hunting group, a centuries-old association among the Malinké and Senoufo ethnic groups in Mali and northern Côte d'Ivoire. *Dozo* hunters had played a significant role fighting crime in northern Ivorian villages since the 1960s.[16] The president of the Korhogo dozoton association explained that while his hunters initially did not want to associate themselves with any faction in the civil war, they were persuaded to work with the FN by Fofié. "When the crisis started, we [the dozo] stopped our activities, we did not want to be mixed up in the fighting ... but the level of crime was still going up here in Korhogo and elsewhere in the region. In time ... Fofié Kouakou Martin, he knew that the dozos did remarkable work before the rebellion, and he called upon us. He called upon us asking to restart our surveillance and patrolling, to patrol and guard against thieves and bandits."[17] This arrangement grew into an important alliance for the dozos. Fofié provided donations of food, money, and vehicles for them and in turn harnessed the hunters' abilities to reduce crime and restore a sense of security in the everyday lives of residents.[18]

Fofié also co-opted a significant portion of the local government machinery to help the FN restore basic services in the city. Repurposing the municipal bureaucracy enabled the FN to continue issuing birth, marriage, and death certificates. In many interviews, civilians pointed to the ability of the rebels to preserve this *état civil* service as an important accomplishment that helped maintain a sense of normalcy.[19] Civil servants at the *mairie* (town hall) also helped Fofié to implement a series of infrastructure repairs in the city, including the refurbishment of local markets and road repairs.[20] As an added benefit, co-opting the municipal government allowed Fofié to cloak the rebels' taxation practices under a semblance of legal legitimacy. Tax collectors who previously worked for the mayoral office were put in the employ of the FN.[21]

Other forms of goods provision under the FN in Korhogo came on a more personalized and ad hoc basis. For example, local university students who volunteered to operate the local primary schools received direct support from FN leaders.[22] Some NGOs and charitable organizations also sought assistance from Fofié directly. As Timité explained, "It was not a written thing, but there were people who approached the com'zone to say, 'We help the orphans, or women, we are located in this area, how can you help us?' It was either bags of rice, or financial help, or sometimes other materials."[23] These small acts of personal assistance by Fofié made a strong impression among many residents that I interviewed. According to Brahima, "The com'zone here supported the population, even the downtown market, the cultural center. . . . Really he made a lot of positive actions."[24] Another resident recalled: "They [the FN] were giving food to the population . . . they gave bags of rice to the most malnourished residents. There were several cases like that. They gave bags of rice to an elderly resident or to families, they even helped people with money."[25]

In addition to goods provision, the FN garnered social support by brokering alliances with local elites in Korhogo. One of Fofié's first priorities upon taking command of the city was to cultivate a partnership with the Coulibaly family, whose patriarch—Coulibaly Drissa Douanier—claimed status as the paramount chief of the Senoufo people.[26] An alliance with the chieftaincy allowed Fofié and his agents to interface more effectively with other gatekeepers in the city considered subordinate to the paramount chief, including the *president des jeunes*, the *presidente des femmes*, and traditional religious authorities.[27] As one interviewee said, "Here, the FN who governed, they quickly realized that in order to have influence and to govern the zone peacefully, it was necessary from the first moment to seek out and work with the traditional *chefferie*."[28] Another resident explained: "They [the FN] were supported strongly by Coulibaly Drissa Douanier, the canton chief. He served as an interface between the population and the FN, and he served as well as a kind of moral surety [*caution morale*]."[29] For their part, customary authorities in Korhogo viewed Fofié as a capable and reliable ally with a reputation for punishing criminals swiftly and harshly. The chief and his advisers hoped that Fofié could restore order to the city, thereby reassuring residents of the competency of the chieftaincy to "navigate the ship through stormy waters."[30]

Rebel rule in Korhogo also involved mechanisms for rebel-civilian dialogue and mediation. Most importantly, Fofié organized regular meetings on a weekly or biweekly basis at the prefecture building. These meetings were open to all residents regardless of age, occupation, or ethnicity, and every resident was in principle free to speak.[31] In some cases, Fofié presided over the gatherings himself, while at other times, this duty was left to one of his delegates. The content of these meetings varied. Some were held for the purposes of disseminating information and propaganda to counteract the "misinformation" coming from government-controlled radio and television outlets. Others were described to me as "meetings of support" that would culminate in a march by pro-FN youth.[32] As one resident explained, "It was all the population who came. Often there were certain military commanders, like Fofié, who arrived to do what they called 'des points de situation.' . . . It alternated, the military officers who spoke to say 'remain confident, we will achieve ultimate victory,' and the civilians who spoke to say 'this is about our dignity and to reestablish our rights within our land.'"[33]

Finally, Fofié strengthened his social support in Korhogo by exerting control over FN elements in the city and limiting abuses against civilians. Residents I interviewed recalled that while rebel soldiers' behavior could be harsh, it was usually predictable. Those interviewees who had managed to cross between rebel- and government-controlled zones during the civil war reflected that they felt comparatively safe in their zone: "When I traveled to Abidjan, there was a lot of anxiety, because at any moment they [government soldiers] could kill you. In our zone, they [rebel soldiers] took money but they did not kill. As long as you did not show yourself to be hostile, they did not kill."[34] Informal mediation between rebels and civilians—often brokered by the chefferie or local politicians—also helped to defuse conflicts that might otherwise have "gone too far."[35] Ultimately, these interlocking practices of inclusive goods provision, power sharing with local elites, mechanisms for rebel-civilian dialogue, and limits on civilian abuse helped the FN to create a relatively robust social contract in Korhogo and won Fofié widespread popularity and respect.

If Korhogo illustrates a paradigmatic case of collaborative wartime rule, then the city of Bouaké provides the relevant counterfactual of predatory rule. Founded as a French administrative outpost in the nineteenth century, Bouaké is Côte d'Ivoire's second largest city and a central transport hub for the north. A diverse mixture of Akan, Malinké, and Voltaic ethnic groups settled in Bouaké over the twentieth century, enjoying relative prosperity within Bouaké La Paix (the city of peace). The rebel takeover in September 2002 of Bouaké, which is geographically closer to the seat of power in Abidjan, encountered stronger government resistance here than it did in Korhogo. In the weeks following the mutineers' failed coup, FANCI forces stationed at the Third Infantry Battalion, the gendarmes, and several loosely organized pro-Gbagbo militia groups in Bouaké attempted to fight back.[36] Armed combat occurred block to block, and hundreds of combatants and civilians were killed.[37] Bullet holes dating from this early phase of the war scar buildings across the city to this day. Nonetheless, by early October

2002, the MPCI/FN rebels had won control of the city and set up command posts in the abandoned FANCI barracks and prefectoral headquarters. Infuriated by this embarrassment, President Gbagbo declared martial law and ordered a new offensive to recapture the city.[38] Advancing pro-Gbagbo forces briefly pushed the rebels out of the city center, but by October 24, the rebels regrouped and captured the telecommunications station.[39] Loyalist forces soon withdrew entirely from Bouaké, and the city remained under FN control for the rest of the war.

Rebel control in Bouaké in the early months of the occupation was fragmented across multiple organizational factions, with a number of prominent mutineer leaders—including Tuo Fozié, Ousmane, and Ibrahim Coulibaly himself—exerting authority in different sections of the city.[40] After the reorganization of the MPCI into the FN in late 2002, Bouaké became the seat of one of the FAFN's ten unified zone commands (zone 3). The first zone commander of the city, Tuo Fozié, was soon promoted to a ministerial position following the Linas-Marcoussis peace accords in 2003.[41] Ousmane (aka Papa Guépard) then became the com'zone of Bouaké. Like Fofié, prior to the rebellion, Ousmane was a key collaborator in the successful 1999 military coup and served as a sergeant in the elite para-commando corps created during Robert Gueï's short-lived military junta. Ousmane's Compagnie Guépard was renowned for its military prowess, and his fighters took a leading role in the FAFN offensive against Liberian mercenaries in western Côte d'Ivoire in 2003.[42]

As in Korhogo, rebel forces in Bouaké under Ousmane established armed patrols around the city, assuming the functions of the police and gendarmerie. Sector and unit commanders in zone 3 operated rudimentary justice systems based on impromptu courts, with more serious cases taken to the zone commander or the FN civilian headquarters for arbitration.[43] Civilian leaders in the FN political branch in Bouaké also organized a handful of public meetings at the prefectoral offices or at the headquarters of the FN secretary general to disseminate propaganda.[44] Outwardly at least, the FN's structures of governance in Bouaké appeared similar to those in Korhogo and other towns in the north.

Yet FN relations with local elites and ordinary residents in Bouaké began to seriously deteriorate as the occupation stretched on. Rather than establishing practices of inclusive goods provision, the FN provided services and material support to the civilian population in Bouaké that rarely rose above a rudimentary level. Rampant criminality in the city had particularly negative consequences for other forms of goods provision. Although youth volunteers operated a basic elementary education system, security conditions were so poor that many parents forbade their children to attend schools.[45] Hospitals and health clinics were thrown into "disequilibrium" due to the lack of security and medical staff.[46] As one deputy mayor of the city told me, "After 2002 . . . it was a time of total chaos. It was like going from the third floor of a building to the tenth floor in the basement . . . there was a moral fracture. There were killings, kidnappings, money being stolen. . . . All were implicated in this destruction."[47] Interviewees even explicitly contrasted Bouaké's lack of security provision with the relatively effective system of crime prevention in Korhogo. As Sidibé said, "Compared to Fofié . . . they [FN rebels in Bouaké] were more about filling their pockets than contributing to the well-being of the population."[48]

Rebel power sharing with local elites and mechanisms for civilian dialogue and participation were also limited in Bouaké. Whereas disputes between residents and occupying rebel forces in Korhogo could be preempted or contained through mediation with customary or religious leaders, local elites in Bouaké found themselves unable to effectively communicate with the FN military hierarchy. As one church leader said, "The most common problems we had to raise with the rebels were abuses . . . the rebels stole from us, but when we went to see the police, nothing happened, they were the same people!"[49] Another student recalled that "the chefferie, the community leaders, they fled the area or remained hidden. The rebels would come and occupy people's houses and steal their things."[50] One of the city's deputy mayors who lived through the occupation in Bouaké explained his own inability to collaborate with the FN: "At first, I wanted to get the population on board with the rebellion. Justice wasn't fair before. . . . However, by 2006, I had begun to lose confidence. They were starting to fight for their personal needs. There were problems with stealing and abuses. Over time I joined the side of the population [against the FN]."[51]

Among the most damaging aspects of rebel rule in Bouaké to the FN's social support was the failure of local commanders under Ousmane to limit the abuse and extortion of civilians.[52] Food and medical supplies were chronically scarce, as the explosion of irregular checkpoints at the entrances and exits of the city made the movement of goods exorbitantly expensive.[53] International NGOs like MSF and UNICEF managed to alleviate the worst of the humanitarian suffering by distributing aid through local churches and mosques, yet even these agencies faced regular theft and extortion at rebel checkpoints.[54] Displaced persons from surrounding villages flooded into the city center seeking shelter from growing lawlessness in the countryside, often only to find conditions worse than where they came from. Overwhelmed by the influx of displaced civilians, Catholic Church leaders at the Bouaké Cathedral were impelled to plea with FN commanders for improved security conditions and an end to civilian abuse by rebel soldiers.[55] Another traditional leader said that during the war, "all the vandals of West Africa came to Bouaké!"[56]

Patterns of rebel rule thus followed quite different trajectories in Korhogo and Bouaké. Survey evidence from residents in the two cities gathered in 2018 confirms a stark difference in perceived wartime security conditions.[57] Nearly 60 percent of respondents in Korhogo reported that order and policing functioned "well" or "very well" during the civil war, while only 21 percent of respondents in Bouaké gave such a positive appraisal.[58] And whereas 42 percent of respondents in Korhogo reported positive evaluations of local institutions resolving property and interpersonal disputes during the war, only 15 percent of respondents in Bouaké did so. Interestingly, evaluations of the quality of education during the civil war appear somewhat more positive in Bouaké than Korhogo, which may reflect the fact that Bouaké was the home base of Ecole Pour Tous, an education NGO that mobilized university students to operate schools throughout FN territory.[59] Ultimately, the empirical realities of any specific case are bound to be complex, and no theoretical schema can be expected to account for every empirical variation. Yet the stark differences in evaluations of the quality of policing, order, and dispute resolution across the two cities, combined with the overwhelming weight of qualitative interview evidence, suggest that patterns of wartime rebel rule in Korhogo and Bouaké followed different trajectories.

The case narratives to this point raise a question: *Why* did patterns of rebel rule diverge under the FN in Korhogo and Bouaké? My case-selection method—which seeks to minimize differences in macrostructural characteristics of each paired comparison—allows us to set aside several possible explanations. As the largest urban centers in FN territory, both Korhogo and Bouaké possessed sizable populations with ample potential for recruitment and taxable economic activity. Both localities, therefore, ought to have generated incentives for rebels to create a social contract to reap the benefits of civilian support.[60] Nor is it likely that FN rebels in Bouaké discounted local support as being unobtainable due to the city's political or ethnic composition: the majority of the city was populated by Malinké, Senoufo, and Baoulé communities, where support for the Gbagbo government was historically weak.[61] And although there is no reliable survey evidence to give us hard statistics about popular support for the rebellion at the beginning of the war, interviewees in both cities reported high levels of initial FN recruitment. Thus, it is difficult to explain different patterns of rebel rule in Korhogo and Bouaké based on differences in prewar political cleavages alone.

One likely reason for the divergence in patterns of wartime governance in Korhogo and Bouaké was the availability of strong local elites who could serve as intermediaries between civilians and rebel occupiers. In Korhogo, the Coulibaly chieftaincy provided Fofié with a relatively powerful and centralized conduit for interfacing with other key gatekeepers in the city.[62] Strong local community institutions enabled the FN to efficiently collect information and exercise authority by co-opting the chefferie, the dozoton, and other municipal bureaucrats who had ties to Korhogo's most powerful families. By comparison, Bouaké's social institutions were weaker and split among a larger number of ethnolinguistic communities who did not share jurisdiction under a single customary authority.[63] Geographic circumstances also played a role, since many traditional leaders and local government elites fled across the cease-fire line in Bouaké in 2002, seeking refuge in the nearby government-held zone.[64] Unlike in Korhogo, therefore, the absence of local elites in the early phases of the rebel occupation may have limited the ability of field commanders like Ousmane to build support via power sharing.

Another factor that potentially affected the divergent trajectories of rebel rule in Korhogo and Bouaké was the cities' proximity to hostile government forces. The Ivorian civil war settled into a prolonged stalemate with limited rebel-government clashes between 2003 and 2010, but rebels' perceptions of the risks of counterinsurgency attacks may still have remained higher in areas adjacent to the cease-fire zone. Although the overall correlation between distance to the cease-fire zone and the quality of rebel rule is weak, Bouaké may be an outlier in this regard. Bouaké was near the front lines of the war and, as the political and military headquarters of the FN, presented many targets for counterinsurgency attacks. Only twenty kilometers to the east and thirty kilometers to the south of the city, progovernment troops were garrisoned behind the UN-monitored cease-fire line. More than once, pro-Gbagbo forces breached the cease-fire agreement and tried to recapture the city.[65] Faced with the specter of armed counterattack, rebel occupiers likely adopted shorter time horizons and thus had weaker incentives to invest in local civilian support.[66] As one former FN soldier in Bouaké told me, "It was really a war zone here. We knew the enemy could attack at any time. This creates a certain mentality, you could say. You cannot get too relaxed."[67] The greater concentration of rebel troops in Bouaké may have also reduced the degree to which rebel commanders relied on the local chefferie to sustain a minimal level of order.[68] In the rear base city of Korhogo, by contrast, FN rebels operated in a context of relative security and could adopt long time horizons. After initial armed clashes with FANCI forces in 2002, the threat of counterinsurgency pressure from the Gbagbo regime was minimal. As the former FN civilian delegate explained, "Korhogo was an area that was considered relatively calm, relatively safe. So a lot of people migrated there."[69] Thus, the simple fact that Bouaké was located much nearer the cease-fire line than Korhogo may have partially shaped rebels' wartime governance.

Finally, differences in wartime governance were likely amplified by dynamics of institutional path dependency. When individuals and groups with limited knowledge of each other are forced to choose some way of interacting, they tend to draw on recent precedent.[70] "Accidents of history" that establish initial mutual expectations, therefore, can prove remarkably durable for organizing human social arrangements, creating a "self-perpetuating system of preferences, expectations, and actions."[71] In Bouaké, initial conditions that worked against collaborative rule—such as heightened fears of armed competition and the flight of local elites who might have served as brokers between the FN and the local populations—may have created a template for predatory rebel rule that became harder to change over time as civilians developed expectations of abuse and withheld cooperation from rebel occupiers.[72]

COMMANDER EMBEDDEDNESS AND POSTWAR RESISTANCE IN KORHOGO AND BOUAKÉ

In the spring of 2011, the FN-RDR political-military coalition completed its victory over the Gbagbo regime. By August of that year, almost all high-ranking FN commanders had integrated into the FRCI in senior military posts. Fofié was named the head of the FRCI's Third Regional Command at the rank of lieutenant colonel.[73] The Ouattara government entrusted Fofié with personally overseeing the custody of Gbagbo—the deposed Ivorian president now facing legal prosecution from the ICC for war crimes and crimes against humanity—in a safe house in Korhogo for eight months before Gbagbo's transfer to The Hague. Ousmane, meanwhile, became the deputy commander of the Groupement de Sécurité de la Présidence de la République (GSPR), a newly formed unit created by Ouattara that served as a praetorian guard.[74] Both commanders appeared poised to play key military leadership roles inside Côte d'Ivoire's new ruling coalition. Yet differences in wartime rebel rule in Korhogo and Bouaké would turn out to have striking effects for these commanders' postwar local ties and their incentives to resist the authority of the new government in Abidjan.

In Korhogo, Fofié's social support proved resilient. In July 2011, Korhogo's deputy mayor, Lanciné Koné, announced that the city could now reestablish regular government administration and the FN would "pass the baton to the state."[75] Like elsewhere in northern Côte d'Ivoire, FN soldiers were split between those selected for insertion into the FRCI and the larger share who drifted back to civilian life, many as part of *démobilisé* associations like Cellule 39 (an association of FN veterans that the Ouattara government viewed as a menace to stability). But even as the FN dismantled its official structures in Korhogo and the regular city administration reassembled itself, Fofié's popular image as a wartime "protector" in Korhogo enabled the former com'zone to sustain connections to a broad set of local social networks and retain status as a legitimate—if informal—guarantor of order in the city. Fofié was regularly invited to important social events among Korhogo's middle and upper classes, such as weddings, funerals, and religious celebrations, where the commander was considered a prestigious guest of honor.[76] Frequent social calls and private visits throughout the city also created opportunities for the former commandant to regenerate ties with local supporters. These visits provided opportunities for Fofié to distribute material gifts (such as bags of sugar, rice, and money) to residents of the city and to assure residents that he would not "forget" about the people of Korhogo.[77]

Local elites in Korhogo also continued to view Fofié as an indispensable partner for controlling crime and violence. The Senoufo canton chief, the head of the dozo hunting association, and the newly deployed prefectoral corps all looked to Fofié to help contain the rising tide of banditry that swept across northern Côte d'Ivoire after the country's reunification.[78] As one resident explained, "When Fofié was integrated into the FRCI, they [the chief and his advisers] still needed Fofié to put fear into the bandits."[79] A prefecture official also remarked, "It was really after 2011 that the *coupeurs de route* became a problem here. Sometimes we would call on the FN commanders to help us resolve these problems. . . . Fofié was often in Korhogo, so naturally he was in contact with his elements around the area."[80]

Fofié's enduring social support and alliances with local elites—founded on the FN's reputation in Korhogo for their effective if harsh methods—in turn enhanced the former commandant's access to social networks and information that could be used to control potential armed supporters and sustain mobilization power. As one interviewee said, "The chefferie and the dozo hunters have received a lot of support from Fofié, and in return they are ready to work together. Today still they are at his disposal."[81] In exchange for Fofié's continued protection, local elites in Korhogo continued to act as go-betweens for Fofié, expanding the ex-rebel commander's potential for organizing collective action in the city. Working in partnership with the police prefect also enabled Fofié to keep his finger on the pulse of Korhogo's criminal underworld, providing information about the activities of ex-combatants, militia members, and armed gangs in the region.[82] Fofié's reputation also made it easier for rank-and-file combatants to continue associating with the former zone commander. As one ex-combatant explained: "It is not easy to be a *démobilisé*. There is a stigma in the eyes of many people. . . . But our *grand-frère* [Fofié] is very respected. He has helped our parents. The population knows this. They know we are helping the commandant."[83] Fofié thus remained deeply embedded in Korhogo's local milieu with access to a broad range of social spaces. Material incentives and patron-client bonds further tethered local démobilisés to Fofié's orbit, as the former zone commander continued to provide material support to former fighters within Cellule 39. One local politician alluded obliquely to these connections: "There has been internal support for them [ex-combatants], there are former rebel commanders like Fofié who provide a certain number of things for them."[84] Some former FN soldiers in Korhogo even received houses provided to them by the former commandant, some of which served as safe houses for Fofié's copious weapons caches.[85] These safe houses reportedly harbored a vast arsenal of mortars, rocket launchers, and machine guns.[86] According to some analysts, Fofié single-handedly amassed as much firepower as the rest of the national army by 2013.[87]

As the initial euphoria of the FN's victory in 2011 began to wane, Fofié's local embeddedness in Korhogo began to fuel more antagonistic relations with regime leaders in Abidjan. From Fofié's perspective, the Ouattara government's plans to reform the postwar security sector by cutting down on "bloated" units filled with ex-FN officers and reestablish the authority of the national police and prefectoral corps across the north posed a direct challenge to Fofié's power base. Fofié also had considerable economic interests in Korhogo through his ties to both legal commercial enterprises and illicit protection schemes for gold-mining operations.[88] He had good reason to fear that Ouattara's allies in Abidjan wished to see those revenues flow to other hands now that the war was over. Though Fofié was a valuable military ally of the regime, his coercive leverage also meant that he could easily threaten to upend political order in Korhogo, align himself with competitors to the president, or even turn his followers directly against the regime. This painted Fofié as a potential threat to the government in Abidjan. As military mutinies and protests among démobilisés increasingly strained relations between the Ouattara government and ex-FN forces, Fofié's influence in Korhogo became a subject of growing concern in the capital. One interviewee claimed that Ouattara became so paranoid as to plant moles in Cellule 39: "Among the local authorities and even up to the highest level [e.g., President Ouattara], one of the major preoccupations, it is really the problem of ex-combatants. . . . They are infiltrated now because they are a latent menace. . . . They are afraid that their enemies will turn them against the government."[89] Such rumors in turn fed more mistrust and fears of betrayal among ex-rebel networks in Korhogo. As an ex-combatant leader in Korhogo described the situation: "We were officially demobilized, yes, but we did not quit the ranks. Me, I do not hide this, it is the truth . . . we ourselves know that if we turn over our arms . . . each of us will pay the price. Therefore it is necessary to stay cohesive to make sure everything goes well."[90]

By 2015, tensions between Fofié and the Ouattara government spilled into public view. Jealous of Fofié's popularity, both President Ouattara and Army Chief Soumaïla Bakayoko plotted ways to reduce his power.[91] In the spring of 2015, Minister of Defense Paul Kofi Kofi ordered that Fofié be reassigned from his command position near Korhogo to a post in Daloa. As one interviewee noted: "The regime more and more wants to weaken the influence of the former zone commanders through the game of musical chairs. When they assign them to zones that they don't totally master, they think that they [the commanders] will have less influence over local armed elements. . . . Some think that in removing Fofié from Korhogo, that will allow them [the government] to take control over these weapons caches . . . to shore up the power of the current regime."[92]

But there was a problem. Unhappy with the relocation order, Fofié initially refused the government's demand. Infuriated, the FRCI chief of staff asked for Fofié's resignation. This order, too, Fofié chose to ignore, forcing Bakayoko and the Defense Ministry to walk back their initial orders in humiliation.[93] Notably, in this episode of commander resistance to the state,

Fofié did not have to make a public "show of arms" to force the government to back down. Government leaders' knowledge of Fofié's coercive power was enough to deter further escalation.[94] While Fofié ultimately accepted reassignment to Daloa as deputy commander of the army's Second Military Region in 2017, the former com'zone kept a strong grip over his affairs in Korhogo. In the aftermath of Guillaume Soro's fallout with the Ouattara regime in 2019, several of Fofié's safehouses in Korhogo were reportedly raided by government agents amid suspicions of Fofié's enduring links to Soro.[95]

In sum, the persistence of strong commander-community ties sustained through repeated interactions and selective forms of service provision enabled Fofié to remain linked to local mobilization networks in Korhogo and maintain the capacity for autonomous collective action. Informal authority relationships and patron-client ties between the former commandant and local networks of youth and ex-combatants remained intact after the demobilization of the FN organization, which endowed Fofié with coercive leverage vis-à-vis the new government in Abidjan and motivated periodic resistance to postwar statebuilding. Fofié's bargaining power was ultimately grounded in a legacy of collaborative wartime rule in Korhogo, which created enduring local alliances and opened a viable pathway for Fofié to resist the demobilization of his private armed networks, remain autonomous from central regime control, and carve out an independent sphere of influence in the postconflict state. Fearful of his enduring power base, the regime in Abidjan attempted to undermine Fofié's authority by relocating him away from his wartime fiefdom. Fofié's local embeddedness both increased his willingness to resist the postwar state and led the Ouattara government to engage in actions against the commander that further eroded ex-rebels' confidence in the regime.

Ousmane, the former zone commander in Bouaké, again provides an instructive counterfactual. Because of the legacy of coercive rebel rule in Bouaké, postwar commander-community ties rapidly declined. Interviewees in Bouaké described an abrupt shift in political order after the end of the civil war in 2011. The governance structures of the FN were dismantled, and the administrative apparatus of the state reasserted itself in the domains of policing, education, and health care. While the redeployed state did not automatically garner trust among the population in Bouaké, few residents wished to see either Ousmane or other FN leaders remain in charge. As one religious leader explained, "The people here [in Bouaké] were not happy about the degradation of services. There is a feeling that the invaders destroyed what they had built."[96] Residents had tolerated the FN presence in Bouaké to a degree while war was ongoing, but this patience evaporated with Ouattara's political victory in 2011. Although Ousmane and his lieutenants were well regarded among their own immediate subordinates who integrated with them into the FRCI, most residents I interviewed in Bouaké were more than happy to see these ex-rebel officers depart the city.

Like Fofié, Ousmane continued to visit his wartime zone of control in an official military capacity in the postwar era and sent his lieutenants to collect tithes from local businesses that remained under the protection of former FN figures.[97] Yet the kinds of social calls, attendance at ceremonial events, and spontaneous cooperation with local elites described by interviewees in Korhogo were almost entirely absent in Bouaké. Responsibility for security and policing largely returned to the redeployed police and gendarmerie forces.[98] In my 2018 survey, 75 percent of respondents in Bouaké indicated that if they were the victim of a crime, they would turn to the police or prefectoral corps for assistance; only a single respondent indicated that they would turn to a former FN commander or combatant. Traditional leaders and members of the municipal government expressed surprise when I asked them if they had ever contacted an ex-rebel commander to help them resolve governance or security problems since the end of the war. As Ismael responded: "The commandants? No. Let me tell you what would happen. You bring your problem before him, and maybe he will just tell you to pay him some money. And that is if you are lucky!"[99] As one church pastor put it simply, "the FN aren't powerful anymore in this city."[100]

Without sustained ties to local elites and popular status as a legitimate guarantor of order in the city, Ousmane's connections to networks of potential collective action in Bouaké diminished after his relocation to Abidjan. Demobilized combatants in Bouaké remained horizontally connected to each other through a series of association-based movements, including the Côte d'Ivoire Association for the Demobilized (ADCI), and Cellule 39 (several of these groups were originally created by FN leaders to control ex-combatant networks and to distribute DDR funds).[101] But the vertical ties between the démobilisés and their former commanders were weak. One demobilized FN member in Bouaké, for example, expressed frustration and a sense of abandonment: "We do not see them, our grand-frères. Where are they now? They have forgotten us."[102] With few postwar linkages to the civilian population in Bouaké, Ousmane and his lieutenants instead attached themselves to political and economic networks in Abidjan, carving out new zones of influence and extortion in the capital's wealthy suburbs.[103] When asked if Ousmane sought to maintain ties with démobilisé networks within Bouaké, one local administrator remarked: "There are a few former soldiers of Chérif [Ousmane] here still loyal to him, but they are not many. The FN leaders here wanted to be close to Abidjan, the center of political power, in order to have their share of the cake."[104] The former zone commander brought an entourage of his most loyal followers with him to the GSPR in Abidjan, but his linkages to broader ex-combatant networks in the north withered.

Weak commander-community ties in Bouaké thus left Ousmane with comparatively little motive or capacity for resistance against the Ouattara

CHAPTER 5

regime. Though Ousmane was considered a competent military tactician, he was neither capable of mobilizing private armed networks on a significant scale nor indispensable for maintaining local order in the north. Resisting the government's schemes for military reconstruction and security-sector reform was therefore a nonstarter. At the same time, Ousmane lacked strong motives to resist the Ouattara regime's statebuilding plans, since those plans did not significantly threaten his power base or parochial interests. Working near the centers of power in Abidjan gave Ousmane better prospects to acquire wealth by establishing control over new commercial networks in the capital city and building closer ties to the president. In 2015, the same year that the Ouattara government unsuccessfully attempted to relocate Fofié, both Ousmane and Issiaka Ouattara (nom de guerre "Wattao," the former zone commander in Séguéla) were sent abroad for an eight-month military training course in Morocco.[105] Referring to Ousmane, one analyst said, "With commanders like that, the government had an easier time. They were military men, and they could be positioned anywhere . . . this gave the president more control."[106] The connotation of being a "military man" was that such commanders were loyal to the FRCI chain of command and possessed fewer outside ties to private armed networks.

The willingness of Ousmane to obey regime orders was also critical for subduing military and ex-combatant protests in 2014 and 2017. Bouaké's central location made it an epicenter for uprisings by rank-and-file ex-FAFN soldiers, who demanded back pay for unpaid wages between 2009 and 2011.[107] Ousmane was among the first military representatives dispatched to confront the mutineers.[108] After several days of negotiation, the uprisings were ultimately resolved without significant bloodshed. In an interview with another former FN commander who worked with Ousmane to talk down the mutineers in 2017, this commander explained to me: "It was our responsibility to manage the difficult situation that was reigning after May 2011. We were inserted into the army, and our duty was to serve the president. . . . So when our brothers were picking up their Kalashnikovs [against the government], we were able to help find a solution, to make our comrades understand."[109] Ousmane's loyalty won him a string of subsequent promotions, attaining the rank of brigadier general and *chef d'état-major* of the land army.

Ousmane's postwar loyalty to the Ouattara regime should not be taken to mean that this ex-rebel commander became a model military professional. Like most former FN commanders, Ousmane and his associates continued to skirt the law and protect their vital business interests after 2011 and participated in illicit businesses and shady protection schemes in the capital city.[110] Yet there is a crucial difference between Ousmane and Fofié in terms of these ex-rebel commanders' relationships to the central postwar state. Whereas Fofié maintained a power base within his wartime zone of control in the context of an increasingly adversarial relationship with the government, fed by mutual suspicion and fears of betrayal, Ousmane cultivated a peacetime career under the umbrella of the president's ruling coalition. With weak ties to former rebel-ruled territory, Ousmane aligned himself with the civilian-led military hierarchy because it was his surest path to survival as a nonembedded commander.

Matched Pair 2: Sangouiné and Mahapleu

This section turns to an in-depth study of Sangouiné and Mahapleu, two adjacent subprefectures in western Côte d'Ivoire that fell under FN control in the Ivorian civil war. These cases offer several distinct advantages for comparison. First, the subprefectures exhibit close similarity across virtually all structural attributes, including geographic position, yet experienced starkly different patterns of wartime rebel rule. The paired comparison of Sangouiné and Mahapleu thus permits an especially strong test of the argument that rebel rule shapes commander embeddedness and postwar ex-rebel resistance. Second, unlike the zone commanders of Korhogo and Bouaké, the local FN commanders in Sangouiné and Mahapleu were mid-level sector commanders with significantly smaller spheres of influence. Studying these localities thus allows me to demonstrate the validity of my commander embeddedness theory at a lower level of territorial aggregation. Finally, unlike in Korhogo and Bouaké, ethnic northerners—the supposed natural political constituency of the FN—were not numerically dominant in Sangouiné and Mahapleu. The cases thus permit a test of the explanatory power of my argument in a context where commanders do not possess coethnic ties to most of the civilian population.

REBEL RULE IN SANGOUINÉ AND MAHAPLEU

During Côte d'Ivoire's agricultural economic boom in the 1960s and 1970s, Sangouiné and Mahapleu both enjoyed a period of relative prosperity driven by coffee and cocoa cultivation. In addition to their Yacouba (Dan-speaking) peoples, a relatively small linguistic group who inhabit western Côte d'Ivoire and northeastern Liberia, the subprefectures also became home to growing numbers of Malinké and Akan migrants from northern and central Côte d'Ivoire.[111] Many of these populations migrated to the west in the early twentieth century as agricultural laborers. By the 1990s, as in many areas in the Great West, intercommunal tensions in the towns grew between "firstcomer" (*autochtone*) and "newcomer" (*allogène*) residents over land access rights.[112]

Civil war came to western Côte d'Ivoire in November 2002, and the region soon became the epicenter of the war's most intense fighting. Fearful of losing economically productive land to the advancing MPCI/FN rebel forces, President Gbagbo and FANCI commanders called for the mobilization of local Krahn and Yacouba youths to form "auto-defense" groups throughout the region.[113] Government leaders also invited mercenaries and militia members from Liberia to help repel the rebel incursions.[114] Confusing matters, MPCI/FN rebels also sponsored the formation of their own proxy militias in the west, including the Mouvement pour la Justice et la Paix (MJP) and the Mouvement Populaire Ivoirien du Grand Ouest (MPIGO), which also recruited Liberian mercenaries.[115] By December, these anti-Gbagbo rebel forces established control over the cities of Man, Danané, and the east–west corridor linking these towns. The subprefectures of Sangouiné and Mahapleu were both within this southern slice of the Tonkpi region, the last stretch of territory to fall under permanent rebel control before the establishment of the *zone de confiance* (cease-fire zone) in the west in May 2003.[116]

Sangouiné and Mahapleu were first captured by the MPIGO militia. These soldiers were mostly Anglophone Liberians who spoke little French. In December 2002, loyalist troops and their hired mercenaries rolled back the rebels' territorial gains, and both towns were recaptured by progovernment forces. This initial period of occupation by pro-rebel and then pro-Gbagbo Liberian fighters was remembered in both towns as a time of brutality and chaos.[117] As the village chief of Sangouiné recounted: "The rebellion came in November 2002. They encircled the village, firing into the air. . . . Then we were taken by the Liberians. All the homes were looted, and property was stolen."[118] FANCI forces conducted security sweeps to round up suspected rebel sympathizers, since "they were very suspicious of the villagers for having helped MPIGO rebels."[119] The situation in Mahapleu was similar. Each time Mahapleu changed hands, another wave of pillage and looting was unleashed. "They all said they were here to protect us," said Ouahi, "but then they started to occupy the houses. . . . Myself, I had a private business, but everything was taken. Many people lost their goods."[120]

By mid-January, rebel reinforcements arrived in the west and installed a semblance of order. Along with allied dozo militia, more disciplined FN units—most comprised of northern Ivorians and soldiers from Burkina Faso—pushed back into the region and "chased out" the Liberian combatants working on behalf of the Gbagbo regime.[121] When the FN leadership in Bouaké established its new administrative system, Sangouiné and Mahapleu were placed under the jurisdiction of the zone commander Losseni Fofana based in the nearby city of Man (zone 6).[122] Fofana in turn appointed his own hand-chosen lieutenants to local command positions throughout the Tonkpi region.[123] Permanent FN control brought a degree of stability and the restoration of basic services that had been nonfunctional since the onset of the conflict. Still, rebel-civilian relations in the west remained tense. Many freshly recruited rebel units lacked discipline or oversight. Heitz-

Tokpa, for example, notes that in the city of Man, "self-proclaimed commanders [COs] . . . roamed the streets with their personal troops and did not necessarily feel they were part of a chain of command."[124] The perceived progovernment sympathies of civilian populations in the west also created friction between residents and FN forces. Many Yacouba in western Côte d'Ivoire had voted for Gbagbo in the 2000 elections, and some local politicians continued to openly align with the Gbagbo regime.[125]

Despite similar initial conditions, patterns of rebel-civilian relations in Sangouiné and Mahapleu began to diverge by late 2003. In Sangouiné, Fofana appointed a Senoufo army officer from Korhogo known only as "Kassero" as the FAFN sector commander. Kassero was born in the Poro region of Korhogo and served in the FANCI army as a corporal prior to the onset of the civil war. During his military career, Kassero grew close to Fofana. The two men fought together in Bouaké to defeat pro-Gbagbo forces in September and October 2002.[126] Kassero subsequently followed his commander west when Fofana was designated as the com'zone of Man in 2003. Initially stationed in Mahapleu as a *chef de poste*, Kassero was soon promoted to the position of sector commander in Sangouiné.

Kassero's arrival, interviewees in Sangouiné agreed, marked the beginning of a positive turn in civilian relations with FN forces. One of Kassero's first priorities upon arriving in Sangouiné was the restoration of an administrative infrastructure capable of meeting local service and material needs. Because many civil servants—including the mayor—had fled the area, the new sector commander hired his own replacements to many positions. "With Kassero, things improved," said the village chief in 2017. "The mairie started to operate again, people started returning to work."[127] Another villager explained, "When they arrived, they established a new government here. All the members of the administration were nominated by them. The mayor himself was in a military fatigue in his office. . . . This was the civilian branch beside the military branch. They took care of paperwork, taxes, that sort of thing for the population."[128] To restore basic health care services, Kassero ordered the medical clinic to be reopened.[129] The head of the clinic recounted, "I presented myself to the CO of the Forces Nouvelles. He said, 'you have to care for the population.' I complained that doctors had to be able to circulate freely. . . . So he granted me a pass that let me travel in the zone."[130] Kassero even provided modest resources to assist in local infrastructure repairs. One member of local government said, "If there was a broken bridge, it was difficult. But the CO would call on his people to go and help organize a team to fix it."[131] Another resident agreed that "if there was something to be done, it was *'vite fait.'*"[132]

Mechanisms for power sharing with local elites and communication between the FN and citizens also facilitated confidence building in Sangouiné. According to one local notable, "Kassero organized meetings, about two times per month. Women, youth, traditional elders, they all participated at these meetings. We explained to them our needs."[133] Another administrative official confirmed that "the rebels worked a lot with the chefferie. The *président des jeunes* was solicited a lot to help organize ceremonies and football tournaments with the villagers and the rebels to improve relations."[134] Even members of Gbagbo's FPI party in Sangouiné acknowledged that Kassero made a special effort to be "available" to local leaders. According to one village notable, who worked as the secretary general of the local FPI branch, "the village leader could mediate with them. Me, as a notable, I could speak with them. There were a lot of other villagers with a privileged relationship who could also go. . . . I had no problem with Kassero personally."[135] Such interactions also provided a communication bridge between residents in Sangouiné and the higher-level FN zone commander in Man, Fofana.[136]

Kassero also made efforts to restore discipline among local FN elements in Sangouiné and reduce the frequency of abuses against civilians that had poisoned popular support for the rebellion in the early months of the war. Rebel soldiers were instructed not to enter or disrupt the churches in the village.[137] As one interviewee said, "I would say that the CO looked after the population well here. In cases of *malcomportement* [indiscipline], we would have a meeting with Kassero, and he would send the offending element elsewhere, or else straighten them out."[138] Visible demonstrations of concern for civilian well-being solidified the sector commanders' popular standing, or at least acceptance, among many residents in Sangouiné.

If Sangouiné illustrates the creation of a strong social contract amid rebel governance in civil war, Mahapleu represents the opposite trajectory. After the rotation of several different outpost commanders, Mahapleu was placed under the shared control of two FN officers in early 2004: "Rodrik" (CO) and "Ondo" (deputy CO). Like Kassero, Rodrik and Ondo were corporals in the FANCI army prior to the rebellion. They were stationed in the Man zone through their connection to Captain "Eddy," the sector commander of Danané and another close associate of Fofana. Along with most of the soldiers in their entourage, both Rodrik and Ondo were ethnic Malinké northerners from the town of Séguéla.[139] Yet interviewees in Mahapleu generally felt that material conditions under the FN were not appreciably different than under the Liberian mercenaries. The village chief recounted that from their arrival in the subprefecture, "they took homes by force, they demanded to be given food. They started to kill people, and there were a lot of cases of pillage. Often they took the beef cattle. . . . We were afraid. They would fire in the middle of the night."[140] Whereas residents in Sangouiné enjoyed a rudimentary system of medical care, health care facilities in Mahapleu remained shuttered. "The [medical] dispensaries were taken by the rebels," Ouahi explained. "They occupied these . . . for their own doctor. But he was only for the rebels. He did not care for the population."[141] Without inclusive health services available, residents in Mahapleu were forced to travel to Danané or Man to seek emergency care.

Power sharing between Rodrik and Ondo and local elites in Mahapleu remained minimal. No routinized system of meetings or dialogue existed. "The FN CO here did not organize meetings with the population or the chefferie. Rodrik organized a few meetings, but they were not regular. They were dominated by the rebels."[142] Other villagers agreed, noting, "It was difficult to communicate with them. As soon as you arrive before them, you don't know how you will be judged or treated."[143] On a few occasions, the FN commanders did reach out to local intermediaries, such as party organizers, to convene gatherings with villagers. Yet descriptions of these meetings did not convey a sense of two-way dialogue or confidence building. One FPI party member I interviewed, for example, recounted his experience working as a spokesperson for the FN: "When they wanted to organize meetings, I would be solicited. It was hard to communicate with them though, you had to pay money each time. . . . This was not really a meeting where the population could say anything to them."[144] Appeals by residents in Mahapleu to discipline or replace abusive FN elements went unheeded.[145]

The absence of effective mediation with local leaders further exacerbated the problem of rebel abuse of civilians in Mahapleu. "Without the chefferie," one civilian said, "the rebels had no knowledge about the needs of the population."[146] When I asked local leaders in Mahapleu about their ability to work with Rodrik and Ondo, the response was often incredulous. "They told us they were here to protect us. But in reality they did not come for that. Those of us who tried to provide security, they mistreated us!"[147] One of the most egregious offenses by FN rebels in the eyes of customary authorities in Mahapleu was the rebels' interference with the ceremonial burial of villagers. According to Mahapleu's village chief, FN soldiers took to demanding paperwork and the payment of a large fee to obtain permission to bury the bodies of the deceased.[148] Such blatant extortion left villagers incensed.

Why did practices of rebel rule look so different in Sangouiné and Mahapleu? Geographic location and armed competition cannot explain the variation in this case. The subprefectures are separated by less than thirty kilometers, and both were proximate to the rebel-government cease-fire zone. The ethnic makeup of each locality was also highly similar—approximately two-thirds Yacouba and the remaining third a mixture of Akan and Mande groups. Thus, there should not have been meaningful differences in the perceived prospects of winning support from the civilian population based on ethnic politics. Given the strategic importance of the western territorial zone, commanders in both subprefectures presumably had incentives to invest in rebel-civilian relations and shore up political support for the rebellion.[149]

While simple idiosyncrasies in the personalities of local FN rebels and their commanders may have played a role, one likely factor that affected the quality of wartime governance was the strength of preexisting local elites. In Sangouiné, a strong local network of business leaders and politicians coalesced in the 1980s and 1990s. This governing elite was headed by the charismatic mayor and regional power broker Siki Blon Blaise (aka "The Bulldozer").[150] Blon Blaise used his economic and political clout in the subprefecture to develop a significant patronage network, install loyal supporters in both local government and the chefferie, and consolidate support for his bids for elected office.[151] When Blon Blaise relocated to Abidjan as an elected member of parliament for the UDPCI party after the 2000–2001 elections, he left behind a still-intact hierarchy of governing elites in Sangouiné.[152] As in Korhogo, the existence of a cohesive set of local gatekeepers likely facilitated Kassero's ability to rule in a collaborative fashion in Sangouiné, enabling the sector commander to gather information and exercise authority through these co-opted intermediaries. In Mahapleu, by contrast, the prewar local elite was comparatively weak. No power broker with comparable stature to Blon Blaise existed, and traditional leaders in the subprefecture were riven by internal conflicts over competing claims to the head of the village chieftaincy.[153] Without a cohesive local elite to work through, Rodrik and Ondo lacked an obvious point of entry to gain influence "from above." This may partly account for why rebels resorted to coercion to enforce civilian obedience in Mahapleu.

COMMANDER EMBEDDEDNESS AND POSTWAR RESISTANCE
IN SANGOUINÉ AND MAHAPLEU

Even in smaller subprefectures like Sangouiné and Mahapleu, local practices of rebel rule had significant consequences for postwar commander-community ties and the willingness of ex-rebels to resist the regime. After Kassero joined the FRCI at the rank of captain at an army base near Man in 2011, the former commandant remained firmly tethered to local affairs and social life in Sangouiné. Enduring social support among ordinary residents and local elites sustained Kassero's ties to his wartime outpost. In the time that I spent conducting research in the region, respondents almost invariably described Kassero as a well-respected and trusted "son of the village." As the village chief told me, "Kassero still comes here. He is like a *fils du village*. He is from Korhogo, he is Senoufo, but he is like a fils du village here."[154] Even the previous (now retired) chief said that "Kassero still comes to greet me here. And he still comes for ceremonies, during holidays."[155] Another interviewee reflected, "He had a good relationship with the population. . . . He helped the population to forget things. That is not soon forgotten."[156] The new mayor, Oulaï Tiémoko Prosper, in a token of recognition of Kassero's service to the community, awarded the former commandant a plot of land at the western edge of town at the road juncture leading to Podiagouine. "We wanted to show our recognition. Thanks to him, our community did not suffer like many others."[157] Kassero "was not like the other commanders," another local notable said.[158]

Kassero's enduring grassroots social support and alliances with local elites in Sangouiné in turn bolstered the ex-commander's ability to sustain relationships with former fighters in the area, keep tabs on ex-combatant networks, and preserve autonomous mobilization power. Most demobilized combatants I interviewed were reluctant to discuss their relationship with Kassero directly, but accounts from other villagers suggested a strong relationship.[159] As one resident explained: "Those who were inserted into the army, when they come back to the village, they don't forget where they came from. They bring some support. Kassero today is an FRCI captain. He was initially a lieutenant but is a captain now. From time to time he comes. When he comes he is still respected by the démobilisés here. He will give some *jettons de la main* [pocket money] for them."[160] Another community leader agreed: "Officially I have not seen Kassero give money in public [to ex-combatants], but among them, among his elements, he gives support. When he comes, they are together, him and the démobilisés."[161] Several ex-combatants were hired by Kassero as laborers for his hotel compound on the land gifted by the mayor. Thus, overlapping bonds—both material and nonmaterial—sustained strong connections between Kassero and local networks of former combatants in Sangouiné.

Although the number of ex-combatants in Sangouiné is small (approximately thirty in the subprefecture) relative to larger cities like Korhogo, Kassero's ability to contact and influence ex-combatants in Sangouiné reinforced the former commandant's status as a legitimate guarantor of order in the community. As one villager said, "He is still in communication with his superiors. If people bother our parents or our elders, you can complain to him. When there are these kinds of complaints against former FN elements, he can resolve it."[162] A member of the mayoral office similarly remarked that "with the *corps préfectorale* and the gendarmes who were redeployed here, there were no major problems. Kassero gave help to them, here. If there was a problem with a former element, Kassero could come."[163] As in other areas in northern Côte d'Ivoire with wartime histories of collaborative rebel rule, the former FN commander continued to function as an important community ally after rebel-military integration.

To what extent did enduring postwar commander-community ties in Sangouiné translate into heightened friction between the former FN sector commander and the central state? Although studying middle-ranking commanders like Kassero is more difficult than examining nationally prominent commanders like Fofié and Ousmane, the degree of participation of ex-rebel commanders' subordinate fighters in the 2017 antiregime mutinies and demobilized rebel protests—the primary subject of chapter 4—provides a meaningful gauge of ex-rebel resistance during an important moment of brinkmanship bargaining. For rank-and-file soldiers and mid-ranking officers like Kassero, the 2017 mutinies were inspired primarily by financial grievances concerning wages, bonus payments, and promotions within the FRCI following military integration in 2011–2012. These former combatants felt that President Ouattara owed his position to the sacrifices of "real" FN veterans like them and were increasingly aggrieved by the government's purported failures to adequately live up to the deal whereby ex-FN elements would be awarded privileged access to postwar state rents.[164]

According to the accounts given to me by multiple demobilized fighters in Sangouiné, ex-rebel participation in the 2017 mutinies was broad-based and organized. On January 7, 2017, one day after mutinying soldiers in the city of Bouaké broke into an armory and seized the police commissariat, a contingent of around two dozen former FN combatants from Sangouiné set out in *baka* minibuses toward the regional capital of Man. For two days, ex-combatants participated in riots at the FRCI barracks alongside their former FN comrades in the army.[165] When the government caved to the mutineers' demands for back pay and bonus payouts, the ex-combatants from Sangouiné were persuaded to return home after Lieutenant Colonel Fofana, the former zone commander of Man, addressed a gathering of mutineer leaders at the prefectoral headquarters. There, Fofana appealed to his former subordinates at the meeting to "call their sons home."[166] According to two interviewees who claimed to be informed about this meeting, Kassero was among the ex-rebel officers who attended.[167] This episode is revealing insofar as it shows qualitative evidence in line with this book's argument: aggrieved by the perceived failures of the Ouattara government to live up to the terms of the postwar bargain between ex-rebels and the state, and equipped with strong ties to ex-combatant networks in Sangouiné, the FRCI captain could participate in antiregime collective action as a meaningful player.

In Mahapleu, by contrast, ex-rebel commanders' ties to the community were cut off after the end of the war. Rodrik passed away shortly after Gbagbo's defeat in 2011, and Ondo was promoted to the rank of captain at an FRCI barracks in Man, less than an hour's drive from Mahapleu. Despite holding the same military rank as Kassero, the former rebel commander rarely visited Mahapleu after the end of the conflict, according to local interviewees.[168] Residents explained Ondo's absence in terms of his lack of grassroots social support and ties to local elites in the community. As one area resident put it, "If you acted bad during war, how can you come to greet the population later? It is impossible."[169] "He does not have a good relationship with the *chef* here," another villager said. "Maybe he still visits with some in the Malinké community, but not us. The former FN commander did not bring us any support here."[170] Another interviewee said, "After 2011 some were recruited to the army, but many were not. When the gendarmes called them [Rodrik and Ondo] to leave, they did not come anymore. Ondo is not welcome here today." One local leader put it simply: "He has no more power here. If he came, the population would not welcome him."[171]

With scant social support among either the population or local elites, Ondo found few opportunities to sustain ties to démobilisés in Mahapleu after his departure from the town. "The démobilisés here are working now," said one civilian. "They have no commandant here who organizes them. They have disarmed."[172] "Here in Mahapleu, démobilisés are here, like everywhere," said another resident. "I cannot really assure you that they are well-integrated, but they have their own means now in the community. Lots of them are implicated in crime, it is true. Insecurity remains. But no former FN commanders give them support. Ondo doesn't come to see them. The rebels don't exist here anymore."[173] Policing and crime prevention in Mahapleu also appeared to have largely reverted to the state. "Now it is the gendarmerie that takes care of security. They [FN] did nothing for us here. Ondo does not cooperate with the gendarmerie. Even if there is a problem with the démobilisés, you have to go to Loss [Fofana]."[174] Without a social conduit to the community or local legitimacy as a guarantor of order, Ondo lost contact with most ex-combatants in Mahapleu.

Ondo's comparatively weak postwar linkages in Mahapleu ultimately meant that, even though ex-rebels from Mahapleu had similar economic grievances against the Ouattara government as those in Sangouiné, he had little capacity or incentive to mobilize his supporters to challenge the state during the 2017 uprisings. Whereas ex-combatants in Sangouiné openly spoke of their involvement in the January 2017 protests, none of the former combatants I interviewed in Mahapleu claimed to have participated. As one démobilisé explained, "Maybe if you have a grand-frère in the army, you will get something. For me, the fight is over. Our grand-frère [Ondo] does not see us."[175] Another demobilized soldier explained that he did not want to leave his farmland to participate in the protests, as he feared that his unguarded property might be stolen.[176] These ex-rebel soldiers felt they had little to gain from participating in the protests without a connection to a senior army officer. Ondo, lacking the ability to generate autonomous collective action by mobilizing ex-combatant networks, played no discernible role in the January 2017 mutinies. According to the sous-préfet of Man, Ondo laid low during the protests and acted as a "loyal officer for the President."[177]

Causal Mechanisms and Alternative Explanations

An important objective of this chapter is to illustrate qualitatively my theory of commander embeddedness in concrete cases and to leverage these controlled comparisons as a test of my argument's micro foundations. Notably, these case studies were selected *after* the bulk of my quantitative data was collected and after an initial sketch of my theory had been formulated. Before concluding, I discuss the extent to which the evidence from these case studies adds confidence to the proposed mechanisms of the theory advanced by this book. I also draw attention to characteristics of each controlled comparison that my research design is unable to hold constant and consider alternative explanations.

The first hypothesis that this book seeks to examine is that postwar commander embeddedness persists in areas where wartime practices of rebel rule are collaborative. This happens because collaborative governance engenders grassroots social support for the field commanders of occupying armed groups and allows commanders to maintain alliances with local elites. Both Korhogo and Sangouiné, where practices of rebel governance closely approximated the ideal type of collaborative rule, support these mechanisms. Almost all residents and local elites that I interviewed in these sites spoke highly and respectfully of the former FN commanders who once governed their communities. People in these areas reported not only that their ex-rebel commander remained influential but also that this influence was legitimate since their commander had already proven through their wartime actions that they were a valuable ally of the community. Such sentiments were not universally shared, of course. A minority of interviewees rejected the authority of ex-rebel commanders in their communities, given that the war was now over. Even these respondents, however, did not deny that ex-rebel commanders did maintain popular support among others in the community. In Bouaké and Mahapleu, by contrast, where rebel rule was more predatory by most measures, ex-rebel commanders appeared to enjoy very little social support among ordinary civilians or local elites. As the local "face" of an armed occupation widely remembered for its brutality and hardships, these commanders rarely won words of respect or appreciation. Indeed, both ordinary civilians and elites in Bouaké and Mahapleu tended to employ an entirely different vocabulary and body language when talking about former FN commanders—one unmistakably marked by resentment and bitterness.

It is possible, of course, that the expressions of social support and moral recognition for ex-rebel commanders that I observed were biased. For instance, if commanders are seen as an important source of patronage resources for a community, then residents might feel pressure to paint these commanders in a positive light, regardless of their actual attitudes. Respondents could also remember wartime events differently because of current socioeconomic circumstances; practices of rebel rule could have been the same everywhere, but people in Bouaké and Mahapleu more readily recalled the predatory aspects of rebel rule because they want somebody to blame for their social or economic problems. While these sources of potential bias cannot be ruled out, several aspects of this study add confidence to the validity of the findings. First, I interviewed a broad cross section of individuals in each case study site, including people from very different socioeconomic stations and with different political inclinations, and heard consistent narratives about local FN commanders in each case. Second, in the cases of Korhogo and Bouaké, I was able to corroborate local accounts with several in-depth interviews with Ivorians in Abidjan who knew each case well but were not themselves residents of these cities. I do not doubt that there are limitations to the oral testimonies provided by respondents, but it is improbable that people from different cities and with different backgrounds would all exhibit the same biases.

The second hypothesis of this book is that local embeddedness affects ex-rebel commanders' likelihood of resistance to the central state after rebel-military integration. The underlying mechanism is that commanders' local embeddedness grants them autonomous coercive power vis-à-vis the central government and strengthens their motivations to resist centralized statebuilding. The case studies show that ex-rebel commanders who governed Korhogo and Sangouiné indeed had autonomous mobilization power that commanders from Bouaké and Mahapleu lacked. Fofié commanded support from a broad swath of influential elites in Korhogo after 2011, maintained contact with and control over a large network of armed fighters, and stashed a vast arsenal of weaponry in caches around the city. The government in Abidjan tolerated Fofié's local influence to a point, only to later attempt to relocate Fofié and dismantle his wartime networks in the north. These actions confirmed Fofié's worst fears about the government's security-sector reform (SSR) agenda and contributed to the erosion of trust between the former Korhogo com'zone and the Abidjan regime. In Kassero's fiefdom of Sangouiné, ex-rebel networks—inspired largely by economic grievances—were mobilized to participate in the 2017 protests against the Ouattara regime, which resulted in financial payoffs to thousands of ex-FN soldiers. Such dynamics of resistance were largely absent in the cases of Ousmane and Ondo. While Bouaké became a hotbed of ex-rebel protest activity, these démobilisé networks operated without the support or control of Ousmane, who had long lost contact with his former foot soldiers by 2017. In Mahapleu, Ondo's lack of communication with or support to former FN soldiers meant that few démobilisés bothered to make the trip to Man to participate when a wave of ex-rebel protests broke out there.

Can the dynamics of ex-rebel resistance in these cases be explained by factors other than commander embeddedness? An account of ex-rebel behavior based on material resources alone—one that ignores the legacies of rebel rule and commanders' social support—is challenged to explain the divergent trajectories of resistance across the cases in this chapter. According to this logic, ex-rebel commanders with access to material resources should be more likely to resist the central state because of their ability to privately purchase armed supporters in a transactional manner. Yet the size of the local economies available for rent extraction cannot easily explain variation across cases. While Sangouiné and Mahapleu were very similar in size, if anything, Bouaké was a comparatively larger commercial center than Korhogo and provided greater opportunities for rebel commanders like Ousmane to collect rents and taxes. Ex-FN commanders' wartime networks of resource extraction often proved brittle after the demobilization of the FN organization. According to the community informant survey, by 2013, only 28 percent of rebel-ruled localities continued to pay taxes to ex-FN members, and by 2017, only 6 percent did so. Ex-rebel commanders who sustained influence and mobilization power in northern Côte d'Ivoire did so primarily because of their enduring social ties to these communities, not because they were rich enough to buy private armies (though modest financial transfers did help to reinforce patron-client ties between commanders and demobilized fighters). Without the pretext of wartime mobilization against the Gbagbo regime, nonembedded commanders like Ousmane and Ondo were incapable of sustaining either sociopolitical or economic influence in their former zones of control.

One alternative explanation that my research design cannot fully account for is the role of personality and leadership. It is possible that the divergent trajectories of commander embeddedness and resistance to the central state in each case reflect the personal ambition of commanders to maintain independent political power or the interpersonal hostilities between these commanders and the Ouattara regime. While the role of leadership and personal psychology among rebel military commanders is a fascinating and under-researched topic, there are reasons to question the explanatory power of such factors here. Both Fofié and Ousmane had a history of close political collaboration with northern politicians in Ouattara's entourage that extended to the 1990s, including participation in the 1999 military putsch and a subsequent coup effort against the Gbagbo government in 2001.[178] Thus, both commanders demonstrated personal political ambitions, and both had preexisting personal ties with figures in the Ouattara government. Fofié himself was sufficiently trusted by the Outtara government to be given custody of Gbagbo in 2011. The deterioration in Fofié's relationship with the Ouattara regime appears to have occurred *after* military integration, when the return of the state administration in Korhogo began to threaten Fofié's parochial interests, and the commanders' independent power marked him as a threat to the regime. In the cases of Kassero and Ondo, both commanders had similar prewar career trajectories within the FANCI, and neither individual appeared to have had any close interactions with senior members of the Ouattara government that would indicate differences in interpersonal ties. Ultimately, no complex outcome has a single explanation, and the idiosyncratic characteristics of commanders like Fofié and Kassero may have played a role in explaining their ability to remain locally embedded and their willingness to challenge the postwar state. But the available evidence indicates that these commanders' local social support also shaped commanders' capacity and motive for resistance.

This chapter presented qualitative evidence from four case studies to illustrate how practices of wartime rebel rule yielded divergent trajectories of ex-rebel commander embeddedness and postwar resistance. Where rebel forces cultivated enduring local ties through collaborative governance, ex-rebel commanders leveraged their social support bases to preserve mobilization power and ultimately to challenge the authority of the postwar regime. Predatory governance, by contrast, curtailed the mobilization power and local legitimacy of rebel commanders after the postwar transition, leading these military actors to align with the central government after rebel-military integration. The stakes of these outcomes are significant. If ex-rebel commanders in a large city like Bouaké had emerged from the civil war with strong local ties, the Ouattara-Soro regime might have soon collapsed under the pressures of armed resistance within its own military.[179] By the same token, weaker local ties among former rebel commanders such as Fofié in Korhogo could have produced a much stronger postwar regime in Côte d'Ivoire.

Beyond testing my theory, the case studies analyzed in this chapter also suggest new insights about the formation of rebels' wartime institutions amid varied preexisting social structures. In particular, the experiences of communities in northern Côte d'Ivoire call into question the assumption of some scholars that in areas with high-quality local institutions, armed groups will abstain from investing in governance institutions because the expected costs of collective resistance are prohibitively high.[180] In Korhogo and Sangouiné, the presence of strong local elites appears to have *enabled* the FN administration to interface more effectively with the population and to subcontract certain governance tasks to existing nonstate actors. The absence of effective and centralized preexisting institutions in Bouaké and Mahapleu, by contrast, left FN rebels without obvious governance partners, resulting in a more authoritarian style of rule and worse outcomes for civilian welfare. At least under certain conditions, such as a minimum level of popular support for armed groups and a willingness among local elites to shift allegiances, the presence of strong communal institutions may sometimes facilitate rather than hinder effective wartime governance.[181]

III. BEYOND CÔTE D'IVOIRE

CHAPTER 6

Commander Resistance after Rebel-Military Integration (1946–2019)

To this point, this book has relied on in-depth research in a single country to build and test a theory of ex-rebel commander embeddedness after civil war. Leveraging comparisons across localities in Côte d'Ivoire, chapters 2–5 illustrated each step in my argument connecting wartime patterns of rebel rule, local commander embeddedness, and postwar resistance. The evidence suggested that where insurgents invested in wartime practices of collaborative rule, field commanders acquired strong local ties in rebel-ruled communities, which in turn endowed them with long-term mobilization power and local legitimacy. These embedded ex-rebel commanders had greater capacity to organize resistance to the postwar regime and stronger motives to disrupt centralized statebuilding. By contrast, in areas that witnessed more predatory wartime rule, rebel field commanders were more likely to see their local ties wither away in the postwar period, leading to cooperation with the central state.

This chapter probes the generalizability of the argument beyond Côte d'Ivoire, leaving behind the advantages of controlled subnational comparisons in exchange for breadth across time and space. To do so, I analyze a novel dataset of sixty cases of rebel-military integration since 1946. Drawing on a broad range of secondary sources, I compare the predictions of my theory against observed outcomes of ex-rebel commander resistance to the state following military integration. I focus on the most impactful and clearly observable form of ex-rebel commander resistance: defection. Defection is conceptualized here as an act of defiance or insubordination that openly challenges the authority of the ruling regime leadership, including acts of violent rebellion, coup attempts, or mutinies. Generalizing the logic of this book's theory to the armed group level, we should expect to see the risks of postwar defection rise among ex-rebel commanders from an integrating armed group when rebels engaged in collaborative wartime rule. By contrast, when rebel groups integrate into state militaries without first engaging in collaborative wartime rule, the chances of postwar defection by commanders from those groups should be reduced. While the challenges of data collection prevent me from testing causal mechanisms directly, I aim to scrutinize an important implication of this book's argument concerning the postconflict behaviors of rebel commanders across a wide historical and geographic sweep.

The core findings of the chapter suggest that the theory has broad explanatory power. Across different decades and world regions, patterns of rebel governance have shaped field commanders' subsequent decisions to resist the postwar state. I show that when integrating armed groups engage in goods provision for civilians during civil war, the predicted likelihood that field commanders from these groups defect from the postwar ruling regime increases substantially. This pattern is present among both victorious rebel groups who defeat their adversaries outright and armed groups that integrate into state militaries following negotiated peace settlements. Other factors, such as regime type and ethnic cleavages, also affect the likelihood of ex-rebel commander defections, but the effects of wartime rebel rule are not washed away by these variables. Overall, the findings presented in this chapter suggest that the roots of instability and security-sector fragmentation in postconflict states often lie in the social legacies of civil wars.

The chapter unfolds in several parts. First, I detail how the dataset of rebel-military integration was constructed and discuss how the main independent and dependent variables (rebel rule and commander defection, respectively) were conceptualized and measured. I also detail several alternative macro-level explanations for rebel-military integration outcomes that are tested in the chapter, including the nature of the armed conflict and its termination, the presence of third-party interveners, state capabilities, ethnic cleavages, ideology, structural characteristics of the military, and regime type. The second part of the chapter analyzes the correlates of ex-rebel commander defection after rebel-military integration since 1946 and includes a discussion of endogeneity concerns and robustness checks. Finally, to demonstrate the utility of the theory to understand contemporary rebel-military integration, I briefly examine two "out of sample" cases: Afghanistan since the Taliban victory in 2021 and the ongoing efforts to rebuild security institutions in the Central African Republic (CAR).

The Data: Rebel-Military Integration since 1946

CASE SELECTION

To assess the external validity of this book's argument beyond Côte d'Ivoire, I collected data on all cases of rebel-military integration since 1946. My unit of analysis is the *integrating rebel group*. Specifically, I analyze all nonstate armed groups that: (1) challenged an incumbent government through sustained armed mobilization and (2) subsequently integrated their military forces, in whole or in part, into the national army of the state. In a break with typical practice among civil war scholars, my analysis joins together two types of conflict termination that are often studied separately: outright victories by rebel groups (where the rebel army becomes the state army) and negotiated settlements that attempt to integrate rebel commanders and soldiers into existing state security forces. By jointly analyzing these cases, I can detect general patterns that cut across different conflict termination contexts while reserving the ability to analyze each type of war-to-peace transition in isolation.

To identify cases of integrating rebel groups, I drew on the list of rebel victories found in the UCDP Conflict Termination Dataset, the list of rebel victories in Monica Toft's dataset of civil war termination,[1] and the list of rebel-military integration agreements compiled by Katherine Glassmyer and Nicholas Sambanis.[2] I then culled from these lists cases that failed to meet the following scope conditions.

First, the nonstate armed group had to be identifiable as a movement or organization that mounted a sustained challenge to the sovereignty of an incumbent government. To meet this criterion, rebels had to be active in fighting with a government that resulted in at least twenty-five casualties within a calendar year and must have had a distinct leadership that made them independent political actors.[3] Given my theoretical interest in the effects of wartime dynamics, I exclude cases of coups d'état where military officers seized power as a fait accompli without first building an independent organization that engaged in organized violence.[4] I do, however, include military putsches that involved a protracted (i.e., at least one month) incumbent-challenger conflict that created an extended "rupture" in state sovereignty.[5] For instance, I include the armed forces who were loyal to General Francois Bozizé in late 2002/early 2003, controlled territory in northern CAR, and engaged in violence against supporters of President Félix Patassé for several months prior to installing Bozizé into power in 2003 and reintegrating into the military.

Second, the armed movement must have attempted to integrate or transform former rebel forces into an incumbent state army. I exclude a handful of cases that appear as rebel victories in the UCDP and Toft lists where armed groups achieve limited regional autonomy or a shift in government policy but do not claim the mantle of independent state rulership. Such cases include the United Wa State Army (UWSA) in northeastern Myanmar, the National Movement for the Liberation of Azawad (MNLA) in Mali, or the Iraqi Kurds in 1991. I also exclude several cases where nonstate armed groups gained physical control of the capital city but made no effort to build a new national army, such as the United Somali Congress (USC) in Somalia in 1991 or the Houthi rebellion in Yemen since 2014. I do include secessionist groups that gained de facto sovereignty and used their rebel armies to build new national armies, such as the Eritrean People's Liberation Front (EPLF), the Sudan People's Liberation Army / Movement (SPLA/M), and the Kosovo Liberation Army (KLA) in Kosovo.

Third, for cases of rebel-military integration via negotiated settlement, there must be evidence of an actual effort to implement the military integration provisions, as demonstrated by events such as swearing-in ceremonies, joint training exercises, and the issuance of new military equipment and attire to rebel armies. I exclude purely nominal and/or shambolic peace settlements that merely acted as cover for belligerents to continue prosecuting war against each other. For instance, I exclude the Lagos Accords in 1979 in Chad, which officially brought the rebel Forces Armées du Nord (FAN, formerly FROLINAT) into the Chadian army under a transitional power-sharing government between Goukouni Oueddei and Hissen Habré. In this case, the peace agreement provided only a brief respite from fighting between pro-Oueddei and pro-Habré forces from August 1979 to January 1980. There is little evidence that any military integration of rebel forces actually occurred in this time, and each faction retained entirely separate organizations. Thus, my analysis aims to capture dynamics of ex-rebel commander resistance in cases where the sovereignty rupture caused by civil war was at least temporarily mended and the military integration process saw some amount of implementation.

Applying these criteria, I identify sixty integrating rebel groups since 1946. The sample includes break-off military factions, anticolonial nationalist movements, revolutionary Marxist insurgencies, and impromptu ethnic militias. While any cross-national data-collection effort of this sort faces limitations, the dataset enables the rigorous study of rebel-military integration outcomes, helping uncover patterns over a range of conflict contexts.

DEPENDENT VARIABLE: EX-REBEL COMMANDER DEFECTION

To gauge ex-rebel commander resistance following military integration, I constructed the dichotomous variable *Defection*. This variable indicates whether any ex-rebel commander (or set of commanders) who formerly belonged to a given rebel group inside the new state army challenged the sovereign authority of the central ruling regime at any point from the start of the military integration process up to a maximum observation window of ten years. I consider the following behaviors to constitute an open challenge to regime authority: (a) attempts to remove or assassinate regime leaders through a coup, (b) the creation of or participation in an antistate rebel group, or (c) the staging of a mutiny to extract monetary or policy concessions. I cast a wide net to construct this variable, process tracing each case using sources such as scholarly histories, NGO reports, news media articles, conflict and military coup databases, and other secondary materials. In total, I document at least one episode of *Defection* among ex-rebel commanders in thirty-one out of sixty cases (52 percent).

One issue with coding defections by ex-rebel commanders after military integration deserves mention here. There is a challenge posed by power-sharing settlements where rebel field commanders enter the state military and become subordinate to a civilian government that includes both leaders from their own political movement and from the old incumbent regime. In such cases, the political leaders of integrating rebel groups may join a power-sharing government or participate in elections but then choose to abandon peaceful politics and drag their field commanders in the military back to war with them. For example, field commanders of the National Union for the Total Independence of Angola (UNITA) integrated into the Angolan military after the 1991 Bicesse Accords but then followed the orders of UNITA leader Jonas Savimbi to resume rebellion against the Angolan state in October 1992, when Savimbi rejected the results of the September elections.[6] Although ex-UNITA field commanders were clearly influenced by political elites, I code such cases as episodes of defection for two reasons. First, conceptually, the logic of rebel-military integration implies that once insurgents merge their armies with the national military, ex-rebel officers ought to shift their allegiance from the leaders of their wartime political movement to the new integrated chain of command. Second, the choices of political leaders of integrating rebel groups are themselves plausibly shaped by the local embeddedness of ex-rebel field commanders. For example, Savimbi likely felt emboldened to return to violent rebellion in 1992 precisely *because* of the local resources and autonomous mobilization power still held by embedded ex-UNITA commanders.[7] In short, I expect that collaborative rebel rule should increase the likelihood of commander defection after both decisive victories and negotiated settlements with power-sharing governments. Nonetheless, as a robustness check, I create an alternative coding of the dependent variable that excludes cases where the impetus for military defection came from the political leadership of the integrating armed group.

INDEPENDENT VARIABLE: REBEL GOODS PROVISION

As a rough-and-ready measure of wartime rebel rule, I code a dichotomous variable, *Rebel goods provision*, which captures whether or not the integrating armed group engaged in significant local goods provision for civilians in rebel-controlled territory. While goods provision is only one element of a broader set of governance practices employed by nonstate armed groups, it is one of the most readily observed aspects of rebel rule and—as my subnational evidence from Côte d'Ivoire illustrates—is strongly correlated with other collaborative governance practices.[8] To measure rebel goods provision, I draw on two main data sources: Reyko Huang's Rebel

Table 6.1. Rebel rule and commander defection after rebel-military integration

	Postwar commander defection[1]	No postwar commander defection
Rebel goods provision[2]	Bolivia 1952 (MNR) Algeria 1963 (FLN) Guinea-Bissau 1973 (PAIGC) Mozambique 1974 (FRELIMO) Angola 1974 (MPLA) Cambodia 1975 (Khmer Rouge) Nicaragua 1979 (FSLN) Chad 1982 (FROLINAT / FAN) Liberia 1997 (NPFL) DRC 1997 (AFDL) Tajikistan 1992 (Popular Front) South Sudan 2005 (SPLA/M) Côte d'Ivoire 2011 (FN) CAR 2013 (Séléka) Angola 1991 (UNITA) Angola 1994 (UNITA) Cambodia 1991 (FUNCIPEC) Cambodia 1991 (Khmer Rouge) Iraq 1970 (KDP) Laos 1973 (Pathet Lao) Sudan 1972 (Anyanya) Zimbabwe 1979 (ZAPU)	China 1949 (PLA) Vietnam 1954 (Viet Minh) Cuba 1959 (M-26-7) Uganda 1986 (NRM) Namibia 1989 (SWAPO) Ethiopia 1991 (TPLF) Eritrea 1991 (EPLF) Afghanistan 1992 (Jamiyat-i-Islam) South Africa 1994 (ANC) Afghanistan 1996 (Taliban) Kosovo 1999 (KLA) Afghanistan 2001 (UIFSA) Bosnia 1995 (Croats / HVO) Mozambique 1992 (RENAMO)
No rebel goods provision	Costa Rica 1948 (NLA) Morocco 1956 (Army of Liberation) South Yemen 1967 (NFL) Uganda 1979 (UNLF) Chad 1990 (MPS)	Indonesia 1954 (Republicans) Guatemala 1954 (Armas) Tunisia 1956 (Fellagha) Iran 1979 (Revolutionary Council) Zimbabwe 1979 (ZANU) Rwanda 1994 (RPF) Congo Brazzaville 1997 (Cobras) Guinea-Bissau 1999 (Mané) Bosnia 1995 (Army of the Republic of Bosnia and Herzegovina) Bosnia 1995 (Serb forces) Djibouti 1994 (FRUD) Dominican Republic 1965 (Constitutionalists) Lebanon 1991 (Lebanese Front) Lebanon 1991 (National Movement) Mali 1995 (Tuaregs) Tajikistan 1997 (UTO) United Kingdom 1998 (IRA)

[1] Defection = Ex-rebel commander defection observed within ten years of military integration
[2] Rebel goods provision = Group provided wartime justice, policing, humanitarian, education, or health services

Governance Dataset and Megan Stewart's Insurgent Social Service Provision Dataset. These data projects represent the most comprehensive efforts to date to measure rebel goods provision cross-nationally, and all sixty rebel groups that meet my scope conditions appear in at least one of these datasets. The Rebel Governance Dataset codes each insurgent group in terms of whether or not the group participated in legal, executive, taxation, tax relief, police, humanitarian aid, education, health care, political propaganda, or diplomacy functions.[9] The Insurgent Social Service Provision Dataset, meanwhile, codes whether a rebel group made efforts to provide health care or education goods to civilians in a broad-based manner (e.g., not only for group members).[10] *Rebel goods provision* is scored 1 if the integrating armed group provided legal, police, humanitarian aid, education, or health care services in the Rebel Governance Dataset and/or if the armed group provided inclusive health care or education in the Insurgent Social Service Provision Dataset, and 0 otherwise. Applying this schema, I code rebel goods provision in thirty-six out of sixty cases (60 percent) of rebel-military integration. Table 6.1 lists the cases that fall in each cell.

ALTERNATIVE ARGUMENTS

In addition to testing this book's theory of commander embeddedness, this chapter also uses the new database of rebel-military integration cases to investigate an array of alternative explanations for ex-rebel commander defection. I concentrate here on eight categories of alternative arguments: the nature of conflict termination, third-party intervention, state resources, ethnic cleavages, the structure of the military, regime type, conflict intensity, and rebel group ideology.

First, as noted earlier, I account for the nature of conflict termination by distinguishing between outright rebel victories and negotiated settlements that include rebel-military integration provisions. It is conventional wisdom that decisive victories yield more resilient settlements to civil wars than stalemates or power-sharing bargains.[11] In this view, winning rebels become effective statebuilders because their organizational capabilities allow them to monopolize violence and deter new challengers.[12] Armed groups that win civil wars outright may also be more cohesive or committed to the "cause" than those that settle for peace agreements. Thus, we might expect that field commanders from victorious integrating armed groups will be more likely to remain loyal to the central state after war's end. *Military victory* is coded 1 if the integrating armed group defeated the incumbent regime outright and 0 if the armed group instead merged into the security forces through a negotiated settlement.

Second, a considerable literature has argued for the importance of third-party interventions and monitoring during war-to-peace transitions.[13] Third-party guarantors may reduce the chances of military defections by offering assurances to former combatants. Since field commanders will be reticent to demobilize existing rebel armies in the absence of an external authority to enforce commitments, foreign states and international organizations can reduce uncertainty and fear by monitoring the demobilization and reconstruction process.[14] Peacebuilding missions can also provide training, advising, and capacity-building programs to bolster professionalism among the armed forces, which may enhance stability.[15] Thus, we might expect that ex-rebel commander defections will be less likely when third-party intervention missions are present. I code a dichotomous variable *Third-party intervention*, indicating whether an external intervener provided security force assistance or on-the-ground monitoring of military reconstruction in the postwar phase.

A third theoretical tradition tells us that military defections may be influenced by the resources available to postwar state leaders. Political rulers with ample financial resources at their disposal are likely to be better positioned to co-opt their military counterparts with generous salaries and payouts, while regimes with fewer resources available for defense spending may face disgruntlement in the military ranks.[16] Well-funded military organizations may also generate higher levels of professionalism and organizational loyalty. I therefore measure the resources available to state leaders using *GDP-per-capita* levels at the beginning of the military integration process as well as levels of *Defense expenditure per capita* to account for the resources allocated to the military.[17]

A fourth alternative argument is that ex-rebel commander resistance may be affected by ethnic cleavages within the postwar military or within the ruling regime. Civil-military relations scholars have long associated ethnic cleavages with civil-military splits.[18] There are two ways that ethnic cleavages could shape ex-rebel commander incentives for defection. First, if the postwar security forces contain multiple rival ethnic groups that previously competed for power with deadly violence (think of the Lebanese military after the 1991 Taif Agreement), this may create risks of intramilitary rivalries and clashes that could escalate to open mutinies, coups, or a return to rebellion. Second, if rebel commanders integrate into the state military in a subordinate position to a state executive from a rival ethnic group, these commanders may fear that the ruler will "stack" the officer corps in favor of their own coethnics, creating incentives for a preventive rebellion.[19] I thus code two variables related to ethnic cleavages. *Ethnic cleavages (within military)* is coded 1 if the officer corps of the postwar military includes multiple politically relevant ethnic groups who previously competed for power in the civil war period. *Ethnic cleavages (military-regime)* is coded 1 if the chief executive of the postwar state hails from a different ethnic group than ex-rebel field commanders from the integrating armed group.

Fifth, structural characteristics of the military could impact the opportunity for antiregime mobilization among ex-rebel commanders. When military forces are divided into several autonomous organizations or the military exists in parallel with extramilitary security forces that operate through separate lines of communication and command, military officers may become more reticent to participate in antiregime actions. Commanders within these "coup-proofed" militaries may face barriers to communication and coordination that inhibit antiregime mobilization, and branches of the military with especially close ties to the state executive may step in to deter would-be coup plotters.[20] To capture the structure of military institutions, I code the variable *Counterbalancing* as the average number of counterbalancing forces employed by the state in the ten-year postwar window.[21] For data on the number of counterbalancing forces, I draw on Erica De Bruin's State Security Forces Dataset.[22]

A sixth alternative argument is that the likelihood of commander defections will be mediated by regime type. Views on the impact of regime type in the civil-military relations literature differ. On the one hand, Staffan Lindberg and John Clark argue that autocratic regimes are more likely to suffer military insubordination and coups due to the inability of these regimes to acquire popular legitimacy.[23] On the other hand, Milan Svolik contends that authoritarian leaders may be better positioned to deter coups.[24] To account for such effects, I code the variable *Democracy* using the electoral democracy index from the Varieties of Democracy (V-Dem) dataset. This index measures the extent to which "the ideal of electoral democracy in its fullest sense" is achieved by the political regime and incorporates subindices of freedom of expression, the extent of political inclusion and suffrage, and the quality of elections.[25] To smooth out year-to-year swings in this index, I use the average score for the electoral democracy index over the ten-year postwar period of observation.

Seventh, levels of postwar hostility among rival belligerents may affect the stability of postwar states and the ability of the new ruling coalition to build new security institutions. Scholars have postulated that civil wars involving especially bloody or protracted fighting may generate deep-seated resentments among belligerents that make future war recurrence more likely.[26] Thus, one might expect that rebel field commanders involved in intense civil wars will be more likely to defect from the postwar ruling regime if that regime includes former adversaries. To account for this possibility, I gauge hostility using measures of conflict intensity based on the UCDP Dyadic Dataset: if dyadic conflict between the armed group and the government resulted in at least a thousand battle deaths in a single year, I score the dichotomous variable *Intense war* as 1, and 0 otherwise. Since hostility among former belligerents should matter most in cases of power-sharing settlements, in my analysis, I explore the interaction between *Military victory* and *Intense war*.

Finally, ex-rebel commander behaviors may be influenced by ideological commitments. Scholarship emphasizing the power of revolutionary beliefs has argued that political ideology can increase militants' personal motivation and loyalty to "the cause" and that revolutionary groups are more likely to invest in centralized, disciplined guerrilla armies.[27] By contrast, armed groups that lack strong ideological motivations may be prone to attract opportunistic members who only aim to maximize personal rents.[28]

CHAPTER 6

Thus, we might expect that ex-rebel commanders from revolutionary movements would be less likely to defect, especially for rebel groups who win outright military victories and attempt to reshape state institutions in their image. I code the dichotomous variable *Ideology* based on whether the leadership of the armed movement adhered to a Marxist-Leninist or an Islamic/jihadist ideology.[29] I also code the variable *Anticolonial war* to capture whether the armed movement was fighting for national independence from European colonial rule. Like ideological rebels, anticolonial insurgents may benefit from a stronger sense of common purpose that makes them less prone to postwar fragmentation.[30] As with the conflict intensity variable, since the stabilizing benefits of revolutionary or anticolonial ideologies may only accrue to victorious armed groups, I separately analyze the interaction between *Military victory* and measures of group ideology.

The Correlates of Ex-Rebel Commander Defections

This section tests my theory of commander embeddedness and competing explanations of ex-rebel commander defection across the sample of sixty integrating armed groups. I start by examining the bivariate relationship between wartime rebel goods provision and postwar commander defection among all rebel-military integration cases. I then introduce a series of increasingly stringent tests to address confounding variables, subsample heterogeneity, and endogeneity concerns.

A FIRST CUT AT THE DATA: BIVARIATE PATTERNS

A simple bivariate comparison of the variables *Rebel goods provision* and *Defection* reveals strong initial support for the generalizability of this book's argument. Across sixty rebel groups that integrated into state militaries since 1945, thirty-six engaged in goods provision to civilians prior to military integration. Of these, twenty-two movements (61 percent) experienced an episode of ex-rebel commander defection. By contrast, seven of twenty-four cases (29 percent) where rebel goods provision was absent saw ex-rebel commander defection. If we knew nothing else about an integrating armed group, therefore, simply knowing that the group engaged in wartime goods provision prior to integrating into a state military would tell us to double the estimated likelihood of ex-rebel commander defection. A two-sample t-test indicates that this difference in means is unlikely to be a mere coincidence ($t = 2.54$; $p < 0.05$). The descriptive evidence thus permits guarded optimism about the explanatory power of this book's theory beyond Côte d'Ivoire. Across a range of conflict contexts, field commanders from armed groups that practice collaborative rule appear to be more likely to resist the postwar state following military integration.

By contrast, the descriptive data do not support several alternative explanations for ex-rebel commander defections. Negotiated power-sharing settlements do not appear to make ex-rebel commander defections more likely compared to military victories. Forty-one cases in the dataset were coded as military victories. Of these, twenty-one experienced ex-rebel commander defection in the postwar period (51 percent). In the remaining nineteen cases of military integration via negotiated settlement, defection occurred in only eight (42 percent) cases. If anything, therefore, victorious rebel groups appear *more* likely to experience ex-rebel commander defection after integrating into the state military compared to armed groups that integrate via peace settlements. Moreover, there is a positive correlation between wartime rebel goods provision and postwar commander defection among both military victories and negotiated settlements, though the association is stronger among negotiated settlements.

Third-party interventions to monitor and assist security-sector reconstruction also do not appear to clearly correlate with ex-rebel commander defections. Half of all cases experienced a third-party intervention; sixteen of these (53 percent) experienced a defection episode. The rate of defection among the remaining thirty cases without a third-party intervention is somewhat lower (43 percent). Explanations based on state resources or structural coup-proofing, meanwhile, appear to have similarly little predictive power. Neither logged *GDP per capita*, *Defense expenditure per capita*, nor *Counterbalancing* show clear correlations with defection outcomes.

Ideology-based explanations appear similarly weak. Among the twenty-five armed groups in the dataset that possessed a revolutionary ideology, fourteen (56 percent) experienced at least one episode of ex-rebel commander defection. Integrating rebels without revolutionary ideologies actually fared somewhat better: fifteen of thirty-five (43 percent) suffered a defection episode. Among *winning* rebel groups, ideological and nonideological groups saw nearly identical postwar defection outcomes: eleven out of twenty-two (50 percent) ideological victors suffered postwar defection, while ten out of nineteen nonideological victors (53 percent) experienced defection. Nor did commanders from anticolonial rebel groups exhibit a different propensity to defect, either among all cases or among military victors only. Eight of fifteen (53 percent) anticolonial rebel groups experienced postwar defection, while twenty-one of forty-five (46 percent) non-anticolonial rebel groups saw defection. Among victorious anticolonial groups, six of thirteen saw commander defection (46 percent), while fifteen of twenty-eight non-anticolonial victors suffered defection. In sum, revolutionary beliefs and anticolonial ideologies appear to tell us surprisingly little about the prospects for military defections among ex-rebel commanders.

Some alternative explanations do find greater purchase. Consistent with priors from the civil-military relations literature, both ethnic cleavages within the postwar military and those between the postwar military officer corps and the chief executive are strongly associated with ex-rebel commander defections. Of the twenty-one armed groups in the dataset where *Ethnic cleavage (military-regime)* was coded as 0, for instance, five (24 percent) experienced a defection episode within ten years. The defection rate jumps to 62 percent among integrating rebel groups where ethnic cleavages between commanders and the chief executive existed.[31] Regime type also appears to meaningfully affect the chances of ex-rebel commander defection. In a bivariate regression, *Democracy* is negatively and significantly correlated with ex-rebel commander defection ($p > 0.01$), suggesting that democratic regimes are better positioned to maintain ex-rebel commander loyalty after war's end. Finally, the intensity of civil war appears to matter, though not in the way anticipated by theories based on "belligerent hostilities." Armed groups that fought intense civil wars (as measured by battle-death counts) were *less* likely to experience defections after integrating into the military, though this correlation appears to be concentrated among winning rebel groups. This finding is consistent with previous research on rebel victories and may be explained by the fact that winning armed groups facing intense civil wars create bonds of cohesion that make postwar state leaders better able to command obedience from ex-rebel commanders.[32]

Overall, the initial descriptive findings support this book's claim that ex-rebel commanders' willingness to resist postwar states is affected by prior variation in practices of wartime rebel rule. However, there is also suggestive support for other explanations of commander behavior based on ethnic cleavages, regime type, and war intensity. To sort out whether wartime rebel rule has explanatory power independent of other confounding factors, I turn to a multivariate regression analysis.

MULTIVARIATE ANALYSIS

In this section, I present a binomial logistic regression model that estimates the correlates of ex-rebel commander defection. The baseline model estimates ex-rebel commander defection as a function of the following variables: *Rebel goods provision, Military victory, Third-party intervention, GDP per capita (log), Defense expenditure per capita, Ethnic cleavage (military-regime), Intense war, Ideology,* and *Democracy*. (I omit the counterbalancing covariate from the baseline model to retain more observations). For ease of interpretation, I consign full regression results to the appendix and focus here on the marginal effects plotted in figure 6.1. The figure shows how the predicted probability of a defection episode changes with shifts in selected explanatory variables, holding other covariates at their mean.

Figure 6.1 shows that, even when accounting for a host of controls, changes in wartime rebel goods provision are associated with substantively significant shifts in the probability of ex-rebel commander defection after

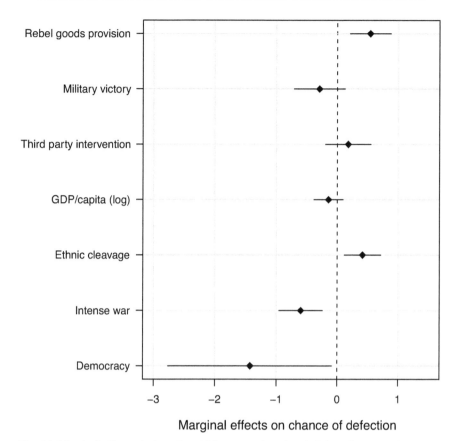

Fig. 6.1. Marginal effects of selected variables on predicted probability of commander defection
Note: Lines show 95 percent confidence intervals. For *Rebel goods provision, Military victory, Third-party intervention, Intense war,* and *Ethnic cleavage,* the figure shows the effect of a change from 0 to 1. For *GDP/capita (log)* and *Democracy,* the effect of a one standard deviation increase is shown.

military integration. Assuming a hypothetical armed group that scored mean values on all other covariates, changing the *Rebel goods provision* variable from 0 to 1 is associated with an impressive fifty-four percentage point increase in the predicted probability that one or more field commanders from that armed group will defect from the ruling regime within ten years of military integration. This association is statistically significant at the 95 percent confidence level ($p < 0.05$) and is substantively larger than most other estimated effects in the model. Among the other variables, ethnic cleavages are also a significant predictor of commander defection, while war intensity and democracy significantly reduce the risk of defection.

CHAPTER 6

Overall, the multivariate model confirms what the raw descriptive data already suggested: there is indeed a link between wartime rebel rule and postwar commander defection among integrating armed groups.

To probe the robustness of this finding, I introduce a series of increasingly stringent tests. Full results appear in appendix I. First, I add an interaction term between *Military victory* and *Intense war* to account for the fact that intense wars that end through power-sharing settlements may face unique risks of ex-rebel commander defections. Second, I interact *Military victory* with *Ideology* to account for the possibility that winning rebels with revolutionary ideological beliefs may be particularly suited to sustaining postwar obedience from commanders. Third, I add covariates for the number of state security forces and the number of counterbalancing forces employed by the state regime. Fourth, I add controls for anticolonial wars and anticolonial victors. Finally, I rerun the analyses using the stricter measure of defection that counts as zero instances where commander defection was precipitated by either open calls for antistate resistance/rebellion by political leaders associated with the integrating armed group (as in Angola 1991) or the withdrawal of political leaders associated with the integrating armed group from the government or peace process (as in Bolivia 1952). Across all specifications, the link between *Rebel goods provision* and *Defection* remains positive, substantively large, and precisely estimated at the 95 percent significance level.

What about potential endogeneity and selection effects? Are rebel groups that engage in local goods provision already systematically different in some way or operating in different kinds of environments that might introduce bias? For instance, perhaps rebel goods provision is more likely to emerge when armed groups fight weak states that have limited penetration into peripheral areas, because rebels can build institutions without fear of counterattack. These weak states may also be more likely, on average, to suffer postwar military defections for reasons unrelated to wartime rebel rule. Though it is difficult to rule out such possibilities without experimentally manipulating armed groups' wartime governance practices, we can partially address concerns about selection effects by looking for balance in rebel goods provision across other covariates. Regressing *Rebel goods provision* on the other variables in the linear regression model reveals no clear patterns that point to such endogeneity problems. *Rebel goods provision* among integrating armed groups is not strongly correlated one way or the other with levels of GDP per capita or levels of defense expenditure, nor is it correlated with the type of conflict termination, the presence of third-party peacekeepers, the presence of ethnic cleavages, or levels of democracy.

Rebel goods provision among integrating armed groups is positively associated with revolutionary ideology, however ($p < 0.01$). The link between rebel governance and ideology would be problematic for my argument under two scenarios. First, if revolutionary ideology is a cause of both collaborative rule and postwar military defection, then the relationship between wartime governance and postwar defection could be spurious. Second, if collaborative governance itself somehow causes groups to become more revolutionary, and revolutionary ideology in turn increases postwar defection, then the observed positive relationship between collaborative wartime governance and postwar commander defection could be explained by a different causal pathway than my theory. Both possibilities seem unlikely. As Megan Stewart argues, revolutionary ideology is much more likely to be a cause of inclusive goods provision than the reverse.[33] Moreover, existing research suggests that revolutionary rebels tend to be *more* effective postwar statebuilders due to increased loyalty, shared norms, and discipline.[34] So it seems doubtful that the relationship between wartime governance and postwar defection is entirely explained by revolutionary ideology. And my empirical analysis shows that collaborative wartime governance is associated with increased postwar defection even when holding constant revolutionary ideology. While my cross-national evidence is admittedly limited and I cannot rule out the possibility that some of the association between rebel rule and postwar commander defection is working through an ideological channel, the more likely explanation is that inclusive rebel goods provision creates embedded commanders with the capacity and motive to defect.

Out of Sample Applications: Rebel-Military Integration in Afghanistan and CAR

For social science research to have value beyond the ivory tower, scholars should use their theories to help shed light on issues of current public concern. As a final empirical application of this book's argument, this section turns to two more cases of postconflict military integration: the military victory of Taliban insurgents in the newly proclaimed Islamic Emirate of Afghanistan and rebel integration in the Central African Republic. Both cases are rapidly evolving situations. Nevertheless, the cases provide an opportunity to employ this book's framework as a tool of theoretical prediction and potential policy guidance. If my arguments' propositions turn out to be borne out by events, it will also increase confidence that the book's theory is not merely an artifact of the Ivorian case.

AFGHANISTAN

In August 2021, after waging a guerrilla insurgency against Western-backed governments for nearly twenty years, the Afghan Taliban seized the capital city of Kabul and proclaimed the restoration of the Islamic Emirate of Afghanistan. As North Atlantic Treaty Organization (NATO) troops scrambled to withdraw from the country, Taliban leaders announced the creation of the Armed Forces of the Islamic Emirate of Afghanistan under the command of Mohammad Yacub Mujahid and other senior Taliban field commanders.[35] Videos were soon released showing uniformed Taliban "marching with military discipline in government facilities."[36] If the Taliban are successful in forging an obedient and cohesive national army, it will bolster the resiliency of their regime in the face of external and domestic threats and empower the Taliban to implement more far-reaching reforms to Afghanistan's society in accordance with the movement's conservative vision of Islam. By contrast, if the Taliban's central leadership faces resistance from their own field commanders as they transition from insurgency to incumbency, the chances of regime destabilization and civil war recurrence will increase.

The predatory nature of Taliban rule in much of rural Afghanistan throughout the movement's insurgency (2003–2021) suggests that field commanders in this movement are likely to have weak social support in the rural hinterlands and thus relatively limited capacity and motive to resist the centralizing ambitions of Taliban political leaders who now control the Afghan state. To be sure, the wartime nationalist appeals of the Taliban found sympathizers among civilians in the face of a foreign military occupation, and rudimentary institution building under the Taliban did occur. Taliban insurgents established a so-called shadow government in their pockets of territorial control, complete with provincial and district governors, taxation, and a system of courts and judges for resolving disputes. Poor governance and endemic corruption by Afghan government institutions encouraged some civilians to turn to these rebel governance structures.[37] The Taliban also attempted to co-opt local elites—particularly mullahs—to act as their representatives and tried to claim credit for services that the government and NGOs provided.[38]

Yet the extent of actual goods provision by the Taliban was minimal. The group exercised little influence over health care and involved itself in education mainly by intimidating teachers and school officials who taught curricula deemed insufficiently Islamic.[39] Crucially, the Taliban relied on enormous amounts of coercion against civilians to root out suspected government collaborators and to regulate social conduct.[40] Wrongdoing and abuses by Taliban members were typically ignored by local commanders, and civilians rarely had recourse to appeal for disciplinary actions against Taliban members. As a result, despite the Taliban's co-optation of NGOs and state services, the group's authoritarian ideology and reliance on violence as a means of control tended to mitigate the legitimacy conferred by its governance performance.[41] Other aspects of the civil war also worked against the ability of Taliban commanders to acquire social support. Intense counterinsurgency pressure by NATO troops and Afghan security forces compelled the Taliban to operate much of its governance structure underground and prevented the insurgents' field commanders from openly interfacing with local communities.[42] Moreover, the Taliban maintained a relatively narrow social base, with almost all senior figures and military commanders being Pashto speakers from the Kandahar area.[43]

Given the patterns uncovered in earlier chapters, we would expect that weak commander-community ties in Afghanistan will limit the autonomous mobilization capacity of Taliban commanders once they leave their zones of wartime control and decrease commander incentives to resist centralized statebuilding after integrating into the military. Early evidence from the initial period of Taliban rule suggests that the local ties and mobilization power of Taliban commanders in Afghanistan's rural hinterlands are already decaying. Military forces have been largely concentrated in the cities, especially Kabul and Panjshir.[44] In outlying districts, the Taliban can only deploy "20–30 men" and are "rarely seen at all in the villages."[45] Former Taliban checkpoints have been left abandoned or are staffed by local men trying to eke out a living. Other armed groups, like Islamic State Khorasan, meanwhile, are reported to be stepping into the vacuum to aggressively recruit from unemployed civilians and ex-Taliban who have drifted away from their commanders.[46]

Certainly, serious challenges to regime survival exist. Internal divisions within the Taliban between the Kandahar faction and the Haqqani network may be a fault line along which field commanders could one day split from the regime and return to war.[47] Edicts issued in 2023 by the emir Sheik Haibatullah Akhundzada that banned women from secondary education have garnered some dissent from other Taliban leaders.[48] And between unintegrated Taliban fighters, unemployed Afghan National Security Forces soldiers, and militants arriving from other countries, there is a large pool of potential recruits in Afghanistan for would-be violence entrepreneurs.[49] At the time of this writing (spring 2024), however, there are few signs of internal resistance or direct challenges by Taliban field commanders to the ruling regime in Kabul. As Andrew Watkins argues, "the Taliban since taking power have thus far managed to retain the cohesion they nurtured so intently through their insurgency."[50] This book's framework suggests that this trend is likely to continue. Opponents of the Taliban should not hold high expectations that the regime will soon collapse of its own accord. While the decline of commander-community ties in rural Afghanistan may ultimately limit the Taliban's ability to enforce its governance vision, it is also likely to bolster regime stability.

CENTRAL AFRICAN REPUBLIC

Since 2003, CAR has experienced recurrent civil conflict and numerous failed attempts at rebel-military integration.[51] A motley alliance of rebel groups of mainly Muslim identity known as the Séléka briefly seized power in 2013, but the coalition soon imploded, and most of its fighters melted back to their home communities in the northeastern hinterlands. State elites in Bangui, now led by the government of Faustin-Archange Touadéra, exercise little authority outside a handful of urban enclaves and rely heavily on foreign mercenaries—including the Russian Wagner Group—for personal protection. The most powerful rebel factions include remnants of the Séléka coalition based in the northeast, like the Front Populaire pour la Renaissance de la Centrafrique (FPRC), as well as Christian militia groups ("anti-balaka") in the southwest who took up arms in 2013 to defend against the perceived threat of Muslim attacks and have yet to put them down.[52] A fifteen-thousand-person-strong UN peacekeeping mission has operated in CAR since 2014 with a broad mandate to protect civilians, bolster government capacity, and support a "transition process" to reach a political settlement to the conflict. In 2019, fourteen different armed groups signed a peace agreement with the Touadéra government that attempted to create a unified military force with mixed security units comprised of 40 percent national army and 60 percent ex-rebels.[53] Few of these mixed units became operational, however, and armed clashes have continued between state security forces and rebel groups over control of territory and resources. By mid-2020, a cascade of defections by ex-rebel forces from the mixed security units left CAR's peace process in limbo.[54] Territorial control remains fragmented across multiple armed groups in the country.

Clearly, the challenges of rebel-military integration in CAR are complex and have no monocausal explanation. But applying this book's theory of commander embeddedness brings an important dimension of the problem into clearer view. To wit, rebel-military integration has proven elusive in CAR in part because some of the most powerful armed factions are led by deeply embedded field commanders with significant capacity for autonomous mobilization.

While it is impossible to make valid generalizations about the nature of rebel governance in such a territorially fragmented country, there is evidence that at least some nonstate armed groups in CAR have engaged in practices of collaborative rule in their zones of control. In the Muslim-majority northeastern region, in particular, armed groups like the FPRC, led by the former CAR military officer Nourredine Adam, exercise wide-ranging governance responsibilities and service provision roles. In the city of Ndele, FPRC control has delivered stability and at least partial access to services including police, prisons, hospitals, water, and forestry management.[55] A regular taxation system supports FPRC rebels in Ndele (who do not earn salaries), and other branches of the preexisting mayoral bureaucracy have been co-opted by the rebel administration. Local elites and self-defense groups are also integrated into rebels' systems of security and village protection.[56] One local FPRC commander credited his group's "community ties" to the ability of rebels to run a parallel state successfully.[57] The ability of groups like the FPRC to invest in governance and goods provision may be attributable to the relative weakness of the central state and the absence of counterinsurgency pressure in peripheral areas. Moreover, unlike the Taliban in Afghanistan, most armed groups in CAR lack a political ideology that necessitates authoritarian levels of control over civilian conduct.[58] As Louise Lombard, one of the foremost scholars of rebellion in eastern CAR, writes: "Most people in the area live unmolested by projects of coercive control."[59]

The theoretical expectation of this book's framework is that the ability of the FPRC and other rebel factions in CAR to establish at least minimally legitimate and effective governance arrangements will in turn grant the field commanders of these armed groups a significant advantage in terms of their capacity for resistance vis-à-vis the central regime in Bangui and strengthen incentives to resist postwar statebuilding. To be sure, commanders like Adam derive patronage power from their control over illicit mining sites and the pervasive system of rebel-operated roadblocks that tax high-volume trade routes.[60] But the FPRC's social support among marginalized Muslim communities in the northeast is equally critical to the group's ability to continually resist the centralizing ambitions of state elites in Bangui. As a result, commanders like Adam can exploit donor funds for DDR and military integration by periodically coming to the negotiating table, confident that they can always defect later if things get rocky. Irregular combatants and youth in rebel-controlled zones, meanwhile, remain firmly tethered to locally embedded commanders as a primary source of patronage and social belonging. Regime leaders in Bangui cannot easily change this situation. In the short run, the central state in CAR is unlikely to replace local armed groups as the most legitimate source of governance for civilian populations in peripheral areas.

Where does this leave the search for peace in CAR? One option is to abandon rebel-military integration as a formula for peacebuilding. Government officials and external interveners in CAR could instead accept that for the foreseeable future, locally embedded armed groups have superior capabilities and popular legitimacy relative to the central state and should be tacitly accepted as autonomous order-providing organizations.[61] Such a policy of coexistence would be at odds with current norms of liberal peacebuilding that prioritize the restoration of uniform central state authority. But it would be more aligned with the pragmatic realities of conflict resolution in spaces of fragmented social control.

Evidence from sixty rebel-military integration cases since 1946 and more tentative evidence from contemporary Afghanistan and CAR point to the generality of this book's argument linking collaborative rebel rule with increased risks of postwar commander resistance. Holding constant a variety of other national- and group-level conditions, ex-rebel commanders from integrating armed groups that engage in local goods provision in civilian communities on their path to power tend to become less reliable agents for regime leaders after civil war. This pattern applies to integrating rebel groups with diverse origins, including anticolonial and revolutionary movements, mutinous military factions that become organized insurgencies, and ethnic militias striving for power in failed states. While the analyses in this chapter do not permit the same level of attention to causal mechanisms or subnational dynamics that earlier chapters provided, they do suggest that the theory of commander embeddedness proposed by this book can be used to understand dynamics of postconflict stability, civil-military relations, and state formation across a variety of historical eras and geographic regions.

The evidence in this chapter revealed that the association between wartime goods provision and postwar commander defection among integrating armed groups is somewhat stronger in cases of negotiated settlements than in cases of outright rebel victories. This points to an important potential caveat for my argument. Previous research has shown that winning rebel groups—particularly those exposed to intense warfare on their path to power—sometimes build strong horizontal ties of cohesion and solidarity among military field commanders and central political leaders.[62] Hence, even if field commanders from these victorious groups are locally embedded and possess significant mobilization capacity, the ruling regime may continue to command obedience from their military counterparts. This may explain why some winning rebel groups that engaged in extensive wartime goods provisions, such as the Tigray People's Liberation Front or the Eritrean People's Liberation Front, did not see ex-rebel commander defections. Strong horizontal solidarity ties within winning rebel movements likely mediate the effects of commander embeddedness on the likelihood of resistance.

The findings of this chapter also raise questions about security-sector reconstruction and the fates of armed movements that go beyond the scope of this book. For instance, one trend that should be concerning to policy makers is that third-party peacekeeping interventions and security-sector assistance do not appear to be particularly helpful for reducing the risks of military defections after rebel-military integration. Why? Perhaps this pattern is driven by a selection effect wherein the very weakest and most fragile states that are "hard cases" for rebel-military integration (e.g., South Sudan, Libya, CAR) also tend to attract third-party intervention for strategic or humanitarian reasons.[63] More speculatively, perhaps external security aid after rebel-military integration actually contributes to the problem of postwar commander defections by helping capital-based regime elites create new special forces and praetorian guards that disturb the balance of power in the ruling coalition and trigger preventive coups.[64] Further research is needed to parse out these possible dynamics.

Conclusion

Field Commanders, War, and the State

The relationship between war and state formation is deeply rooted in political theory. Charles Tilly's observation that "war made the state" was based on the recognition that medieval rulers exploited warfare to acquire the allegiance of diverse warlords, barons, militia leaders, and regional violence entrepreneurs. Binding these field commanders to a centralized authority was a crucial step in the consolidation of territorial polities that extended beyond city-states. It seems natural to expect modern civil wars to fulfill a similar statebuilding function. Yet it often seems they do not. Even with external assistance to build, train, and equip state security forces, postconflict governments often wield little influence beyond the capital and struggle to control local military strongmen. Rebel field commanders can repurpose the resources and local ties they acquired during war to become influential power brokers in peacetime. While these commanders provide valuable services to the communities they are embedded in, they also pose a vexing problem for regime leaders who wish to rebuild centralized military institutions and consolidate state authority across national territory.

The evidence presented in this book suggests that one central aspect of civil war—insurgent governance of civilians—has a counterintuitive relationship with state formation. When civil wars break out, rebel groups seek to obtain civilian compliance in territories they control. If rebels govern collaboratively and provide essential goods for civilians, local commanders can acquire ties to communities that outlast the war itself. Once integrated into the postwar military, ex-rebel commanders with local mobilization power and legitimacy in former rebel-ruled territory are difficult for central regime leaders to control. Endowed with coercive leverage and fearful for their security during the rebel-military integration process, locally embedded commanders often resist postwar statebuilding or even defect from the state entirely and return to rebellion. Ironically, the same governance practices that increase civilian welfare during civil wars can end up creating more fragmented and unstable states that are prone to crises and conflict recurrence.

This final chapter has three goals. First, I address caveats that may restrict the scope of my argument. Second, I consider the implications of this work for scholarship on the legacies of rebel rule and the politics of coercive institutions in weak states. Finally, I discuss implications for policy makers focused on peacebuilding and security-sector reform in war-torn societies.

Caveats and Scope Conditions

This book's theory of commander embeddedness applies to civil wars where armed groups contest an incumbent government and then integrate into the national military. The logic of the argument is expected to operate regardless of the nature of the war's cleavage (e.g., ethnicity or ideology) and of rebels' political aims (e.g., center-seeking or secessionist). Evidence presented in chapter 6 supported this claim to generality by showing a robust association between wartime goods provision and postwar commander defection across sixty cases of rebel-military integration since 1946.

This is not to say that other aspects of armed groups or the terms of conflict termination do not matter. Other conditions may affect the explanatory variables in my theory. While wartime governance is an important reason why field commanders become locally embedded (or not) in rebel-ruled communities, it is not necessarily the only one. Ideological proximity to the population, ethnic and religious ties, the personal charisma of individual commanders, and available patronage resources may all be factors that either reinforce or dilute the link between rebels' governance performance and postwar commander-community ties. My subnational research design in Côte d'Ivoire allowed me to hold constant most of these factors and isolate the relationship between rebel rule and postwar commander embeddedness. Yet it still may be the case that under wartime conditions different than those found in Côte d'Ivoire—for example, when the state administration retains a foothold in contested territory and preserves a governance role—rebels' governance practices may translate differently into local social support among civilians. Further research that gathers detailed subnational data on armed group–community ties both during and after civil wars in cases beyond Côte d'Ivoire will be required to test more nuanced theories of the causes of commander embeddedness.

The relationship between field commander embeddedness and resistance to postwar statebuilding may also be mediated by other aspects of the war-to-peace transition. As noted in chapter 6, for example, military integration following rebel victories appears to follow a different logic than integration following negotiated settlements. Winning rebel groups that face intense warfare and acute threats to survival on their paths to power—such as the People's Liberation Army in China or the Rwandan Patriotic Front—may be particularly likely to forge strong solidarity ties between the political elites who take up executive state offices and the field commanders who integrate into the military.[1] Field commanders with strong horizontal ties to new regime leaders may be unlikely to mobilize resistance to the central state even if they possess the capacity to do so, because they trust that regime leaders will make good on their promises. Coethnic or ideological ties between regime leaders and ex-rebel commanders may also increase commanders' willingness to cooperate with centralized statebuilding. Even in these cases, understanding how the local support bases of ex-rebel commanders affect their capacity and motive for antistate mobilization is important. If initial postwar regime leaders are elected out of office or otherwise lose power, then ex-rebel commanders may once again fear exclusion and seek to mobilize resistance.[2]

Spirals of mistrust and hostile escalation between ex-rebel commanders and regime leaders could also be triggered by commanders with expansionist postwar goals. For example, field commanders might try to exploit the war-to-peace transition and the weakness of yet-to-be-redeployed state institutions to broaden their spheres of influence into additional economic sectors and territorial areas. Such belligerent actions could mark the commander as a threatening rival in the eyes of civilian leaders or bring the commander into conflict with other allies of the central regime. This type of bald expansionist behavior was uncommon among ex-rebel commanders in Côte d'Ivoire, but it may occur more frequently in other contexts. For example, when integrating armed groups rely heavily on the exploitation of natural resources or lack effective processes to select and promote members, more "greed"-driven individuals may rise internally to senior command positions.[3] Future research could usefully investigate cross-group and within-group variation in field commanders' goals.

The explanatory power of my argument is likely to have a limited shelf life. I expect my theory to have the most purchase in the first decade following military integration, though commander-community ties may endure even longer in some cases. Embedded commanders may eventually lose their local ties as the wartime governance performance of armed groups recedes into memory. Regime leaders can pursue statebuilding and development policies that crowd out the local governance services of ex-rebel commanders in former rebel-ruled territories. Aging commanders may decide to exit public life. New domestic coalitions may emerge that redefine the contours of politics, and local elites may decide to switch alliances and partner with the central state to push embedded commanders out of their communities. Further research is needed to better understand when and how commander-community relationships end.

Implications for Scholarship

Civil war processes and postconflict politics are often studied in a vacuum by social scientists, and insights from one field of research rarely fertilize the other. While there now exists a significant literature on rebel governance and the organizational structures of armed groups, as well as research on the effects of political violence and victimization, relatively few studies have attempted to connect wartime institution building with longer-term outcomes after conflict termination.[4] This book joins a small but growing body of scholarship that underscores how paying attention to wartime processes—both violent and nonviolent—can yield important theoretical dividends for understanding what is likely to happen after the fighting stops and formal declarations of peace are made. In particular, understanding how rebel rule shapes the social ties between occupied communities and nonstate armed groups provides important avenues for research at both the local and macro levels.

At the local level, patterns of wartime rebel governance are likely to shape how formerly rebel-ruled communities generate social order and provide core public goods well after insurgent groups demobilize and state authorities redeploy to the area. Field commanders and warlords who acquire social support and political legitimacy during civil conflicts can continue to exercise a wide range of informal governance functions, especially in the security domain. Communities that experience predatory wartime rule, by contrast, are more likely to revert to alternative governance providers in times of peace. While this book focuses on the field commanders of rebel groups, other types of nonstate actors—including customary authorities, business leaders, or criminal organizations—may also acquire new governance roles during armed conflict that persist over time.[5] And whether field commanders working inside state militaries can also acquire independent power bases during counterinsurgency campaigns (one thinks of General Mohammed Dagalo in Sudan) is a fascinating question that merits further research.

The normative consequences of locally embedded field commanders also warrant deeper theorization. On the one hand, local power brokers with the capacity to mobilize armed networks often play central, if largely informal, roles in the maintenance of basic civilian protections and goods provision in fragile states. These "benevolent warlords" can help to shield civilians from violent crime and sustain the everyday predictability necessary for economic recovery.[6] Removing these embedded commanders from their informal governance roles—especially in areas where formal law enforcement and justice structures are ineffective or mistrusted by local populations—may lead to worse security conditions in the short run. On the other hand, even the most popular and socially embedded field commanders remain, in essence, violence entrepreneurs who are not democratically elected, who face only indirect accountability for their actions, and who sit atop power structures that are typically dominated by violent men. To the extent that meaningful peacebuilding depends not just on a "negative peace" but also on the strengthening of transparent and inclusive structures of democratic governance, embedded commanders present a thorny normative problem for postconflict politics. Ultimately, the basic protections and local order provided by ex-rebel commanders are not easy to evaluate in isolation. Rather, these goods must be assessed relative to whatever alternatives are available to conflict-affected communities, including the governance offered by the postwar state. Such comparisons are necessarily context-specific; former rebel-ruled communities may or may not be better off with embedded commanders. This depends on the capacity and legitimacy of other governance providers.

One important next step for scholars is to gather more systematic empirical data to better understand how such transformations to local social orders affect other downstream political and development outcomes. For example, political scientists seeking to better understand electoral democracy in postconflict contexts might ask whether citizens in communities that remain socially tethered to popular field commanders or warlords also exhibit differences in political engagement or voting behaviors. Voters may seek to reward parties that are aligned with local guarantors of security or punish parties seen as tainted by the wartime abuses and neglect of predatory armed groups.[7] Ex-rebel commanders might also wield their local ties to influence voter turnout or the types of candidates who compete for government office.

Furthermore, while strong commander-community ties may increase human security in the short run by providing more effective and locally legitimate forms of order, the broader consequences for development are much murkier. Some research suggests that strong rebel-community ties reduce government incentives to invest in postwar local goods provision.[8] Communities where youth and ex-combatant networks remain linked to their former commanders may be at higher risk of suffering crime and extortion at the hands of these irregular elements.[9] And the inability of states to establish mechanisms of dispute resolution independent of the influence of local armed groups may create opportunities for new rebel factions or paramilitary groups to emerge.[10] There is still much to learn. Though these dynamics may turn out to be highly context-specific, scholars of civil war and peacebuilding should remain committed to explaining postconflict phenomena in terms of the prior wartime processes that shape local social orders.

Scaling up to the macro level, one implication of this work is that the local governance structures that arise during civil wars can have unanticipated consequences for centralized statebuilding. Effective rebel institution building can produce socially embedded military actors who are exceptionally difficult for regime elites at the center to control. This is because these military actors can efficiently access local social networks and sustain ties to armed supporters that are beyond the control of the government. Wartime processes have a significant impact on the ability of states to consolidate authority over space. This book therefore challenges the prevailing assumption that wartime institution building will translate into more capable and effective postwar statebuilding. Scholars should not assume that local wartime institutions will easily aggregate up to the national level. Instead, we should seek more refined theories about the local, organizational, and national conditions that mediate how wartime institutions affect the centralizing projects of postwar states.

In a related vein, this work carries implications for understanding the problem of persistent state weakness in postcolonial societies. Previous research has pointed to factors like low population densities, arbitrary colonial-era boundaries, and a lack of interstate warfare to explain why some postcolonial countries—particularly those in Africa—have struggled to develop strong and viable states.[11] This book suggests that the centralization of political and military power has proven elusive in many postcolonial states not only because of political demography or incoherent borders, but also because civil conflict itself has yielded a cohort of regionally embedded military elites who are too powerful to be reliably co-opted by central political rulers. Whereas Africa's postindependence states in the 1960s and 1970s staffed their national armies with professional career officers who came up through colonial military systems, many national armies are today patchwork quilts stitched together from insurgent factions, former rebel commanders, and regional strongmen who draw their power from territory and populations in the rural hinterlands. In a few cases, such as Ethiopia and Eritrea, victorious rebel movements have been able to turn these embedded commanders into reliable agents of the postwar regime. More often, however, embedded military commanders hamstring the ability of ruling political elites to command more than token obedience from their armed forces. In countries like South Sudan and the Central African Republic, large numbers of uniformed soldiers answer to regionally based mid-level commanders and power brokers rather than to formal chains of command controlled by the president or the minister of defense. The principal statebuilding challenge in these countries is not that national militaries lack training or technical capacity. Rather, the problem is that large segments of the security apparatus are managed by individuals who cannot be realistically controlled by elected leaders in the capital. Understanding persistent state weakness in these cases demands an appreciation of how locally embedded actors wield their mobilization power and legitimacy to challenge and defy central state leaders.

This book also points to new directions for scholarship on civil war and regime type. It challenges the claim that strong social contracts between rebels and civilians developed during war will lead to more robust democracy because citizens become mobilized and demand accountability from the postwar regime.[12] There are additional pathways that connect rebel institution building to postwar democratization. For instance, if field commanders do remain obedient to the postwar military hierarchy, then strong commander-community linkages may *increase* the coercive power and authoritarian potential of new ruling regimes. This may neutralize any prodemocracy effects of rebel governance that occur through the mechanism of civilian political mobilization and make the establishment of a strong one-party state more likely. The Eritrean People's Liberation Front (EPLF) or the People's Liberation Army (PLA) in China are potential examples of this dynamic of "embedded authoritarianism" after civil war. On the other hand, it is also possible that strong commander-community linkages could be employed to thwart the authority of the central state, acting as a de facto constraint on executive power. Locally embedded state agents may also be less willing to repress populations on behalf of the regime.[13] It is worth noting that while this book has presented postwar politics in Côte d'Ivoire in a pessimistic light from the point of view of military obedience, ex-rebel commander resistance to the Outtara government has plausibly delayed the emergence of a dominant single-party state of the kind seen in postwar Zimbabwe or Rwanda. Such constraints on executive power may decay over time as commander-community ties weaken—indeed, there are worrying signs of democratic backsliding in Côte d'Ivoire.[14] Future research on civil war and democratization should look beyond mechanisms of citizen mobilization; the incentives and capacities of ex-rebel commanders may also shape the prospects for the consolidation of democracy or autocracy.

Finally, the findings in this book contribute to scholarship on civil-military relations and coercive institutions in weak and postconflict states. There is a particular need for scholars in this field to expand their focus beyond extreme military behaviors like coups. Research on coercive institutions ought to encompass a broader range of phenomena, including brinkmanship bargaining by military elites through mutinies and protests and the preservation of private armed networks by commanders with positions inside the state apparatus. While these outcomes are hard to observe, they are critical for grappling with the quality of civilian control over the military and the constraints that political rulers face as they seek to rebuild security institutions after war. Greater attention to the informal governance roles of military commanders that go beyond their official duties—including local policing, material goods provision, and the maintenance of irregular armed networks—can also help scholars to build more nuanced theories about the nexus between civil-military relations and other political and development outcomes.

One topic ripe for further research is the strategies regime leaders employ to manage and control field commanders after rebel-military integration.[15] To date, most theoretical work on rulers' strategies to control military elites has assumed a context of a strongly institutionalized autocracy.[16] These frameworks may prove less useful in postwar contexts, where political authority is fragmented and networks of armed combatants are extremely difficult for the central regime to monitor. Future research could explore why regime strategies vary across time and individual commanders. *Why* do regime leaders accommodate the demands of ex-rebel commanders in some cases and not others? Under what conditions do regime leaders try to co-opt ex-rebel networks into the state, shuffle commanders away from their local fiefdoms, or eliminate commanders through purging? How and why do regime strategies change over time? In the Ivorian case, for instance, what explains the shift by the Ouattara government away from its initial strategy of accommodating ex-rebels toward more aggressive tactics, including issuing arrest warrants against disloyal ex–Forces Nouvelles (FN) leaders?

Although these questions go beyond this book's core focus, two factors may help to explain this cross-time variation in regime strategy. First, the rising threat of jihadist extremist groups in West Africa has elevated Côte d'Ivoire as a partner in international counterterrorism efforts. Accordingly, the Ouattara government has received significant international resources to shore up border security and pursue more aggressive efforts to strengthen central state institutions and erode the autonomy of ex-FN actors in the north.[17] Second, the consolidation of single-party rule in Côte d'Ivoire under the Rassemblement des Républicains (RDR) / Rassemblement des Houphouëtists pour la Démocratie et la Paix (RHDP) appears to have emboldened the Ouattara government to pursue more aggressive actions against former FN elements. In some northern areas—including Korhogo—the central state has resurrected its alliances with local elites and powerful family heads to entrench alternative political patronage networks that bypass the wartime networks controlled by ex-FN commanders.[18] To be clear, these explanations for regime strategy are tentative. Yet they point to new directions for cross-national and subnational research on regime governance strategies after rebel-military integration.

Ultimately, efforts to understand the development of coercive institutions after civil war in Côte d'Ivoire or elsewhere must simultaneously grapple with the governance strategies pursued by capital-based regime leaders and the interests and capacities of local violence entrepreneurs to resist those strategies. This book underscores that warlords and ex-rebel field commanders, who often stand at the center of the security apparatus in fragile states, cannot be taken as a homogeneous set of actors. The local legacies of conflict and the evolution of coercive institutions are deeply intertwined.

Implications for Policy

Building obedient militaries and consolidating central state authority in war-torn societies is an enduring security problem in international politics. Since the end of the Cold War, approximately 20 percent of the countries in the world have experienced an ongoing civil war in any given year.[19] In response, Western governments and international peacebuilding organizations often turn to security-sector reconstruction and the integration of ex-rebel forces as an expedient means of ending civil wars and creating new state institutions in their wake. Indeed, security-sector reform is the most common state-related provision included in peace agreements and peace processes related to internal conflict.[20]

The argument advanced in this book suggests that there are important limits on the abilities of external interveners to shape the course of rebel-military integration after civil war. Turning militant groups and their field commanders into effective agents of the state is not merely a box on a peacebuilding checklist but rather a long-term challenge that goes to the heart of state consolidation. Stability and civil-military cohesion after civil war are first and foremost products of internal bargains among domestic power brokers. Military entrepreneurs who command armed networks inside and outside of the regular army play kingmakers for capital-based political elites. Sometimes these commanders will support ruling coalitions and hold states together. In other cases, commanders will defect and allow states to unravel. When ex-rebel commanders possess both motive and capacity for autonomous mobilization, even well-resourced peacebuilding programs will struggle to ensure stability and support state consolidation. Security-sector assistance may even be counterproductive if local military partners divert aid to bolster their private armed networks. By the same token, some postconflict states will be perfectly capable of stabilizing on their own, without significant external support.

External interveners should thus act with humility. The international community's approach to stabilization in postconflict societies, though long criticized by scholars and citizens in countries that experience intervention, continues to privilege the (re)construction of rational-legal, Weberian bureaucratic states with security institutions that are subordinate to democratically elected civilian leaders. This approach to peacebuilding assumes that the state security apparatus can and should be quickly reformed to fit such a centralized model and that local military actors who agree to the initial terms of peace settlements can also be expected to continue cooperating with centralized statebuilding throughout the transition process. The experiences of Côte d'Ivoire and other cases of peacebuilding via rebel-military integration belie these assumptions. The consolidation of cohesive security institutions and uniform state authority in postconflict societies is, at bottom, a deeply political and contentious process. This process is likely to be resilient to externally sponsored tinkering with institutional design or technocratic fixes. If local military actors fear that centralized statebuilding represents a threat to their core interests and these actors have autonomous bases of support that allow them to mobilize coercive power through channels that are not controlled by capital-based regime leaders, these actors can be expected to "dilute, alter, and instrumentalize" statebuilding efforts.[21] This book thus joins other works in concluding that international interventions in postconflict societies are often unlikely to result in the types of states that interveners hope to create.

This is not to say that external actors do not have any agency or that improving the practice of international peacebuilding is not a normatively worthwhile objective. Interveners can affect outcomes at the margins—for example, by supplying resources that allow regime leaders to buy off their commanders and maintain peace in the short run. Donors can also help to reintegrate ex-combatants into their home communities and secure gainful employment, thereby shrinking the pool of individuals who are available for remobilization by their former commanders. Such demobilization and reintegration efforts ought to adopt a community-centric approach that identifies and works through the local elites who often mediate external access to social networks in the communities where ex-combatants live. Foreign military advisers, meanwhile, could encourage partner governments to assign ex-rebel commanders to positions that are geographically distant enough from their territorial strongholds that commander-community ties will wither over time but are not so disconnected that commanders view the shuffling process as an obvious threat to their power. Alternatively, donors can invest in foreign military-training programs that allow partner governments to send their commanders abroad for prestigious programs that simultaneously weaken commanders' local capacity for autonomous mobilization.

Above all, the policies of external interveners ought to be informed by realistic assumptions about the ability of partner governments to override resistance from locally embedded military actors. Policy makers should appreciate that rebels' wartime networks of command and control are often highly resilient. Tailored approaches to disarmament, demobilization, and reintegration (DDR) and military reconstruction must take the local embeddedness of armed groups and their commanders into account. When ex-rebel commanders have strong local ties and significant mobilization power, policy makers could avoid initiatives that threaten these actors' interests—such as military downsizing—and that may push them to mobilize collective resistance to the state. Efforts to dismantle commanders' private armed networks over relatively short time horizons may be impractical and impossible to enforce and end up fostering cynicism about the peace process if ex-rebel commanders fail to adhere to the demobilization timeline. When armed groups and commanders are nonembedded, by contrast, more aggressive security-sector reform policies from the center may be more feasible. In these cases, ex-rebel military actors are more likely to be successfully co-opted and threatened with legal sanctions for noncompliance. Even in these cases, however, policy makers should be cautious about disrupting whatever local balance of power allowed peace to emerge in the first place.

For postwar governments, there are a variety of ways that peacebuilding processes can be manipulated to the regime's advantage during rebel-military integration. The easiest policy in the short run is for regime leaders to offer preemptive concessions to commanders through a strategy of accommodation. Under this approach, ex-rebel commanders and their subordinate armed networks are imported directly into the state and given access to state rents. Regime leaders can simply turn a blind eye toward military officers who continue to operate autonomous chains of command and illicit protection schemes and hope that these military actors will help to keep the peace by keeping a lid on organized violence, monitoring the criminal underworld, and coming to the aid of the government in the event of a crisis. This approach can minimize antiregime grievances among ex-rebels, though at the cost of enabling field commanders to preserve capacity for autonomous mobilization.

In the long run regime leaders are unlikely to remain satisfied with arrangements that leave ex-rebel commanders' independent power bases intact. Ex-rebel commanders may choose at any time to leverage the threat of violence to renegotiate the price of stability. An alternative strategy, therefore, is for postwar regime leaders to reduce ex-rebel commanders' capacity for autonomous mobilization by undercutting or destroying their local ties in rebel-ruled areas. By cutting off ex-rebel commanders in the military from private armed networks and alternative revenue streams, regime leaders can hope to either marginalize these violence entrepreneurs or later co-opt them with selective incentives.[22] This strategy may be accomplished through technical-administrative measures under the guise of security-sector reform. In Côte d'Ivoire, for example, the Ouattara government has tried to weaken ex-FN commanders' domestic ties by "promoting out" a number of these officers, sending them to specialized military training schools abroad, posting them to foreign embassies, or offering them new commissions that require permanent relocation to the capital in Abidjan.[23] By physically separating commanders from their zones of control, regime leaders hope to diminish their local influence and allow redeployed state authorities to take root. As an interviewee in Korhogo put it, "The regime more and more wants to weaken the influence of the former commanders through the game of musical chairs. When they assign them to zones that they don't totally master, they think that they will have less influence over local armed elements."[24] The Ouattara government also implemented customs administration policies designed to shut down cross-border flows of

CONCLUSION

illicit mineral trading linked to ex-rebel networks.[25] And in 2015, the government deployed a newly created antiracketeering force to disrupt illegal extraction sites.[26]

These regime strategies of control have had mixed success in Côte d'Ivoire. As of this writing, the Ouattara government remains entrenched in power. In the aftermath of the 2017 wave of military mutinies, a number of prominent ex-FN leaders in the Forces Républicaines de Côte d'Ivoire (FRCI), including the former FN military chief Soumaila Bakayoko, were relieved of their commands and replaced with non-FN officers viewed as more loyal to Ouattara. The Ouattara regime also pursued a strategy of coup-proofing by creating parallel security units that answered directly to the president. In 2019, following a dramatic political break between former FN Secretary General Guillaume Soro and President Ouattara, the government announced criminal charges against the former FN chief on allegations of embezzlement and money laundering. In an escalatory move in November 2020, after Ouattara was reelected to a third term in power, Soro called on the FRCI to mobilize against Ouattara to "restore democracy." Soro's call to arms went largely unheeded, however, and the Ouattara government retaliated by piling on additional criminal charges against Soro for conspiring to destabilize the government.[27] As of this writing (spring 2024), the ex-FN chief remains exiled in Europe, unable to return to the country he aspires to rule, with only long-distance contact with his former wartime rebel comrades inside the Ivorian military.[28]

Yet the government's tactics to isolate and contain ex-rebel military threats have not resolved underlying sources of civil-military dysfunction. Ex-FN commanders are still among the most powerful military leaders in the country. Given the risks of retaliation from ex-rebel commanders who maintain significant mobilization power, the civilian regime in Abidjan remains something of a prisoner to its nominal ex-rebel allies. Experts in the Ivorian mining sector, for example, express doubts that government interventions impacted the most lucrative networks connected to military leaders.[29] In the event that a credible challenger to the Ouattara government emerges in the future—whether under the leadership of Guillaume Soro or somebody else—these commanders could defect from the regime, remobilize irregular armed networks, and fight to create a new political order. Postwar politics in Côte d'Ivoire continue to play out against the backdrop of fragility, security-sector fragmentation, and a ruling regime with incomplete control over its own coercive institutions.

This book underscores the importance of understanding how armed actors become socially embedded during periods of organized violence and the consequences of these local ties for postwar politics. It illustrates that effective governance and concern for civilian welfare help to sustain commanders' local mobilization power and legitimacy during war-to-peace transitions. Commander-community ties, in turn, shape military actors' capacity and motive for resistance in the face of centralized statebuilding efforts. Wartime processes and postwar politics are fundamentally intertwined in ways that are often overlooked. Efforts to secure peace and stability after the fighting stops must contend with the social legacies of war and the creation of new local orders.

Finally, I hope that this book contributes to a better understanding of the course and consequences of the civil war in Côte d'Ivoire. While the FN officially disbanded in August 2011, the influence of its members in northern Côte d'Ivoire has persisted in myriad ways. Dozens of FN commanders retained broad social and political connections to their areas of wartime control; many of these linkages persist to this day. Though the Ivorian government is certainly aware of the power and influence that former FN commanders wield, international donors appear to be largely unaware of these connections. Ex-rebel commanders can have positive impacts in postwar communities, serving as powerful allies to communities that need—and deserve—access to security. Yet these commander-community linkages come at a price. Ex-rebel officers who retain strong ties to armed networks outside of the regular army are often a threat to the very regimes they help to install. As in many postconflict states, politics in Côte d'Ivoire remains indelibly marked by the legacies of war.

APPENDIX A

Interviews

Between 2015 and 2018, I conducted structured and semistructured interviews and focus groups with a wide range of individuals in Côte d'Ivoire. Table A.1 provides general information on these interviews. The list does not include the structured interviews conducted by the author or research assistants for the community informant survey in 2017, or the interviews conducted by enumerators for the citizen survey in 2018.

Table A.1. Interviews

No.	Category	Location
1	Foreign researcher	Abidjan
2	Foreign researcher	Abidjan
3	Businessman	Abidjan
4	Former police chief	Abidjan
5	Foreign researcher	Abidjan
6	Local researcher; Head of Institute for Human Rights	Abidjan
7	Director, CERAP-INDES program	Abidjan
8	Journalist	Abidjan
9	Local researcher	Abidjan
10	Businessman	Abidjan
11	Local researcher	Abidjan
12	Community member	Abidjan
13	Canadian embassy official	Abidjan
14	US embassy attaché	Abidjan
15	Former FN member	Abidjan
16	Commander of ONUCI Forces	Abidjan
17	Program manager, UNMAS Côte d'Ivoire	Abidjan
18	Former FN member	Abidjan
19	Head of SSR, ONUCI	Abidjan
20	Operations manager, HALO Trust	Abidjan
21	FRCI officer, former FN member	Abidjan
22	FRCI officer, former FN member	Abidjan
23	FRCI officer, former FN member	Abidjan
24	Traditional leader	Abidjan
25	Assistant to the sous-préfet of Bouaké	Bouaké
26	Student	Bouaké
27	Resident, Air France quartier	Bouaké

(continued)

APPENDIX A

(continued)

No.	Category	Location
28	Resident, Dar es Salaam quartier	Bouaké
29	Resident, Dar es Salaam quartier	Bouaké
30	School director	Bouaké
31	Catholic priest	Bouaké
32	Catholic priest	Bouaké
33	Sous-préfet of Bouaké	Bouaké
34	Interim director, Regional Health Office	Bouaké
35	Charge d'études, City Hall	Bouaké
36	Chef du cabinet, City Hall	Bouaké
37	Pastor, Air France 2 quartier	Bouaké
38	Former FN official, member of La Centrale	Bouaké
39	Deputy mayor	Bouaké
40	Chef de tribune	Bouaké
41	Deputy secretary, National Security Council	Abidjan
42	Former minister of defense	Abidjan
43	Head of evaluation for SSR, National Security Council	Abidjan
44	Independent analyst in natural resource governance sector	Abidjan
45	Journalist	Abidjan
46	3 former FN members, Angré	Abidjan
47	Ministry of interior official	Abidjan
48	EU SSR adviser	Abidjan
49	Local researcher	Abidjan
50	FN spokesperson	Abidjan
51	FN spokesperson	Abidjan
52	Member of Parliament, former FN civilian delegate	Abidjan
53	Former commander of Gendarmerie forces	Bouaké
54	Chef de quartier, Sokoura	Bouaké
55	Head of the Republican Guard, former FN com'zone	Abidjan
56	Civil society leader	Bouaké
57	Civil society leader	Bouaké
58	Mayor of Diabo	Diabo
59	Chef de canton, Botro	Botro
60	Civil society leader	Bouaké
61	Deputy mayor	Katiola
62	Civil society leader	Katiola
63	Municipal government member	Katiola
64	Official, Office of Parks and Forest Protection	Dabakala
65	Civil society leader	Dabakala
66	Municipal government member	Foumbolo
67	Sous-préfet of Brobo	Brobo
68	Member of Parliament, former FN civilian delegate	Bouaké
69	Former FN civilian delegate	Mankono
70	Civil society leader	Mankono
71	Sous-préfet of Mankono	Mankono
72	Sous-préfet of Bobi	Bobi
73	General secretary of prefecture, Séguéla	Séguéla
74	President of women's association	Séguéla
75	Municipal government members	Séguéla
76	President of ex-combatant association	Séguéla
77	Préfet of Vavoua	Vavoua
78	Former FN members (4)	Vavoua
79	Municipal government member	Man
80	Sous-préfet of Man	Man
81	Civil society member	Man

(continued)

No.	Category	Location
82	Political party member	Abidjan
83	Civil society members	Korhogo
84	Journalist	Korhogo
85	Journalist	Korhogo
86	Deputy mayor	Korhogo
87	Deputy mayor	Korhogo
88	Regional councillor	Korhogo
89	Chef de Canton	Korhogo
90	President of dozo association	Korhogo
91	Secretary general of dozo association	Korhogo
92	Spokesperson of dozo association	Korhogo
93	Religious leader	Korhogo
94	Deputy mayor	Korhogo
95	Traditional leader	Ferkessedougou
96	Former FN member, leader of Cellule 39	Korhogo
97	Resident	Man
98	Chef de village, Sangouiné	Sangouiné
99	Medical doctor	Sangouiné
100	Civil society leader	Sangouiné
101	Former village chief	Sangouiné
102	Chef de quartier	Mahapleu
103	Chef de village	Mahapleu
104	Président de jeunes	Mahapleu
105	Resident	Mahapleu
106	RDR secretary general	Sangouiné
107	FPI secretary general	Mahapleu
108	Mayor, Sangouiné	Sangouiné
109	Former FN soldiers (4)	Sangouiné
110	Former FN soldiers (3)	Mahapleu
111	Former FN commander	Bouaké

APPENDIX B

Community Informant Survey

The community informant survey was fielded between July and November 2017 in northern Côte d'Ivoire. The sampling frame consisted of the 219 current subprefectures in areas that were controlled by the Forces Nouvelles (FN) between January 2003 and April 2011. To create a map of FN territory, I relied on administrative maps provided by the Ivorian National Institute of Statistics (INS) in Abidjan. In a small number of cases, I added corrections based on interviews with local officials.

To create the sample, I first compiled a list of departments (one level higher than subprefectures) with data on the electoral vote share for Alassane Ouattara in the first round of presidential elections in 2010. More recent electoral data in Côte d'Ivoire is problematic as a measure of underlying political partisanship, because Front Populaire Ivoirien (FPI) leaders called for electoral boycotts after the arrest of Laurent Gbagbo in 2011. I used data from the 2010 elections because all three major political parties at the time—the Rassemblement des Républicains (RDR), the FPI, and the Parti Démocratique de Côte d'Ivoire (PDCI)—competed on the ballot. Information about voting outcomes was important because I expected political partisanship to influence community support for FN insurgents. I then ordered the departments within each district by vote share for Ouattara and selected one department in the bottom third of electoral support, one department in the top third of electoral support, and one department in the middle. Within each bin, the department was selected randomly, with the exception that departments in the district that included former FN zone capitals (i.e., the cities where the FN com'zones were based, usually the seat of the district capital) were always selected. The goal of this approach was to achieve a sample of localities that would be reasonably representative in terms of political partisanship but that also included the rebel zone capitals—locations I needed to visit in order to obtain necessary permissions and collect contacts for other areas.

Once these thirty-three departments were chosen, I selected two to four subprefectures to visit within each department for survey enumeration. I selected these locations on the basis of convenience sampling, taking into account considerations such as weather conditions, road quality, security risks, and respondent availability while also making efforts to include a mix of accessible and more isolated subprefectures. After obtaining prior permission from the Ivorian Ministry of Interior in Abidjan, I first visited the seat of the prefecture in the regional capital accompanied by an Ivorian research assistant in order to explain the purpose of the research project. The prefect (or another official) then contacted the subprefectures we planned to visit to notify them of our presence in the area.

In two cases, selected subprefectures had to be replaced with alternatives due to unforeseen challenges; in one instance, a subprefecture was dropped due to recent reports of violent banditry along the main access route, and in another instance, the local sous-préfet was unwilling to grant us permission to carry out the survey. It is worth emphasizing that, especially given the sensitive nature of some survey questions, it was imperative to obtain these official forms of approval—often at multiple levels of administration—before conducting the interviews. Moreover, given the generally low quality of road infrastructure in northern Côte d'Ivoire and the geographic isolation of some subprefectures, a sampling strategy based on pure random selection would not have been logistically practical. In addition to the ninety subprefectures in the sample, I also carried out surveys in three urban quartiers in the city of Bouaké and two quartiers in the city of Korhogo. Each quartier in the city has a population roughly equivalent to an average subprefecture and is represented by a chef de quartier. Urban quartiers were generally governed by an FN sector commander.

The surveyed localities varied significantly in terms of the presence of basic government and commercial services, such as a police or gendarmerie post (55 percent), a mayoral office building (60 percent), a hospital or health clinic (95 percent), a secondary school (70 percent), and a bank (25 percent). Forty-seven of ninety-five localities (49.5 percent) enjoyed paved road access.

Table A.2 compares subprefectures from which I collected data to those from which I did not. Data are taken from the Commission Électorale Indépendante (CEI) and the 2008 and 2014 Quality of Life Household Survey (Enquete niveau de vie des ménages en Côte d'Ivoire, or ENV) carried out by the National Institute of Statistics. There is no statistically significant difference in terms of population size, the vote share for President Ouattara's RDR party in the 2010 elections, the average level of household poverty, the level of household exposure to conflict-related losses, or ethnic composition.

Table A.2. Comparing in-sample and out-of-sample subprefectures in FN territory

Covariates	In sample (n = 93)	Not in sample (n = 129)	P-value from t-test (two-sided)
Population (log)	9.94	9.82	0.28
Vote share RDR (%)	0.52	0.48	0.12
Households in poverty (%)	0.51	0.54	0.48
Material losses from conflict per household	2.74	2.63	0.72
Ethnicity—Senoufo (%)	0.28	0.22	0.20
Ethnicity—Malinke (%)	0.16	0.13	0.40

APPENDIX C

Political Transition and Inclusion Survey

The Political Transition and Inclusion Survey was funded by the United States Agency for International Development (USAID) Côte d'Ivoire in the context of the Political Transition and Inclusion initiative, a component of USAID Côte d'Ivoire's Political Inclusion and Accountability project, which aims to improve inclusion and government responsiveness to citizens' interests and grievances. A key purpose of the survey was to gauge citizen attitudes about governance, citizenship, and local political inclusion in formerly conflict-affected areas of the country, which were identified by USAID Côte d'Ivoire as priority areas for the PIA project in the lead-up to the 2020 national elections. The PTI Survey was administered by the author and two collaborators (Giulia Piccolino and Jeremy Speight) in partnership with a local survey firm, the Center for Research and Training for Integrated Development (CREFDI). CREFDI is the Afrobarometer partner in Côte d'Ivoire.

The base sampling frame for the survey consisted of all subprefectures and communes in Côte d'Ivoire that were controlled by the FN rebel group during the 2002–2011 civil war. An additional five regions from the government-controlled zone—all of which were adjacent to the rebel zone—were also included in a supplementary sampling frame to enable comparative analyses of respondents in former rebel- and government-controlled areas. In total, the survey reached 1,200 respondents across 120 enumeration sites.

In preparation for implementing the survey in the field, CREFDI recruited twenty Ivorian interviewers with previous experience conducting survey research with them, with an even gender split. For logistical and security reasons, the interviewers were divided into four field teams with a supervisor and a 4x4 vehicle each. Along with CREFDI staff, two researchers helped to facilitate a five-day training in August 2018 with the interviewers and team supervisors and implemented a pilot survey in Bingerville, a suburb of Abidjan.

In line with standard Afrobarometer polling methodology, a random-walk grid method was used to identify households for survey enumeration, with an even split between male and female respondents. Informed consent was obtained from each respondent prior to the survey interview. Surveys were conducted in person with the assistance of computer tablets. The survey was administered in two languages, French and Dioula, which are the most widely spoken in Côte d'Ivoire. The survey instrument was designed by the authors in collaboration with USAID and incorporated extensive feedback from CREFDI staff as well as local Ivorian researchers. CREFDI staff translated the questionnaire into Dioula and uploaded both versions onto tablets using the software SurveyToGo.

APPENDIX D

Variable Descriptions

Subprefecture Level

- Policing / criminal justice: Binary indicator for whether FN were responsible for policing and administering criminal justice from 2002 to 2011. Source: Community informant survey.
- Protect from external threats: Binary indicator for whether FN were responsible for protecting community members from external armed attacks from 2002 to 2011. Source: Community informant survey.
- Dispute resolution (e.g., land): Binary indicator for whether FN were responsible for resolving disputes over property and land from 2002 to 2011. Source: Community informant survey.
- Education: Binary indicator for whether FN were responsible for reopening schools and ensuring the functioning of education services from 2002 to 2011. Source: Community informant survey.
- Health: Binary indicator for whether FN were responsible for reopening health clinics and ensuring the functioning of health services from 2002 to 2011. Source: Community informant survey.
- Infrastructure: Binary indicator for whether FN were responsible for infrastructure repairs (e.g., roads) from 2002 to 2011. Source: Community informant survey.
- Loans: Binary indicator for whether FN were responsible for providing credit and/or loans to community members from 2002 to 2011. Source: Community informant survey.
- Rebel goods provision: Index ranging from 0 to 6 that scores one point for each of Policing / criminal justice, Protect from external threats, Dispute resolution, Education, Health, Infrastructure, and Loans.
- Leaders cooperated: Binary indicator for whether local elites cooperated with FN to provide public goods, to mediate disputes between FN and civilians, or helped FN commanders identify recruits. Source: Community informant survey.
- Leaders excluded: Binary indicator for whether Leaders Cooperated == 0 or local elites resisted FN rule. Source: Community informant survey.
- Organized meetings: Binary indicator for whether the FN organized public meetings in the locality. Source: Community informant survey.

- Civilians physically victimized by rebels: Binary indicator for whether FN rebels physically abused civilians between 2002 and 2011. Source: Community informant survey.
- Civilian property pillaged by rebels: Binary indicator for whether FN rebels were responsible for looting between 2002 and 2011. Source: Community informant survey.
- Tensions due to violent actions: Binary indicator for whether tensions occurred occasionally or frequently between FN rebels and civilians due to violence by rebel soldiers. Source: Community informant survey.
- Coercion: Index ranging from 0 to 3 that receives one point for each of: Civilians physically victimized, Civilian property pillaged, and Tensions due to violent actions.
- Collaborative rule: Index ranging from −1 to +2. Receives one point for each of: at least two forms of Inclusive rebel goods provision, Leaders cooperated, and Organized meetings. One point is subtracted if any form of rebel abuse of civilians was reported.
- Commander visits: Binary indicator of whether the former FN commander visited the locality in a nonofficial capacity after 2011. Source: Community informant survey.
- Material support: Binary indicator of whether former FN commanders/leaders provided private material assistance to members of the community or ex-combatants within the sous-prefecture since the end of the war in 2011. Source: Community informant survey.
- Provides order: Binary indicator of whether FN rebels who operated in the sous-prefecture between 2002 and 2011 continued to be involved in any aspects of governance in the first two years after the end of the war in 2011. Source: Community informant survey.
- Political position: Binary indicator of whether a former FN member held any political position within the sous-prefecture since 2011. Source: Community informant survey.
- Postwar commander influence: Index from 0 to 4 that receives one point for each of: Commander visits community, Material support, Provides order, and Political position.
- Mining site: Binary indicator of whether gold or diamond mining is a significant economic activity in the subprefecture. Source: Community informant survey.
- Commander native: Binary indicator of whether the FN commander who controlled the subprefecture from 2002 to 2011 was a resident of the department prior to the onset of the conflict. Source: Community informant survey.
- Ethnicity northern: Binary indicator of whether the subprefecture is primarily inhabited by members of a nordiste ethnicity (e.g., north Mande or Voltaic). Source: ENV 2008, National Institute of Statistics.
- Logged population: Log of the subprefecture population. Source: ENV 2014, National Institute of Statistics.
- Infrastructure index: Index of services available in subprefecture, ranging from 0 to 6, including: prefecture, *mairie*, police/gendarmes post, health clinic, secondary school, and a bank. Source: Community informant survey.

APPENDIX D

- Paved road: Binary indicator of whether the locality is accessible by paved road. Source: Author coding.
- Combat: Binary indicator of whether armed combat between FN rebels and government soldiers occurred in the subprefecture between 2002 and 2011. Source: Community informant survey.
- Recruitment: Binary indicator of whether the FN recruited soldiers within the subprefecture. Source: Community informant survey.
- Logged distance to cease-fire line: Distance of subprefecture to cease-fire line in kilometers (logged). Source: Google Maps.
- Social capital index: An aggregate index of social capital in May 2002, averaged across households at the department level. Index receives 1 point if the household head reported receiving financial assistance from a community organization or credit cooperative in the last twelve months, if the household head reported receiving a loan from a neighbor in the last twelve months, or if the household would be willing to take in a nonfamilial child in crisis. Source: ENV 2002, National Institute of Statistics.
- Ethnicity northern (percentage): Proportion of residents in subprefecture belonging to nordiste ethnic group. Source: ENV 2008, National Institute of Statistics.
- Household poverty: Proportion of residents in subprefecture below national poverty line. Source: ENV 2008, National Institute of Statistics.
- Household victimization: Average number of conflict-related harms experienced by individual households in the subprefecture. Source: ENV 2008, National Institute of Statistics.
- Block voting index: Average margin of victory in subprefecture for candidates in 2011 legislative and 2013 municipal elections. Source: CEI.
- Com'zone rank: Dummy variable for whether the local FN field commander held the rank of zone commander. Source: Community informant survey.
- Mutiny: Number of military mutinies by ex-FN soldiers that occurred in the subprefecture between May 2011 and May 2020. Source: Author coding.
- Demobilized rebel protest: Number of antigovernment protests by demobilized FN combatants that occurred in the subprefecture between May 2011 and May 2020. Source: Author coding.

Department Level

- Violent victimization: Proportion of respondents who reported experiencing violent victimization during the 2002–2011 conflict. Source: Political Transition and Inclusion Survey.
- Local recruitment: Proportion of respondents who reported that FN rebels were recruited in their community. Source: Political Transition and Inclusion Survey.
- Taxed by armed group: Proportion of respondents who reported paying taxes to FN rebels during 2002–2011 conflict. Source: Political Transition and Inclusion Survey.

APPENDIX D

- Perceived order: Proportion of respondents who reported that security and order provision was "good" or "very good" during the 2002–2011 conflict. Source: Political Transition and Inclusion Survey.
- Support FN: Proportion of respondents who reported that the FN played a positive or very positive role in their community during the 2002–2011 conflict. Source: Political Transition and Inclusion Survey.
- Support gov militia: Proportion of respondents who reported that progovernment militias played a positive or very positive role in their community during the 2002–2011 conflict. Source: Political Transition and Inclusion Survey.
- Support army: Proportion of respondents who reported that the army played a positive or very positive role in their community during the 2002–2011 conflict. Source: Political Transition and Inclusion Survey.
- Education (dep): A department-level measure of educational attainment in May 2002, averaged across all households (0 = No formal education, 1 = Primary education, 2 = Secondary education, 3 = Postsecondary education). Source: ENV 2002, National Institute of Statistics.
- Poverty (dep): A department-level measure of poverty rates in May 2002, averaged across all households. Households receive a score of 1 if their per capita household expenditures fell below the national poverty line in 2002 (183, 450 CFA [Communauté Financière Africaine]), and 0 otherwise. Source: ENV 2002, National Institute of Statistics.

Individual Level

- Wartime services quality: Ordinal variable ranging from 0 to 3 that receives a point for each of the following services that respondents indicated was present in their community during the 2002–2011 period under FN rule: order and crime prevention, health care, and education. Source: Political Transition and Inclusion Survey
- Age: Age of respondent in years. Source: Political Transition and Inclusion Survey.
- Female: Dummy variable for female. Source: Political Transition and Inclusion Survey.
- Christian: Dummy variable, respondent reported belonging to a Christian denomination. Source: Political Transition and Inclusion Survey.
- Nordiste: Dummy variable, respondent reported belonging to northern Mande or Voltaic ethnic group. Source: Political Transition and Inclusion Survey.
- Urban: Dummy variable, respondent resides in urban area. Source: Political Transition and Inclusion Survey.
- Crime assistance choice: Nominal variable indicating which actor respondent would turn to for assistance if they were the victim of a crime. Options include police or gendarmes, family member, traditional or religious leader, ex-commander or combatant, nongovernmental organization (NGO), and other. Source: Political Transition and Inclusion Survey.

- Visit police: Binary measures of whether anybody in the household reported having previously visited the police commissariat to seek services in the last twelve months. Source: ENV 2014, National Institute of Statistics.
- Visit prefecture: Binary measures of whether anybody in the household reported having previously visited the government prefecture office to seek services in the last twelve months. Source: ENV 2014, National Institute of Statistics.

APPENDIX E

Appendix to Chapter 2

This section presents the analyses of the determinants of wartime rebel rule in Côte d'Ivoire described in chapter 2.

Table A.3. Comparing collaborative and predatory localities (sample means)

Covariates	Collaborative	Predatory	P-value from t-test (two-sided)
Ethnicity northern	0.50	0.52	0.79
Logged population	10.30	9.80	0.03
Mining site	0.16	0.05	0.11
Logged distance to cease-fire line	1.33	1.22	0.58
Social capital index	1.34	1.32	0.45
Paved road	0.56	0.40	0.12
Combat	0.25	0.25	0.96
Commander native	0.16	0.05	0.06

Cluster Analysis

The theoretical framework described in chapter 1 posited that wartime governance by armed groups can be usefully conceptualized along a spectrum from predatory to collaborative rule. Four indicators of insurgent governance—inclusive goods provision, power sharing with local elites, civilian participation, and restraints on civilian abuse—are assumed to co-vary together along this spectrum, due to the self-reinforcing logic of local institution building and path dependencies of order creation. To what extent did governance practices in FN-ruled localities actually cluster together in this way? To gauge the extent to which my theoretical framework fits the evidence, I employ a k-means cluster analysis to identify two clusters of observations in the data. I use four indicators of rebel rule: a summary index for Rebel goods provision (scaled from 0 to 1) and three dummy variables for Leaders cooperated, Organized meetings, and Restraint on abuses (coded 1 if informants did not identify the FN as being responsible for abuses during the war). Higher values on each indicator thus suggest more collaborative rebel rule.

The results confirm that these indicators do tend to covary in a coherent manner. There is a positive correlation between the mean values of each indicator of rebel rule within each cluster and a negative correlation between each indicator across clusters. In other words, rebel rule in northern Côte d'Ivoire tended to be either collaborative (with higher values across each indicator) or predatory (with lower values across each indicator). Notably, however, even for subprefectures within the "predatory" rebel rule cluster (thirty-nine of ninety-three cases), cooperation from local elites was fairly common (mean = 64 percent). Moreover, localities categorized as having "collaborative" rebel rule (fifty-four of ninety-three) also witnessed their share of rebel abuse of civilians (mean = 59 percent). Thus, while the predatory-collaborative rule spectrum does a reasonable job of classifying rebel-ruled localities in northern Côte d'Ivoire in the aggregate, there is variance in insurgent governance practices within types and a subset of localities that exist in between each end of the spectrum.

APPENDIX F

Appendix to Chapter 3

This section presents the full results and robustness checks for the analysis of postwar commander-community ties described in chapter 3.

Table A.4. Determinants of postwar commander influence (OLS)

	(1)	(2)	(3)	(4)	(5)	(6)	(7)	(8)	(9)	(10)
Collaborative rule	0.667*** (0.180)				0.426*** (0.156)	0.417** (0.194)	0.454*** (0.161)	0.590*** (0.131)	0.583*** (0.144)	0.599*** (0.184)
Rebel goods provision		0.492** (0.147)								
Organized meetings			1.071*** (0.294)							
Coercion				-0.051 (0.147)						
Logged population	0.351* (0.173)	0.280 (0.186)	0.547** (0.164)	0.543** (0.188)	0.485** (0.218)	0.877*** (0.305)	0.181 (0.222)	0.203 (0.148)	0.287* (0.147)	0.184 (0.206)
Paved road	0.484 (0.388)	0.166 (0.396)	0.213 (0.388)	0.365 (0.449)	0.015 (0.314)	-0.862* (0.475)	-0.458 (0.336)	-0.152 (0.321)	0.081 (0.312)	0.483 (0.384)
Combat	-0.329 (0.365)	-0.544 (0.383)	-0.302 (0.366)	-0.205 (0.416)	-0.422 (0.309)	-0.187 (0.468)	-0.482 (0.337)			-0.340 (0.362)
Recruitment	0.503 (0.436)	0.500 (0.449)	0.589 (0.431)	1.042* (0.461)	0.247 (0.479)	0.391 (0.756)	0.672 (0.442)			0.644 (0.443)
Mining site	0.062 (0.594)	0.312 (0.592)	0.256 (0.585)	0.633 (0.645)						0.148 (0.591)
Commander native	-0.135 (0.460)	-0.130 (0.469)	0.033 (0.461)	0.001 (0.528)						-0.181 (0.456)
Ethnicity northern	-0.580 (0.605)	-0.352 (0.614)	-0.282 (0.605)	-0.428 (0.687)		-0.340 (0.449)	-0.141 (0.335)	-0.344 (0.271)	-0.377 (0.237)	-0.866 (0.630)
Ethnicity northern (%)					-0.587* (0.342)					
Household poverty						-0.689 (0.753)				
Distance to cease-fire zone							-0.430* (0.228)			
Taxed by armed group (Dep)								1.478** (0.712)		
Support FN (Dep)									-0.124 (0.916)	
Com'zone rank										0.848 (0.586)
Department FE	Yes	Yes	Yes	Yes	Yes	Yes	Yes	Yes	Yes	Yes
R-squared	0.655	0.642	0.652	0.566	0.475	0.546	0.507	0.493	0.464	0.668
N	93	93	93	93	75	46	45	82	82	93

Significance: *** = p < 0.01; ** = p < 0.05; * = p < 0.1

Table A.5. Disaggregating postwar commander-community ties (OLS)

	Dependent variable					
	Mobilization power	Legitimacy	Mobilization power	Legitimacy	Mobilization power	Legitimacy
Collaborative rule	0.190* (0.072)	0.125 (0.077)				
Rebel goods provision			0.135* (0.059)	0.119 (0.061)		
Organized meetings					0.293* (0.119)	0.257* (0.123)
Additional covariates	Yes	Yes	Yes	Yes	Yes	Yes
Department FE	Yes	Yes	Yes	Yes	Yes	Yes
R-squared	0.600	0.532	0.590	0.542	0.595	0.546
N	93	93	93	93	93	93

Significance: *** = $p < 0.01$; ** = $p < 0.05$; * = $p < 0.1$

Table A.6. Heckman selection models (probit)

	Variables included in selection equation		
	Combat	Combat + Victimization	Combat + Distance to cease-fire zone
Organized meetings	1.786** (0.815)	2.132*** (0.674)	2.091*** (0.686)
Additional covariates	Yes	Yes	Yes
Department FE	Yes	Yes	Yes
N	93	82	64
Log likelihood	−181.02	−158.49	−121.266

Significance: *** = $p < 0.01$; ** = $p < 0.05$; * = $p < 0.1$; DV = Postwar commander influence

APPENDIX F

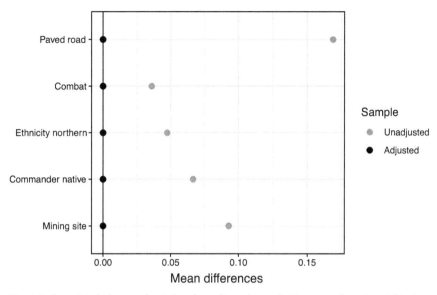

Fig. A.1. Covariate balance, adjusted and unadjusted samples (coarsened exact matching)

Table A.7. Matching models

	Matching method		
	Coarsened exact	Nearest neighbor	Genetic
Organized meetings	0.526**	0.643*	0.643*
	(0.686)	(0.674)	(0.815)
Additional covariates	Yes	Yes	Yes
Department FE	Yes	Yes	Yes
N	86	76	76

Significance: *** = p < 0.01; ** = p < 0.05; * = p < 0.1; DV = Postwar commander influence

APPENDIX F

Table A.8. Rebel rule and postwar civilian perceptions of ex-rebels (negative binomial)

	Dependent variable	
	Armed groups positive today	*Armed groups influential today*
Wartime services quality	0.019**	0.020
	(0.008)	(0.012)
Age	−0.000	−0.002*
	(0.001)	(0.001)
Female	−0.020	−0.040
	(0.019)	(0.028)
Christian	−0.026	−0.038
	(0.023)	(0.034)
Nordiste	0.029	−0.075**
	(0.022)	(0.032)
Urban	0.019	0.035
	(0.020)	(0.029)
Poverty	0.010	−0.011
	(0.020)	(0.029)
N	900	900

Significance: *** = $p < 0.01$; ** = $p < 0.05$; * = $p < 0.1$

APPENDIX G

Appendix to Chapter 4

This section presents full results for the analyses of military mutinies, ex-rebel protests, and police-citizen relations described in chapter 4.

Table A.9. Determinants of mutinies and ex-rebel protest events (negative binomial)

	Dependent variable					
	Mutiny			Demobilized rebel protest		
Collaborative rule	0.922***			0.456**		
	(0.116)			(0.200)		
Rebel goods provision		0.459***			0.738***	
		(0.049)			(0.076)	
Organized meetings			0.507***			1.294***
			(0.142)			(0.347)
Postwar commander influence				0.173**		1.507***
				(0.088)		(0.234)
Logged population	3.071***	3.268***	2.922***	2.832***	1.231***	1.493***	1.306***	1.297***
	(0.105)	(0.108)	(0.090)	(0.088)	(0.136)	(0.140)	(0.120)	(0.140)
Paved road	17.226	17.495	17.780	17.962	18.090	16.920	17.689	16.392
	(1,006.281)	(928.279)	(986.617)	(949.589)	(1,633.577)	(1,189.161)	(1,511.557)	(1,180.159)
Combat	−0.412***	1.072***	0.042	−0.259**	0.236	−0.674**	0.806***	0.266
	(0.112)	(0.145)	(0.137)	(0.107)	(0.311)	(0.272)	(0.306)	(0.247)
Recruitment	−1.079***	−0.319*	−0.364*	−0.141	−1.144**	−1.523***	−1.763***	−3.599***
	(0.223)	(0.167)	(0.218)	(0.226)	(0.464)	(0.334)	(0.484)	(0.585)
Ethnicity northern	0.942***	0.431	0.704***	0.429***	−0.213	−0.418*	0.199	0.378
	(0.136)	(0.116)	(0.142)	(0.112)	(0.275)	(0.215)	(0.281)	(0.247)
Mining site	−19.437	−18.545	−18.755	−18.757	−18.391	−17.491	−17.934	−18.896
	(2,390.689)	(2,473.774)	(2,366.718)	(2,421.064)	(3,650.279)	(2,755.118)	(3,376.629)	(2,692.211)
Commander native	−19.842	−19.579	−19.299	−19.580	−18.681	−18.403	−18.038	−18.762
	(2,152.740)	(2,196.384)	(2,161.023)	(2,171.259)	(3,331.361)	(2,434.669)	(3,051.668)	(2,360.442)
Prior event	−1.779***	−1.754***	−1.408***	−1.165***	−0.164	−0.164	−0.270	−0.091
	(0.195)	(0.178)	(0.178)	(0.172)	(0.391)	(0.285)	(0.353)	(0.258)
N	837	837	837	837	837	837	837	837
Year FE	Yes	Yes	Yes	Yes	Yes	Yes	Yes	Yes

Significance: *** = p < 0.01; ** = p < 0.05; * = p < 0.1

Table A.10. Determinants of mutinies and ex-rebel protests (zero-inflated negative binomial)

	Dependent variable			
	Mutiny		Demobilized rebel protest	
Zero-inflation				
Collaborative rule	−0.948*** (0.360)		−1.744 (1.406)	
Postwar commander influence		−0.802*** (0.235)		3.253 (2.109)
Constant	5.038*** (0.555)	5.852*** (0.734)	4.899*** (1.469)	−10.167 (8.640)
Count				
Collaborative rule	−0.093 (0.241)		−0.777 (1.294)	
Postwar commander influence		−0.094 (0.254)		2.144*** (0.664)
Constant	1.409*** (0.348)	1.557*** (0.745)	−0.535 (1.561)	−9.217*** (1.872)
N	837	837	837	837
Additional covariates	No	No	No	No
Year FE	No	No	No	No

Significance: *** = $p < 0.01$; ** = $p < 0.05$; * = $p < 0.01$

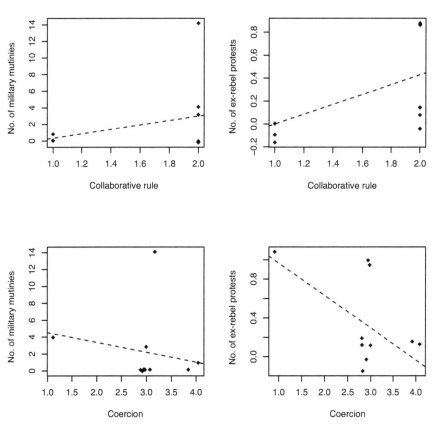

Fig. A.2. Rebel rule, postwar mutinies, and ex-rebel protests in former FN zone capitals

APPENDIX G

Table A.11. Rebel rule and postwar police-citizen relations (multinomial logit)

	Dependent variable: Crime assistance choice (reference category = police/gendarmes)				
	Family member	Traditional or religious leader	Ex-combatant or commander	Other	NGO
Wartime services quality	0.032	0.209**	0.398**	0.268	0.090
	(0.099)	(0.083)	(0.162)	(0.435)	(0.252)
Age	−0.009	−0.007	−0.028**	0.042	−0.019
	(0.009)	(0.007)	(0.014)	(0.032)	(0.026)
Female	1.011***	0.003	−0.273	−1.045	0.589
	(0.239)	(0.189)	(0.338)	(1.170)	(0.602)
Christian	−0.549*	−0.323	−1.295**	0.094	−0.116
	(0.299)	(0.299)	(0.504)	(1.375)	(0.667)
Nordiste	0.201	−0.107	−0.366	1.587	−1.103
	(0.263)	(0.216)	(0.361)	(1.025)	(0.754)
Urban	−0.812***	−3.100***	−0.526	0.146	−0.777
	(0.242)	(0.277)	(0.348)	(1.025)	(0.629)
Poverty	0.120	0.363*	0.775**	1.544	0.034
	(0.235)	(0.201)	(0.372)	(1.188)	(0.605)
Education	−0.591***	−0.348***	−0.628***	0.312	0.180
	(0.132)	(0.107)	(0.198)	(0.462)	(0.316)
N	900	900	900	900	900

Significance: *** = $p < 0.01$; ** = $p < 0.05$; * = $p < 0.01$

Table A.12. Household-level visit to police commissariat (logistic regression)

	Dependent variable: Visit Police		
Postwar commander influence	−0.232***		
	(0.072)		
Collaborative rule		−0.109**	
		(0.053)	
Coercion			0.215***
			(0.046)
Age	−0.001	−0.000	−0.001
	(0.003)	(0.003)	(0.003)
Nordiste	0.558***	0.614***	0.616***
	(0.106)	(0.106)	(0.106)
Muslim	−0.053	−0.028	−0.091
	(0.105)	(0.104)	(0.106)
Rural	1.108***	1.064***	1.139***
	(0.123)	(0.120)	(0.127)
Female	0.150	0.148	0.162
	(0.114)	(0.114)	(0.114)
Aware market	2.068***	2.026***	2.027***
	(0.135)	(0.134)	(0.133)
Infrastructure	0.112	0.066	0.027
	(0.074)	(0.071)	(0.072)
Combat	0.094	0.132	0.095
	(0.121)	(0.132)	(0.118)

(continued)

	Dependent variable: Visit Police		
RDR vote share	0.027***	0.030***	0.019***
	(0.004)	(0.004)	(0.004)
Ethnicity northern	0.072	−0.003	0.515***
	(0.122)	(0.128)	(0.157)
N	2724	2724	2724

Significance: *** = p < 0.01; ** = p < 0.05; * = p < 0.01

APPENDIX H

Appendix to Chapter 5

I used a statistical matching approach to select paired cases for in-depth research in chapter 5. Case selection was determined in October 2017, after a substantial portion (roughly three-quarters) of my community informant interviews were completed and a preliminary dataset had been compiled. I employed matching to select partner cases for two localities of interest: Korhogo in northern Côte d'Ivoire and Sangouiné in western Côte d'Ivoire. These cases are noteworthy because they illustrate the persistence of commander-community linkages under different strategic conditions and at different levels of aggregation. Korhogo was a stronghold FN city situated far from the front lines of the war. It was also inhabited by a nordiste population that broadly sympathized with the aims of the rebellion. Sangouiné, by contrast, was a smaller town located only kilometers from the cease-fire boundary in one of the most violent regions of the country. Local Yacouba (Dan) residents held much more ambivalent views about the political project of the FN insurgency. Yet in both localities, ex-rebel commanders sustained strong local ties and mobilization power after war's end. By studying these cases, I aimed to understand whether wartime governance practices provided the key to explaining similar postwar outcomes in these otherwise different localities.

I used Rich Nielsen's case.Match() algorithm to identify appropriate counterfactuals for each case. The set of matching covariates included the same set of variables that appear as controls in the regression analyses in chapter 3: Population (log), Paved road, Northern ethnicity, Infrastructure index, Combat, and Recruitment (a potential concern is that Recruitment could be argued to be "post-treatment," meaning it might be impacted by the existence of collaborative governance by the FN in the locality. However, the same matched pairs are obtained even when dropping Recruitment from the algorithm). The algorithm calculated a pairwise Mahalanobis distance score for each potential paired case in my dataset, only considering cases with a different treatment value. For simplicity, I used Organized meetings as the binary treatment variable. Intuitively, this score is a measure of the total degree of difference between units, calibrating among all the matching covariates.

The best available match for Korhogo (central) is Bouaké (central), an urban quartier in the most populous city controlled by the FN. In addition to their large populations, both Korhogo and Bouaké enjoyed relatively high levels of infrastructure and development prior to the war. Both localities experienced armed combat in the early phases of the conflict (with Bouaké experiencing more sustained fighting) as well as extensive local recruitment by the Forces Armées des Forces Nouvelles (FAFN) rebel army. The central quartier in Bouaké is demographically dominated by ethnic Malinkes (Dyulas) and Akan, while the central quartier in Korhogo is also mostly inhabited by northern Senoufos and Malinkes. Both localities delivered victories to RDR party candidates in the 2011 and 2016 legislative elections, and both supported Alassane Ouattara in the 2010 presidential elections by significant margins. Nevertheless, the quality of wartime governance institutions in Bouaké scored markedly lower than in Korhogo. In addition to the absence of Organized meetings in Bouaké (central), the locality scored two points lower than Korhogo (central) on the Rebel goods provision index.

For Sangouiné, the best available match is the adjacent subprefecture of Mahapleu. Both localities possess midrange population sizes (approximately forty thousand) and intermediate levels of infrastructure. Both towns experienced similar bouts of violence and combat during the fierce fighting in the west between rebels, government forces, and foreign militias. Both towns, moreover, are dominated by ethnic Yacouba (Dan-speaking) residents, with smaller pockets of allogènes living in the periphery of the town. Compared to Korhogo and Bouaké, the ruling RDR party and President Ouattara are relatively unpopular. Ouattara garnered only 23 percent of the vote in Sangouiné and 14 percent in Mahapleu in the 2010 elections. Despite these close similarities, metrics of wartime governance institutions diverged considerably, with Sangouiné scoring higher in terms of goods provisions and rebel-civilian dialogue.

APPENDIX I

Appendix to Chapter 6

This section presents full results and robustness checks for the analysis of commander defection after rebel-military integration described in chapter 6.

Table A.13. Determinants of ex-rebel commander defection since 1946 (logistic regression)

	Dependent variable					
	Defection					Defection (strict)
Rebel goods provision	2.567**	2.525**	2.791**	2.862**	2.695**	2.503**	1.896**
	(1.074)	(1.067)	(1.222)	(1.273)	(1.047)	(1.031)	(0.870)
Military victory	-1.216	17.091	-0.286	-0.457	-1.094		-0.509
	(0.932)	(2,583.290)	(1.043)	(1.138)	(0.941)		(0.854)
Third-party intervention	0.733	0.316	0.870	1.175	0.620	0.717	0.663
	(0.797)	(0.891)	(0.847)	(1.088)	(0.796)	(0.799)	(0.718)
Intense war	-2.823**	15.804	-3.116**	-3.661**	-2.727**	-2.431**	-2.002**
	(1.161)	(2,583.291)	(1.322)	(1.449)	(1.135)	(1.054)	(0.960)
Logged GDP per cap	-0.586	-0.656	-0.797	-0.685	-0.592	-0.693	-0.482
	(0.495)	(0.520)	(0.538)	(0.662)	(0.483)	(0.498)	(0.440)
Defense expenditure per cap	0.451	0.627	0.554	0.635	0.453	0.505	0.390
	(0.373)	(0.411)	(0.393)	(0.526)	(0.365)	(0.364)	(0.330)
Ethnic cleavage (mil-regime)	1.899**	1.846**	2.181**	2.431*	1.821**	2.113**	1.347*
	(0.855)	(0.933)	(0.951)	(1.397)	(0.835)	(0.874)	(0.742)
Democracy	-5.790**	-6.033**	-4.895**	-5.387	-6.372**	-6.228**	-4.402**
	(2.799)	(2.851)	(2.850)	(3.286)	(2.962)	(2.963)	(2.507)
Ideology	0.537	0.517	18.684	0.371			
	(0.848)	(0.893)	(2,004.408)	(1.030)			
Anticolonial					-0.365		
					(0.852)		
Anticolonial victor						-1.518	
						(0.971)	
Military victory X Intense war		-19.653					
		(2,583.291)					
Military victory X Ideology			-18.775				
			(2,004.408)				
Counterbalancing				-19.734			
				(1,802.341)			
Constant	0.122	-18.353	-0.500	16.965	0.470	-0.169	-0.377
	(2.533)	(2,583.292)	(2.678)	(1,802.342)	(2.517)	(2.370)	(2.359)
N	60	60	60	34	60	60	60

Significance: *** = $p < 0.01$; ** = $p < 0.05$; * = $p < 0.01$

Notes

Introduction: Rebels, Commanders, and Military Integration after War

1. The FN is sometimes referred to as the Forces Armées des Forces Nouvelles (FAFN), the Mouvement Patriotique de Côte d'Ivoire (MPCI), or the Forces Républicaines de Côte d'Ivoire (FRCI), depending on the time period in question. For consistency, I use the acronym *FN* throughout this book.
2. Interview with Ali, Korhogo, October 2017.
3. Sean Lyngaas and Dionne Searcey, "Soldiers Mutiny in Ivory Coast, Reviving Memories of Civil War," *New York Times*, January 6, 2017, accessed November 14, 2023, https://www.nytimes.com/2017/01/06/world/africa/soldiers-mutiny-ivory-coast.html.
4. Ange Aboa, "Gunmen Attack Military Bases in Ivory Coast Cities Abidjan, Korhogo," Reuters, July 15, 2017, accessed November 13, 2023, https://www.reuters.com/article/us-ivorycoast-military-idUSKBN1A00CA.
5. "Peacekeeping Mission to Leave Côte d'Ivoire after 14 Years, Mission Chief Tells Security Council, Citing Peaceful Polls, Referendum Success," United Nations Press, February 8, 2017, accessed November 14, 2023, https://press.un.org/en/2017/sc12711.doc.htm.
6. Collier et al., *Breaking the Conflict Trap*; Walter, "Critical Barrier"; Fearon "Why Do Some Civil Wars Last So Much Longer than Others?"; Toft, "Ending Civil Wars."
7. Licklider, *New Armies from Old*; Krebs and Licklider, "United They Fall," 93–94.
8. Huntington, *Political Order in Changing Societies*; McMahon and Slantchev, "The Guardianship Dilemma."
9. Horowitz, *Ethnic Groups in Conflict*. On military splits and authoritarian collapse, see also Slater, *Ordering Power*; and O'Donnell and Schmitter, *Transitions from Authoritarian Rule*.
10. De Bruin, *How to Prevent Coups d'État*; Driscoll, *Warlords and Coalition Politics*.
11. Sambanis and Schulhofer-Wohl count 167 civil war termination cases in this period (using the criteria of a sustained "sovereignty rupture" in the polity as the primary definition of a civil war), with 43 ending in rebel victory. Glassmyer and Sambanis, meanwhile, count 34 cases of military integration agreements since 1945 that brought rebel armies into existing state militaries. This creates a combined 77 out of 167 instances of civil war termination that involved rebel-to-military integration. See Sambanis and Schulhofer-Wohl, "Civil War as Sovereignty Rupture"; Glassmyer and Sambanis, "Rebel-Military Integration."

12. I prefer the term *field commander* or simply *commander* to designate these actors, since the term *warlord* tends to carry pejorative connotations. Some work attempts to rehabilitate warlords as legitimate political actors. See Blair and Kalmanovitz, "On the Rights of Warlords."

13. Christine Lagarde, "Toward a Second Ivoirien Miracle," International Monetary Fund, January 7, 2013, accessed November 14, 2023, https://www.imf.org/en/News/Articles/2015/09/28/04/53/sp010713#:~:text=The%20Ivoirien%20economic%20miracle%20was,fragmentation%20to%20unity%20and%20reconciliation; Manning, "Whatever Happened to 'Marxist Terrorist' Mugabe?"

14. Levitsky and Way, "Beyond Patronage," 874–876.

15. Even the 2017 military putsch against Mugabe represented an effort by ex-ZANU army leaders to preserve the political dominance of their movement, rather than a fracturing of the party-state itself. See Martin, "Why Zimbabwe's Military Abandoned Mugabe."

16. Joe Bavier, "Army Mutiny Exposes Cracks in Ivory Coast Success Story," Reuters, January 19, 2017.

17. Interview with Reuters journalist, Abidjan, June 2015.

18. Straus and Waldorf, *Remaking Rwanda*.

19. Vu, *Paths to Development in Asia*; Fravel, *Active Defense*.

20. Klein, *A Concise History of Bolivia*; Chabal, *Amilcar Cabral*; Lombard, *State of Rebellion*.

21. Driscoll, *Warlords and Coalition Politics*.

22. Licklider, "The Consequences of Negotiated Settlements"; Walter, "Bargaining Failures"; Mason et al., "When Civil Wars Recur"; Toft, *Securing the Peace*; Levitsky and Way, "Beyond Patronage"; Lyons, "The Importance of Winning."

23. Hartzell and Hoddie, *Crafting Peace*; Jarstad and Nilsson, "From Words to Deeds"; Glassmyer and Sambanis, "Rebel-Military Integration."

24. Arjona, *Rebelocracy*; Mampilly, *Rebel Rulers*; Metelits, *Inside Insurgency*; Staniland, *Networks of Rebellion*; Stewart, *Governing for Revolution*; Weinstein, *Inside Rebellion*; Wickham-Crowley, *Guerrillas and Revolution in Latin America*; Zukerman Daly, *Organized Violence after Civil War*.

25. Stewart, "Civil War as State-Making."

26. Huang, *The Wartime Origins of Democratization*, 47. See also Toft, *Securing the Peace*, 114–115.

27. Lyons, "The Importance of Winning," 170.

28. Skocpol, "Review Article," 363.

29. For recent work along similar lines, see Rickard and Bakke, "Legacies of Wartime Order."

30. Migdal, *Strong Societies and Weak States*.

31. Kalyvas, *The Logic of Violence in Civil War*, 111–115; Staniland *Networks of Rebellion*, 22–25; Zukerman Daly, *Organized Violence after Civil War*.

32. Themnér, "Former Military Networks."

33. Marten, *Warlords*; Malejacq, *Warlord Survival*; Mukhopadhyay, *Warlords*; Driscoll, *Warlords and Coalition Politics*.

34. Nordlinger, *Soldiers in Politics*, 78.

35. Malejacq, *Warlord Survival*; Reno, *Warlord Politics and African States*.

36. Banks and Wilson, "Cross-National Time-Series Data Archive."

37. Jowell, "Cohesion Through Socialization."

38. De Bruin, *How to Prevent Coups d'État*; Greitens, *Dictators and Their Secret Police*; Talmadge, *The Dictator's Army*.

39. Decalo, *Coups and Army Rule in Africa*.

40. Roessler, *Ethnic Politics and State Power in Africa*, 48–51.

41. Roessler, *Ethnic Politics and State Power in Africa*, 92–93; Harkness, *When Soldiers Rebel*.

42. Fortna, *Does Peacekeeping Work?*; Matanock, *Electing Peace*; Doyle and Sambanis, *Making War and Building Peace*; Paris and Sisk, *Dilemmas of State-Building*.

43. Downes, "The Problem with Negotiated Settlements"; Licklider, "The Consequences of Negotiated Settlements"; Wagner, "The Causes of Peace."

44. Lyons, "The Importance of Winning"; Slater, *Ordering Power*; Levitsky and Way, "Beyond Patronage"; Thaler, "From Insurgent to Incumbent"; Toft, "Ending Civil Wars"; Huang, *The Wartime Origins of Democratization*; Weinstein, "Autonomous Recovery."

45. Hartzell and Hoddie, *Crafting Peace*; DeRouen Jr., Lea, and Wallensteen, "The Duration of Civil War Peace Agreements"; Jarstad and Nilsson, "From Words to Deeds."

46. Biddle, Macdonald, and Baker, "Small Footprint, Small Payoff"; Krebs and Licklider, "United They Fall."

47. Marten, *Warlords*, 26.

48. The literature on war and statebuilding is vast. For a partial introduction, see Barkey and Parikh, "Comparative Perspectives on the State"; Centeno, *Blood and Debt*; Herbst, *States and Power in Africa*; Hintze, *Historical Essays*; Karaman and Pamuk, "Different Paths to the Modern State in Europe"; Mann, *States, War, and Capitalism*; Tilly, *The Formation of National States in Western Europe*; Wimmer, *Waves of War*.

49. Important exceptions include Huang, *The Wartime Origins of Democratization*; Zukerman Daly, *Organized Violence after Civil War*; and Cheng, *Extralegal Groups in Post-Conflict Liberia*.

50. For a critical review of this literature, see Autesserre, *Peaceland*, 75–79.

51. Lee, "International Statebuilding and the Domestic Politics of State Development," 1–11.

52. Biddle, Macdonald, and Baker, "Small Footprint, Small Payoff"; Kleinfeld, *Fragility and Security Sector Reform*; Krebs and Licklider, "United They Fall"; McNerney et al., *Assessing Security Cooperation as a Preventive Tool*; Watts et al., *Building Security in Africa*.

53. Martin Chulov, Fazel Hawramy, and Spencer Ackerman, "Iraq Army Capitulates to Isis Militants in Four Cities," *The Guardian*, June 11, 2014, accessed November 14, 2023, https://www.theguardian.com/world/2014/jun/11/mosul-isis-gunmen-middle-east-states?CMP=twt_gu; Daniel Howden, "South Sudan: The State that Fell Apart in a Week," *The Guardian*, December 23, 2013, accessed November 14, 2023, https://www.theguardian.com/world/2013/dec/23/south-sudan-state-that-fell-apart-in-a-week.

54. For a similar perspective, see Barma, *The Peacebuilding Puzzle*.

55. Blair and Kalmanovitz, "On the Rights of Warlords"; Cheng, *Extralegal Groups in Post-Conflict Liberia*.

56. Cunningham, Gleditsch, and Salehyan, "Non-state Actors in Civil Wars"; Stewart, "Civil War as State-Making."

57. De Bruin, "Mapping Coercive Institutions"; White, "The Perils of Peace."

58. See, for example, Soro, *Pourqoui je suis devenu un rebelle*.

59. Interview with former FN director of communications, Abidjan, June 2017.

60. For example, the exact series of events that led to Guillaume Soro's ascension within the MPCI/FN hierarchy and his fallout with the (now deceased) rebel leader Ibrahim Coulibaly, as well as the identities of the organizing leaders of the military mutinies among ex-FN members in 2017, remain difficult to discern.

61. Most scholarship on the Ivorian crisis and civil war has focused on the armed militia groups in government-controlled territory or on national-level political actors who participated in peace negotiations rather than on the FN as a political-military organization. Exceptions include the work of Kathrin Heitz-Tokpa, Jeremy Speight, Moussa Fofana, Camille Popineau, and Sebastian van Baalen.

62. Driscoll's discussion of these issues in the context of studying state consolidation in Central Asia rings true for me. See Driscoll, *Warlords and Coalition Politics*, 17–22.

1. A Theory of Commander Embeddedness

1. Driscoll, *Warlords and Coalition Politics*, 34–35.

2. Conceptualizing the relationship between political rulers and domestic violence entrepreneurs in this way is useful across a broad historical period. Considering the dynamics between European monarchs and military barons in the feudal ages, for example, Lisa Blaydes and Eric Chaney observed that "the independent military power of the barons allowed for a degree of bargaining strength vis-à-vis the monarchy as barons could either rebel against the king or support an opposition figure who might meet their demands in exchange for support." Blaydes and Chayney, "The Feudal Revolution and Europe's Rise," 21–22.

3. Driscoll offers a similar and more formalized framework applied to warlords and civilian rulers exiting anarchy. See Driscoll, *Warlords and Coalition Politics*, 30–45.

4. Here I build on Roessler's understanding of weak states as a subset of "natural" states. Roessler, *Ethnic Politics and State Power in Africa*, 44–46. On natural states, see North, Wallis, and Weingast, *Violence and Social Orders*, 32–39.

5. Christia, *Alliance Formation in Civil Wars*, 11.

6. Huntington, *Political Order in Changing Societies*, 213; Talmadge, *The Dictator's Army*, 14.

7. Malejacq, *Warlord Survival*, 21–23.

8. Zoltan Barany, *The Soldier and the Changing State*, 40; Talmadge, *The Dictator's Army*, 13–15.

9. Roessler, "The Enemy Within," 308–311.

10. Walter, "Critical Barrier"; Fearon, "Why Do Some Civil Wars Last So Much Longer than Others?" On the general problem of credible commitment between chief executives and other social actors in weak states, see Weingast and North, "Constitutions and Commitment," 803–832; Walter, "Why Bad Governance Leads to Repeat Civil War," 1242–1272; and Roessler, "The Enemy Within," 301–302. While existing scholarship has used the commitment problem concept to explain why military integration of competing armed forces is dangerous, my theory extends this logic to the intracoalitional commitment problems inside victorious rebel armies.

11. In cases of rebel victory, remnants of the incumbent officer corps may be kept on because they possess technical skills needed to operate advanced military equipment and keep existing logistics networks functional. Even Lenin agreed to incorporate Imperial Army specialist officers (the voenspetsy) into the Soviet Red Army. Reese, *The Soviet Military Experience*, 20–21.

12. On power shifts and commitment problems in general, see Powell, "War as a Commitment Problem," 181.

13. Zolberg, *Creating Political Order*; Arriola, *Multiethnic Coalitions in Africa*.

14. See Driscoll, *Warlords and Coalition Politics*, chapter 2, for a similar argument.

15. On the importance of multilateral recognition for civil war combatants, see Landau-Wells, "High Stakes and Low Bars," 100–137.

16. The post-Gaddafi government in Libya, for example, faced international pressure to purge rebel brigade commanders who were connected to criminal and jihadist networks. The President of the General National Congress (GNC) Mohamed al-Magariaf acceded to this pressure by (unsuccessfully) ordering the disarmament of several major militias in 2012. Chivvis and Martini, *Libya after Qaddafi*, 20.

17. Cheng, *Extralegal Groups in Post-Conflict Liberia*, 88.

18. In Zimbabwe, for example, some ex-rebel commanders initially threatened to turn on Robert Mugabe and other ZANU party elites early in the rebel-military integration process in 1980–1981 because they perceived ZANU elites to be cutting too many deals with members of the (much hated) ancien regime. Kriger, *Guerrilla Veterans in Post-war Zimbabwe*, 79–97.

19. Rationalist models of military behavior in transitional states have conceptualized a similar distinction between cooperation and resistance. See Snyder, "Explaining Transitions from Neopatrimonial Dictatorships," 379–399; McLaughlin, "Loyalty Strategies and Military Defection in Rebellion," 333–350; Bellin, "Reconsidering the Robustness of Authoritarianism in the Middle East," 127–149; Albrecht and Ohl, "Exit, Resistance, Loyalty," 38–52. Albrecht and Ohl propose that military behavior should be categorized in terms of loyalty, resistance, and exit (the latter being a passive reaction, wherein soldiers fail to act to subdue regime challengers).

20. Themnér, "Former Military Networks," 334–353. Some civil wars produce a professional mercenary class of fighters and atomized insurgents who remain in the permanent employ of wealthy commanders and warlords. Yet because such mobile mercenaries can also be easily co-opted by regime elites and relatively few ex-rebel commanders are likely to be wealthy enough to purchase large entourages, such mercenary fighters may not be sufficient to sustain commanders' capacity for resistance over time.

21. Like the irregular militias often employed by governments, commanders' parallel armed networks "complement the work of regular forces and provide important efficiency and information gains," including better access to local intelligence. Carey, Colaresi, and Mitchell, "Risk Mitigation, Regime Security, and Militias," 59.

22. The field commander Klim Voroshilov in the region of Tsaritsin (later Stalingrad), for example, wary of Lenin and Trotsky's efforts to consolidate central Bolshevik control over the Red Army in the early 1920s, built extensive extramilitary networks among local peasant militiamen in his region. These networks made Voroshilov indispensable to the Bolshevik leadership while at the same time permitting him to disregard orders from the Revolutionary Military Council that Voroshilov viewed as a threat to his own position. Wollenberg, *The Red Army*, chapter 1.

23. Arjona, *Rebelocracy*; Tilly, *From Mobilization to Revolution*; Olson, "Dictatorship, Democracy, and Development," 567–576.

24. Kalyvas, *The Logic of Violence in Civil War*; Zedong, *On Guerrilla Warfare*; Stewart, "Rebel Governance," 16–38.

25. Way and Levitsky, "The Dynamics of Autocratic Coercion after the Cold War," 387–410.

26. Weingast and North, "Constitutions and Commitment"; Weinstein, *Inside Rebellion*, 167–171.

27. Arjona, *Rebelocracy*; Mampilly and Stewart, "A Typology of Rebel Political Institutional Arrangements," 164–167.

28. Predatory rebel rule may be understood in similar terms to predatory states. As Peter Evans writes, "Some . . . apparatuses consume the surplus they extract, encourage private actors to shift from productive activities to unproductive rent seeking, and fail to provide collective goods. They have no more regard for their societies than a predator does for its prey." Evans, "The State as Problem and Solution," 389.

29. On the difference between inclusive and exclusive service provision by insurgents, see Stewart, "Civil War as State-Making."

30. Scholars have categorized this mode of rebel governance using different terminology, including *rebelocracy*, *rebel power sharing*, and *rebel statebuilding*. While one could use any of these terms, I prefer the term *collaborative rule* in order to underscore the reciprocal bargain at the heart of this form of political order. Collaborative rule trades "order for compliance," wherein rebel groups build authority through "an exchange between governor and governed in which A provides a political order of value to B sufficient to offset the loss of freedom incurred by his subordination to A, and B confers the right on A to exert the restraints on his behavior necessary to provide that order." Lake, "Rightful Rulers," 595.

31. The concept of collaborative rule may also be thought of as a form of "coproduction," or the synergistic relationship between service producers and local clients. See Ostrom, "Crossing the Great Divide," 1073–1087; Weinstein similarly refers to systems of "comanagement" between rebels and civilians. Weinstein, *Inside Rebellion*, 165.

32. It is also possible that occupying insurgents can form a social contract with local populations but only intervene narrowly in local governance and goods provision. This is what Arjona calls "Aliocracy." For analytical simplicity, I conceptualize collaborative and predatory rule along a single continuum. In chapter 3, I show microstatistical evidence that broad rebel intervention in local governance and goods provision was necessary for ex-rebel commanders to sustain strong postwar ties in northern Côte d'Ivoire.

33. Mampilly and Stewart include in their typology an additional dimension—"innovation"—that captures the degree to which rebels seek to transform political structures. I omit this dimension in part because I see no obvious way of mapping it onto the collaborative-predatory spectrum; collaborative governance may occur when rebels introduce completely new systems or when rebels work with and empower existing institutions. Thus, I expect my framework to apply to both revolutionary and nonrevolutionary armed groups. Mampilly and Stewart, "A Typology of Rebel Political Institutional Arrangements."

34. Weinstein, *Inside Rebellion*, 169–170.

35. Close-range studies of rebel rule have found that military field commanders play important roles in the functioning of rebel governance systems, even if a separate political wing of the movement also engages in civilian governance. See, for example, the cases in Mampilly, *Rebel Rulers*, chapters 4–6.

36. I borrow the term *embeddedness* from Granovetter, "Economic Action and Social Structure," 481–510.

37. This definition builds on existing theories of collective action and resource mobilization. See, for example, Tilly, *From Mobilization to Revolution*; McCarthy and Zald, "Resource Mobilization and Social Movements," 1212–1241.

38. Zukerman Daly observes a similar pattern in Colombia; areas where commanders and foot soldiers remained in geographic and social proximity after war were more likely to retain remobilization capacity due to stronger norms of reciprocity, improved monitoring, and dense commander-combatant bonds. Zukerman Daly, *Organized Violence after Civil War*, 21–23; McCarthy and Zald, "Resource Mobilization and Social Movements," 1225; Zukerman Daly, "Organizational Legacies of Violence," 477. Since irregular armed networks are less likely to be deployed outside their local zone of recruitment, these types of armed units are especially valuable to ex-rebel commanders for purposes of postwar remobilization.

39. On the importance of local elites for governance and political brokerage in nonconflict contexts, see Baldwin, "Why Vote with the Chief?" 795–796; Stokes, Dunning, Nazareno, and Busco, *Brokers, Voters, and Clientelism*. On the mobilization power of local elites in rebel-ruled areas, see Van Baalen, "Guns and Governance," 21–26.

40. Themnér and Utas, "Governance through Brokerage," 256–257.

41. Hoffman, "The City as Barracks," 413.

42. Carreras, "The Impact of Criminal Violence on Regime Legitimacy in Latin America," 85–107; Pérez, "Democratic Legitimacy and Public Insecurity," 627–644.

43. Tsai, "Solidary Groups," 356.

44. Zukerman Daly, *Organized Violence after Civil War*, 28.

45. This basic proposition has long been appreciated by rebel leaders seeking to win civilian hearts and minds. See, for example, Guevara, *Guerrilla Warfare*; Zedong, *On Guerrilla Warfare*. Other studies in the insurgency and counterinsurgency literature suggest mixed but overall positive empirical support for this proposition. See, for example, Berman, Shapiro, and Felter, "Can Hearts and Minds Be Bought?" 766–819; Beath, Christia, and Enikolopov, "Winning Hearts and Minds through Development Aid."

46. Studying the "social acceptance" of ex-combatants after civil war, Yuhki Tajima notes that "ex-combatants who enjoy intrinsic acceptance may be better able to establish trust and positive relationships with civilians . . . civilians with greater reservoirs of trust can forge more productive relationships with ex-combatants, rather than be in fear of ex-combatants in their communities." Tajima, "When Do Communities Accept or Aid Former Combatants?" 7.

47. For evidence that exposure to rebel rule reduces citizens' perceptions of state and police legitimacy, see Martin, Piccolino, and Speight, "The Political Legacies of Rebel Rule."

48. Arjona, "Civilian Cooperation and Non-Cooperation," 768.

49. Elisabeth Wood similarly observes that "the militarization of local authority often displaces prewar governance networks . . . the new governance network may be directed by civilians but usually relies on armed actors for their coercive authority and sometimes their legitimacy." Wood, "The Social Processes of Civil War," 552.

50. Macartan Humphreys and Jeremy Weinstein find that ex-combatants in Sierra Leone from units who committed more wartime abuses of civilians were less likely to be accepted by their communities. Humphreys and Weinstein, "Demobilization and Reintegration," 531–567. Using survey evidence from postwar Indonesia, Tajima similarly finds that wartime violence creates "intensified antipathy" toward ex-combatants within communities. Tajima, "When Do Communities Accept or Aid Former Combatants?"

51. Kaplan and Nussio, "Community Counts," 132–153.

52. Even predatory and unpopular commanders might purchase armed supporters in a purely transactional manner. Most midranking commanders, however, are unlikely to possess enough resources to easily support sizable armed networks in this way. For many military officers, mobilization capacity is not based on resource transactions alone but also on their social connections to communities where potential supporters live. Without such local political capital, it is not easy for commanders to mobilize supporters hundreds of kilometers away.

53. Marten, *Warlords*, 29.

54. Levi, "The Predatory Theory of Rule," 439.

55. Quinlivan, "Coup-Proofing: Its Practice and Consequences in the Middle East," 131–165; Belkin and Schofer, "Coup Risk, Counterbalancing, and International Conflict," 140–177; De Bruin, "Preventing Coup d'état," 1433–1458; Harkness, *When Soldiers Rebel*.

56. In a similar fashion, rulers seek to exclude ethnic groups that are particularly threatening challengers rather than risk including them in sensitive state positions from which they could launch coups. Exclusion then increases grievances and raises the likelihood of rebellion. See Roessler, "The Enemy Within," 312–316.

57. On regime-shuffling strategies, see Carter and Hassan, "Regional Governance in Divided Societies"; Woldense, "The Ruler's Game of Musical Chairs."

58. On the spiral model of conflict, see Jervis, *Perception and Misperception*, chapter 3; and Kydd, "Game Theory and the Spiral Model," 384–386. For an application of the spiral model to civil-military relations, see Roessler, "The Enemy Within," 308–311.

59. Zukerman Daly, *Organized Violence after Civil War*, 253–254.

60. Here I agree with Richard Snyder that the military's "capacity for autonomous action" is a critical enabling condition for military resistance and defection. Snyder, "Explaining Transitions from Neopatrimonial Dictatorships," 382. Snyder leaves the sources of this capacity unexplained.

61. Meng and Paine, "Power Sharing and Authoritarian Durability," 1211–1212. At the same time, intense armed competition may reduce the likelihood of collaborative rebel rule by shortening rebels' time horizons. See Martin, "Insurgent Armies," 98–100; Arjona, *Rebelocracy*, 48–55.

62. van Baalen, "Guns and Governance," 28–31; Of course, strong prewar institutions need not always increase rebels' incentives to practice collaborative rule. When communities with strong institutions and community leaders have the capacity to resist rebel occupiers, rebels may decide to limit the scope of their involvement in these communities. See Arjona, *Rebelocracy*, 70–72; and Rubin, "Rebel Territorial Control," 459–489.

63. van Baalen, "Local Elites," 931.

64. Raleigh and De Bruijne, "Where Rebels Dare to Tread," 1237–1239.

65. Bratton and Van de Walle, "Neopatrimonial Regimes."

66. Boone, "Africa's New Territorial Politics," 70–72; Boone, *Political Topographies*; Zolberg, *Creating Political Order*.

67. Banégas and Popineau, "The 2020 Ivorian Election," 7–10.

68. Huang, *The Wartime Origins of Democratization*, 9.

69. Weinstein, *Inside Rebellion*, 7–11.

70. Arjona, *Rebelocracy*, 53–55; Axelrod and Keohane, "Achieving Cooperation Under Anarchy," 226–254.

71. Kalyvas, *The Logic of Violence in Civil War*, 118–132.

72. I present evidence for this dynamic in Martin, "Insurgent Armies." In chapter 6, I adjust for the effects of wartime threat intensity and find that it does not wash out the independent effects of rebel rule.

73. Balcells, *Rivalry and Revenge*.

74. Lilja and Hultman, "Intraethnic Dominance and Control," 171–197.

75. Mampilly and Stewart, "A Typology of Rebel Political Institutional Arrangements," 27; Stewart, *Governing for Revolution*.

76. Mampilly and Stewart, "A Typology of Rebel Political Institutional Arrangements," 28–29.

2. Rebel Rule in the Ivorian Civil War (2002–2011)

1. Pigeaud, *France Côte d'Ivoire*, 36–37.

2. Hecht, "The Ivory Coast Economic 'Miracle,'" 25–53.

3. Côte d'Ivoire is administratively divided into 31 regions, 109 departments, and 509 sub-prefectures.

4. This term comes from Mampilly, *Rebel Rulers*, chapter 3.

5. Some analysts categorize the Ivorian conflict as two separate civil wars: the first occurring between 2002 and 2005, and the second following the postelection crisis from December 2010 to April 2011. Throughout this book, I group these periods together as a single civil war, for two reasons. First, in agreement with Nicholas Sambanis and Jonah Schulhofer-Wohl, I consider the essence of a civil war to be the presence of a "sovereignty rupture," wherein the ruling authority of the incumbent state is contested in a sustained way by a domestic armed organization. From this perspective, neither the key actors in the Ivorian conflict nor the nature of their dispute over the sovereignty of the Ivorian state in northern Côte d'Ivoire changed from September 2002 to April 2011. See Sambanis and Schulhofer-Wohl, "Civil War as Sovereignty Rupture." The second reason is that, in my experience, most Ivorians themselves conceive of the conflict as a single historical episode.

6. Akindès, "Côte d'Ivoire: Socio-political Crises, 'Ivoirité' and the Course of History"; Choi, *La Crise Ivoirienne*; Pigeaud, *France Côte d'Ivoire*; McGovern, *Making War in Côte d'Ivoire*; Ogwang, "The Root Causes of the Conflict in Ivory Coast"; Langer, "Horizontal Inequalities and Violent Group Mobilization in Côte d'Ivoire."

7. Zolberg, *One-Party Government in the Ivory Coast*. The Ethnic Power Relations (EPR) dataset records the following constellation of power from 1960 to 1993: Baoulé (Senior Partner), Northerners (Junior Partner), Other Akans (Junior Partner), Kru (Powerless). From 1994 to 2002, Northerners are downgraded to Discriminated, while the Kru are elevated to Senior Partners after the election of Gbagbo and the Front Populaire Ivorien in 2000.

8. Rabinowitz, *Coups, Rivals, and the Modern State*, 140–168.

9. Crowder, ed., *West African Chiefs*, 70; MacLean, "Constructing a Social Safety Net in Africa," 64–90.

10. Akindès, Fofana, and Koné, "Côte d'Ivoire: insurrection et contre-insurrection," 93–97; McGovern, *Making War in Côte d'Ivoire*.

11. Akindès, "Côte d'Ivoire: Socio-political Crises, 'Ivoirité' and the Course of History," 23.

12. The catchall term *Dioula* is invoked to refer to northern Ivorians, particularly Muslims, despite the ethnolinguistic diversity of Côte d'Ivoire's northern populations. The Muslim-Christian cleavage is also a generalization that papers over a more complicated set of overlapping identity groups. For example, many have noted the presence of Catholic Christians within the northern axis, including the FN leader Soro. Despite these complexities, thinking about the conflict in terms of a "north-south" cleavage—which partially overlaps with other ethnic, linguistic, and religious divisions—provides a reasonably accurate shorthand.

13. Rabinowitz, *Coups, Rivals, and the Modern State*, 205.

14. Rabinowitz, *Coups, Rivals, and the Modern State*, 214.

15. Akindès, Fofana, and Koné, "Côte d'Ivoire: insurrection et contre-insurrection," 94.

16. Le Pape and Vidal, *Côte d'Ivoire*. For a history of the Ivorian armed forces in the colonial and postcolonial era, see Banga, *La coopération militaire entre la France et la Côte d'Ivoire*; Akindes, "Côte d'Ivoire: The Military, Ruling Elites, and Political Power."

17. "Military Uprising in Côte d'Ivoire," Agence France Presse, December 23, 1999.

18. Rabinowitz, *Coups, Rivals, and the Modern State*, 221.

19. Amnesty International, *Amnesty International Report 2001*, 82.

20. "Un mois après le début des hostilités les causes de la rebellion resent mystérieuses," *Le Nouveau Réveil*, October 12, 2002, National Library Archives, Abidjan.

21. "Une rébellion a trois têtes," *Le Nouveau Réveil*, October 28, 2002, National Library Archives, Abidjan.

22. Excellent works on the pro-Gbagbo youth militias in Cote d'Ivoire include Koné, *Les Jeunes Patriotes*; Akindès, "Côte d'Ivoire: de la Stabilité Politique à la Crise."

23. Interview with former defense official, Abidjan, October 2016.

24. "Cessez-le-feu fragile en Côte d'Ivoire," *La Nouveau Réveil*, October 19, 2002, National Library Archives, Abidjan.

25. The FN army continued to grow throughout the war, fluctuating between eight thousand and ten thousand core members but reaching a peak at around forty thousand fighters in 2011. The upper estimate includes a broader coalition of anti-Gbagbo militias that bandwag-

NOTES TO PAGES 49–52

oned with Ouattara in the closing months of the war. Estimates taken from the Non-state Actors Dataset, v. 3.4. Cunningham, Gleditsch, Salehyan, "Non-state Actors in Civil Wars."

26. The MPIGO and MJP factions were more peripheral actors within the rebels' organizational hierarchy, which remained dominated by the original core of MPCI members. Interview with former member of the FN civilian cabinet, Man, August 4, 2017. See also Koné, *Les Jeunes Patriotes*, 66.

27. Balcells, *Rivalry and Revenge*, 151–170.

28. Interview with former defense minister, Abidjan, November 2016.

29. International Crisis Group, *Côte d'Ivoire: "The War is Not Yet Over,"* 17–18.

30. Koné, *Les Jeunes Patriotes*, 44–48.

31. Charbonneau, "War and Peace in Côte d'Ivoire," 513.

32. "L'armée française campe sur la ligne de front," *La Nouveau Réveil*, October 4, 2002, National Library Archives, Abidjan.

33. By late October 2002, French forces were complemented by 1,200 troops from the Economic Community of West African States (ECOWAS).

34. Lydia Polgreen, "France is Cast as the Villain in Ivory Coast," *New York Times*, November 15, 2004, accessed November 14, 2023, https://www.nytimes.com/2004/11/21/world/france-is-cast-as-the-villain-in-ivory-coast.html.

35. MINUCI would later be replaced by the United Nations Operation in Côte d'Ivoire (ONUCI).

36. Interviews with ONUCI official, Abidjan, October 2016.

37. International Crisis Group, *Côte d'Ivoire: "The War is Not Yet Over,"* 14.

38. Other factors may have contributed to the dissipation of the war's violence. Scott Straus, for example, has argued that Côte d'Ivoire's civil war was tamed by the national "founding narrative" of interethnic peace and inclusion that dated to Houphouët-Boigny's regime, which prevented the use of greater counterinsurgency force at key moments of potential escalation. Straus, *Making and Unmaking Nations*, 150–159.

39. Balcells, *Rivalry and Revenge*, 151–170; Straus, "'It's Sheer Horror Here,'" 481–489; Allouche and Zadi Zadi, "The Dynamics of Restraint in Côte d'Ivoire," 72–86.

40. Uppsala Conflict Data Program, accessed February 11, 2020, UCDP Conflict Encyclopedia. The lion's share of the killing in Côte d'Ivoire that did occur was not meted out by state counterinsurgency forces but rather by lesser-organized militias that arose in contested and ethnically intermixed areas. Chelpi-den Hamer, "Militarized Youth in Western Côte d'Ivoire," 21–45. Findings from my community informant survey also suggest that one-sided violence against civilians by irregular militias and rebel forces account for the largest proportion of conflict-related fatalities.

41. On the ethnic exclusion theory of rebellion, see Wimmer, *Waves of War*, 28–31; Cederman, Wimmer, and Min, "Why Do Ethnic Groups Rebel?" 87–119.

42. Akindès, "Côte d'Ivoire: Socio-political Crises, 'Ivoirité' and the Course of History," 17.

43. Roessler, *Ethnic Politics and State Power in Africa*, 6.

44. Reporting on the FN has sometimes adopted this framing. See International Crisis Group, *A Critical Period for Ensuring Stability in Côte d'Ivoire*; Marco Chown Oved, "Ivory Coast's Warlords Obstacle to Reconciliation," Associated Press, July 29, 2011.

45. For a more general critique of the ideological-versus-self-interested rebellion distinction, see Kalyvas, "'New' and 'Old' Civil Wars," 99–118.

46. Arjona, *Rebelocracy*, 44–45.

47. Interview with former FN communications officer, Abidjan, June 2017.

48. This section draws on both my own interviews and several important qualitative works on rebel governance in Côte d'Ivoire, including Fofana, "Ethnographie des Trajectoires Sociales"; Förster, "Dialogue Direct," 203–225; Heitz-Tokpa, "Trust and Distrust in Rebel-Held Côte d'Ivoire"; Speight, "Big-Men Coalitions and Political Order in Northern Côte d'Ivoire (2002–2013)"; and Popineau, "Prendre la craie," 27–48.

49. "L'école ivorienne est divisée en deux," *Le Nouveau Reveil*, October 12, 2002, National Library Archives, Abidjan. In July 2003, the internally displaced persons (IDP) unit of the UN

Office for the Coordination of Humanitarian Affairs (OCHA) estimated that the war had resulted in seven hundred thousand to a million internally displaced persons.

50. Heitz-Tokpa, "The Onset of War as a Novel Experience," 419.

51. "La delegation des mutins recue à diner à Lomé," *La Nouveau Reveil*, October 28, 2002, National Library Archives, Abidjan; "Qui est le chef des rebelles?" *La Nouveau Réveil*, October 26, 2002, National Library Archives, Abidjan.

52. Soro's civilian arm was initially small and fledgling, mostly staffed by student and labor union organizers introduced to Coulibaly through Soro during their time in Burkina Faso. Others—such as Louis-André Dacoury-Tabley, Kanigui Soro, Affousy Bamba, Mamadou Koné, Sidiki Konaté, and Amadou Koné—were associates of Soro from his time as president of the FESCI student union and as a candidate for the RDR during the 2000 parliamentary elections. Koné, *Les Jeunes Patriotes*, 62–66; interview with former FN information minister, Abidjan, Côte d'Ivoire, June 2017.

53. Interview with sous-préfet in Bouaké, Côte d'Ivoire, November 2016.

54. Interviews with former FN administrative officials, Bouaké, November 2016.

55. Interview with former FN administrative official, Bouaké, November 2016. See also Guichauoua and Lomax, "Fleeing, Staying Put, Working With Rebel Rulers"; Förster, "Insurgent Nationalism," 20; Speight, "Rebel Organization and Local Politics," 233.

56. Subprefectures in Côte d'Ivoire are roughly akin to municipalities in size and function, with a median population size of 23,117. In a few cases, multiple subprefectures fell under the control of a single sector commander, and in the larger cities of Bouaké and Korhogo, different sector commanders were responsible for different quartiers of the city.

57. Interviews with various ex-FN members, Bouaké, Man, Korhogo, Abidjan, 2016 and 2017.

58. Interview with Issiaka Ouattara, former FN zone commander, Abidjan, 2017. Data on the ethnic identity of commanders collected through my informant survey confirms this assessment.

59. Heitz-Tokpa, "Power-Sharing in the Local Arena," 115.

60. Heitz-Tokpa, "Power-Sharing in the Local Arena," 116.

61. Speight, "Rebel Organization and Local Politics," 227.

62. Förster, "Dialogue Direct," 203–225.

63. van Baalen, "Local Elites," 6, 10.

64. Boone, *Political Topographies*, 243–281.

65. Baldwin, "When Politicians Cede Control of Resources," 253–271.

66. Baldwin, "When Politicians Cede Control of Resources," 253–271; MacLean, *Informal Institutions and Citizenship in Rural Africa*.

67. Boone, "Electoral Populism Where Property Rights are Weak," 189.

68. Interview with traditional leader in Bouaké, November 2016; interview with CSO leader in Bouaké, November 2016.

69. Interviews with traditional leaders and local bureaucrats in Bouaké, Man, and Korhogo, October–November 2016 and July–November 2017. For an excellent analysis of the mobilization of volunteer school teachers under the FN, see Popineau, "Prendre la craie."

70. Interviews with traditional leaders in Man and Katiola, July 2017.

71. van Baalen, "Local Elites."

72. Overall, less than 50 percent of the population in rebel-ruled territory in northern Côte d'Ivoire identified as Malinke or Senoufo, the ethnic groups that constituted nearly 100 percent of the FAFN officer corps.

73. Fofana, "Ethnographie des Trajectoires Sociales," 77–78.

74. Fofana, "Ethnographie des Trajectoires Sociales," 81.

75. van Baalen, "Local Elites," 6.

76. Fofana, "Ethnographie des Trajectoires Sociales," 82.

77. van Baalen, "Local Elites," 10.

78. van Baalen, "Local Elites," 9–10.

79. The case of Kpata is discussed further in Martin, Piccolino, and Speight, "Ex-Rebel Authority After Civil War," 219–220.

80. van Baalen, "Local Elites," 6.
81. Soro, *Pourquoi je suis devenu rebelle*, 86–87.
82. The community informant survey is further described in Martin, "Commander-Community Ties after Civil War," 778–793. I am grateful to Giulia Piccolino and Jeremy Speight for their collaboration on both the community informant and citizen surveys.
83. There have been several rich ethnographic studies of individual towns under FN control. However, none have gathered data systematically across a larger number of localities. See, for example, Fofana, "Ethnographie des Trajectoires Sociales"; Heitz-Tokpa, "Trust and Distrust in Rebel-Held Côte d'Ivoire"; Speight, "Big-Men Coalitions and Political Order in Northern Côte d'Ivoire (2002–2013)."
84. I relied on administrative maps provided by the Ivoirian National Institute of Statistics (INS) in Abidjan. In a small number of cases, I added corrections based on interviews with local officials.
85. For a dated but comprehensive overview of the key informant interview method, see Tremblay, "The Key Informant Technique," 688–701.
86. In two cases, selected subprefectures had to be replaced with alternatives due to unforeseen challenges; in one instance, a subprefecture was dropped due to reports of violent banditry along the main access route, and in another instance, the local sous-préfet was unwilling to grant us permission to carry out the survey.
87. I am grateful to Abel Gbala, Bakary Soro, Arthur Banga, Joseph Koné, Francois Defourny, and the Centre de Recherche et de Formation sur le Développement Intégré in Abidjan.
88. Kathrin Heitz-Tokpa, interview with the author, Bingerville, Côte d'Ivoire, November 2017.
89. Election data in Côte d'Ivoire are problematic to use in this context. The RDR candidate—Alassane Ouattara—was banned from running in the 1995 and 2000 elections, leading to a general boycott among many pro-RDR communities of both national-level and municipal-level elections. The same problem is true for the use of election data after 2011, when FPI leaders called for general election boycotts.
90. In cases where more than one field commander was stationed in a locality, I use data on the commander who spent the most time in charge of that sector or zone.
91. United Nations Security Council, "Final Report of the Group of Experts on Côte d'Ivoire."
92. Interview with four former FN soldiers, Yopougon, November 2016.
93. van Baalen, "Local Elites."
94. Boone, "Africa's New Territorial Politics," 70–72; Banegas and Popineau, "The 2020 Ivorian Election," 7–10.

3. Commander Embeddedness in Postwar Côte d'Ivoire (2011–2017)

1. Interview with Bernard, Sangouiné, November 2017.
2. Interview with Eric, Mahapleu, November 2017.
3. For a detailed overview of the events of the 2010 election, see Choi, *La Crise Ivoirienne*; and Carter Center, "Final Report."
4. The head of the UN mission in Côte d'Ivoire, Young-Jin Choi, along with five independent election observation missions, reaffirmed the result. These included the African Union, ECOWAS, the European Union, the International Organization of La Francophonie, and the Carter Center.
5. These included the departments of Beoumi, Bouaké, Boundiali, Dabakala, Ferkéssedougou, Katiola, Korhogo, and Sakassou.
6. Decision no. CI-2010-EP-34/03-12/CC/SG of December 3, 2010. In a subsequent analysis of the available polling data from the second round results and the locations of the anecdotal claims of violence and intimidation leveled by the government in its appeal to the Constitutional Council, the Carter Center concluded that "it appears that Ouattara's victory was largely decided by the vote in the south of the country and not, as the presidential camp al-

leged, in the departments of the north where Ouattara enjoys an indisputable historic hegemony." Carter Center, "Final Report," 62. In other words, while it is likely that voting irregularities and intimidation did occur in the northern departments in question, there is not convincing evidence that these irregularities decided the final outcome of the election.

7. Straus, "'It's Sheer Horror Here,'" 481–489.

8. Allouche and Zadi Zadi, "The Dynamics of Restraint in Côte d'Ivoire," 78; Balcells, *Rivalry and Revenge*, 164–169.

9. These included up to five thousand fighters under the command of Coulibaly—the "Invisible Commandos." Coulibaly had secretly returned to Côte d'Ivoire in 2010 following his exile from the FN in 2004.

10. Fofana, "Des Forces Nouvelles aux Forces Républicaines de Côte d'Ivoire," 161–178.

11. Adam Nossiter, Scott Sayare, and Dan Bilefsky, "Leader's Arrest in Ivory Coast Ends Standoff," *New York Times*, April 11, 2011, accessed November 14, 2023, https://www.nytimes.com/2011/04/12/world/africa/12ivory.html.

12. Piccolino, "Peacebuilding and Statebuilding in Post-2011 Côte d'Ivoire," 485–508.

13. As one government official put it, "Rwanda has been one country that has served as a model. Our people have gone to study their army, there were military exchanges. . . . The idea was to follow that kind of example." Interview with former CNS official, Abidjan, November 2016.

14. Author interview with foreign military adviser, Abidjan, November 2016. See also Fofana, "Des Forces Nouvelles Aux Forces Républicaines de Côte d'Ivoire."

15. Speight and Wittig, "Pathways from Rebellion," 21–43. A number of FN political leaders also ran as independent candidates.

16. Christine Lagard, "Toward a Second Ivoirien Miracle," International Monetary Fund, January 7, 2013, accessed November 14, 2023, https://www.imf.org/en/News/Articles/2015/09/28/04/53/sp010713#:~:text=The%20Ivoirien%20economic%20miracle%20was,fragmentation%20to%20unity%20and%20reconciliation; Piccolino, "David against Goliath in Côte d'Ivoire?" 1–23.

17. Between 2011 and 2016, Côte d'Ivoire received an average of over $1.13 billion USD annually in Official Development Assistance (ODA) from foreign partners. OECD, "Development Aid at a Glance." Over the 2012–2016 period, France and the United States spent tens of millions of dollars on security-sector assistance, including numerous programs aimed at promoting increased cohesion and command and control. Wyss, "The Gendarme Stay in Africa," 81–111; Security Assistance Monitor, "Côte d'Ivoire."

18. Piccolino, "Peacebuilding and Statebuilding in Post-2011 Côte d'Ivoire," 493–494.

19. de Tessières, "Enquête nationale," 27.

20. "Organisation de la nouvelle armée: le sort réservé aux chefs de guerre," *L'Inter*, June 28, 2011, accessed November 13, 2023, http://news.abidjan.net/h/402804.html.

21. Fofana, "Des Forces Nouvelles aux Forces Republicaines," 175. The commander of the pro-Gbagbo FDS forces, General Philippe Mangou, pledged allegiance to Ouattara after Gbagbo's arrest on April 12, 2011. General Fermin Detoh Letoh, commander of the FDS land army, was appointed by Outtara as FRCI deputy chief of staff under Soumaïla Bakayoko.

22. Interview with ex-FAFN members (ranks of sergeant and lieutenant) in Yopougon, Abidjan, October 22, 2016.

23. International Crisis Group, *A Critical Period for Ensuring Stability in Côte d'Ivoire*, 5.

24. "President Tells New Ivorian Army Chiefs to 'Clean Up' Ranks," *Jane's Country Risk Daily Report* 18, no. 146 (July 2011).

25. Hillebrecht and Straus, "Who Pursues the Perpetrators?" 179.

26. "Enquête de la CPI contre pro-Gbagbo et pro-Ouattara—Le Président Ouattara a donné son accord," *Le Nouveau Reveil*, June 29, 2011, National Library Archives, Abidjan.

27. Piccolino, "Peacebuilding and Statebuilding in Post-2011 Côte d'Ivoire," 494; United Nations Security Council, "Final Report of the Group of Experts," paragraph 10.

28. The former FAFN chief of security and com'zone Martin Kouakou Fofié, for example, was placed under UN sanctions in 2006 in response to allegations of recruitment of child soldiers, abductions, and extrajudicial killings. "Côte d'Ivoire: Interview with Sanctioned Rebel,

Martin Kouakou Fofie," *IRIN News*, March 29, 2006, accessed November 13, 2023, https://reliefweb.int/report/c%C3%B4te-divoire/cote-divoire-interview-sanctioned-rebel-martin-kouakou-fofie.

29. Soro himself had already demonstrated his willingness to purge ex-FN allies from the new regime. In May 2011, only weeks after the arrest of Gbagbo, FRCI forces loyal to Soro killed Coulibaly in a firefight in an Abidjan suburb. Coulibaly's assassination is assumed to stem from bad blood between Coulibaly and Soro due to disagreements over the FN's wartime strategy and a failed attempt on Soro's life by Coulibaly in 2003. The violent death of Coulibaly—one of the original military *formateurs* behind the anti-Gbagbo rebellion—reverberated throughout ex-rebel networks.

30. Interview with Issiaka Ouattara, Presidential Residence, Abidjan, July 2017. See also International Crisis Group, *A Critical Period for Ensuring Stability in Côte d'Ivoire*, 4–5.

31. Martin, Piccolino, and Speight, "The Political Legacies of Rebel Rule."

32. Focus group with members of civil society organization, Katiola, July 2017.

33. Interview with second deputy mayor, Katiola, July 2017.

34. Interview with second deputy mayor, Katiola, July 2017.

35. Interview with teacher's union coordinator, Katiola, July 2017.

36. Interview with former commandant of gendarmerie forces, Bouaké region, July 2017.

37. Interview with traditional chief, Katiola, July 2017.

38. Interview with ONUCI SSR official, Abidjan, November 2016.

39. Themnér, "Wealth in Ex-Combatants," 526–544.

40. Kriger, *Zimbabwe's Guerrilla War*; Driscoll, *Warlords and Coalition Politics*; Marten, *Warlords*.

41. This index ranges from 0 to 3 and scores a point for each measure listed under "Abuse of Civilians."

42. Collier and Hoeffler, "Greed and Grievance"; Reno, *Warfare in Independent Africa*, 163–205.

43. Staniland, *Networks of Rebellion*; Humphreys and Weinstein, "Handling and Manhandling Civilians," 429–447.

44. It is worth noting that commanding FN officers within surveyed subprefectures were usually outsiders to the communities they controlled; in only 12 percent of localities did informants identify the rebel commander as a native of the department. Moreover, while the recruitment of foot soldiers into the rebellion was nearly ubiquitous (87 percent), in many localities (66 percent) informants indicated that the rebel forces who manned outposts and checkpoints were not native to the area but rather were recruits sent from another region. These patterns are important because they suggest a deliberate strategy by FN leaders to station officers and units outside of their home areas, most likely to disrupt social and familial bonds between soldiers and communities that could undermine discipline and command authority. This technique is a long-standing strategy of political rule in northern Côte d'Ivoire, previously practiced via the rotation of state officials in the prefectoral corps. Thanks to Kathrin Heitz-Tokpa for raising this point.

45. For a discussion of the strengths and limitations of this method, see Simmons and Hopkins, "Constraining Power of International Treaties."

46. Existing theory has linked armed competition to rebel governance and coercion. See Kalyvas, *The Logic of Violence in Civil War*; and Arjona, *Rebelocracy*. The assumption is that these variables may influence wartime governance type but are not related to the error term in the second-stage equation.

47. Further details about the survey methodology are described in the appendix. See also Martin, Piccolino, and Speight, "The Political Legacies of Rebel Rule."

4. Ex-Rebel Commanders and the Ivorian State

1. Schiel, Powell, and Faulkner, "Mutiny in Africa, 1950–2018," 1–19; Dwyer, "Tactical Communication," 5–23.

2. Schiel, Powell, and Faulkner, "Mutiny in Africa, 1950–2018."

3. Schiel, Powell, and Faulkner, "Mutiny in Côte d'Ivoire," 103–115.

4. Albrecht and Ohl, "Exit, Resistance, Loyalty"; Huntington, *Political Order in Changing Societies.*

5. Interview with ex-FAFN members (ranks of sergeant and lieutenant) in Yopougon, Abidjan, October 2016.

6. Schiel, Faulkner, and Powell, "Mutiny in Côte d'Ivoire."

7. "Ivorian President Orders Army Back to Barracks," *Jane's Country Risk Daily Report* 18, no. 254 (December 21, 2011).

8. It is hard to discern the legitimacy of claims to "war veteran" status in Côte d'Ivoire. Many individuals who lacked combat roles in the 2002–2011 conflict have sought to obtain material gains from claiming the title.

9. Demobilized combatants are organized through a series of association-based movements, including the Côte d'Ivoire Association for the Demobilised, the Côte d'Ivoire Association for the Demobilised, and Cellule 39. Many of these groups were originally created by FN leaders to control ex-combatant networks and to distribute DDR funds. Diallo, "La Cellule 39 en Côte d'Ivoire," 173.

10. Interviews with ex-combatants in Bouaké, Korhogo, Man, and Katiola, 2017. See also Moody, "Reaching for the Impossible?" 127; Moody, "Ex-combatants Thinking Differently," 732–734.

11. Moody, "Reaching for the Impossible?" 127; Diallo, "La Cellule 39 en Côte d'Ivoire."

12. Leboeuf, *La réforme du secteur de sécurité à 'Ivoirienne*, 34–35.

13. Interview with four FRCI soldiers, Yopougon, July 2017; interview with five ex-FN demobilized combatants, Korhogo, October 2017; interview with ex-FN demobilized combatants, Man, November 2017. For their part, the two former FN zone commanders that I interviewed during my field research both denied any direct involvement in orchestrating the mutinies but expressed sympathy with those who participated.

14. Interview with EU security adviser, Abidjan, June 2017; interview with US security attaché, Abidjan, June 2017; interview with Ministry of Interior official, Abidjan, June 2017.

15. Interview with EU security adviser, Abidjan, July 2017.

16. Interview with Reuters journalist, Abidjan, June 2017.

17. Schiel, Powell, and Faulkner, "Mutiny in Africa, 1950–2018."

18. Schiel, Powell, and Faulkner, "Mutiny in Africa, 1950–2018," 494.

19. The variance-to-mean ratio of the *Mutiny* outcome variable is 6.8, and it is 1.2 for the *Demobilized rebel protest* variable.

20. The inclusion of additional covariates often caused the zero-inflated models to fail to converge.

21. On focal points in coordination games, see Schelling, *The Strategy of Conflict*. For an empirical application of the focal points concept to protest events, see Dahlum and Wig, "Chaos on Campus," 3–32.

22. The Gendarmerie Nationale (Camp Commando) and the Groupement Mobile d'Intervention de Bouaké are both stationed in the city.

23. Leboeuf, *La réforme du secteur de sécurité a l'ivoirienne*, 5.

24. Beck, Gleditsch, and Beardsley, "Space Is More than Geography," 27–44.

25. The p value of the Moran's I statistic is 0.39 for military mutinies and 0.28 for demobilized rebel protests.

26. On the centrality of internal policing to state formation, see Bayley, "The Police and Political Development in Europe." On postconflict policing in weak states, see Blair, Karim, and Morse, "Establishing the Rule of Law in Weak and War-Torn States," 641–657; Dow, "Policing in a Post-Conflict State." On rebel governance and postconflict policing, see Richard and Bakke, "Legacies of Wartime Order."

27. See Albrecht and Buur, "An Uneasy Marriage," 390–405; Cammett and MacLean, "Introduction," 1–21.

28. Ricard, "Faire de «l'ordre»."

29. Ricard, "Faire de «l'ordre»," 157–158. Hellweg, *Hunting the Ethical State.*

30. Ricard, "Faire de «l'ordre»," 192.

31. The specific question asked: "Who would you turn to today if you had to [get back something stolen from you or seek justice after being harmed as the victim of a crime]?"

32. Hamm, Trinkner, and Carr, "Fair Process, Trust, and Cooperation," 1183–1212; Jackson and Bradford, "Measuring Public Attitudes towards the Police."

33. In the case of police commissariats, households were asked how long it takes to travel to get there. A large proportion of respondents (nearly one-half) answered that either they "never go there" or that the police/gendarmes "do not exist," even considering only those subprefectures where a commissariat did in fact exist in 2014. Conditional on the existence of a police commissariat, we can infer that either of these responses indicate that households likely do not make use of police services.

34. Estimates obtained using ten thousand Monte Carlo simulations, moving *Postwar commander influence* from its minimum to its maximum, holding other variables at their mean.

35. On the difficulties of challenges prediction in conflict studies, see Cederman and Wiedmann, "Predicting Armed Conflict."

36. Schiel, Powell, and Faulkner, "Mutiny in Côte d'Ivoire," 112.

37. Schiel, Powell, and Faulkner, "Mutiny in Côte d'Ivoire," 106–109.

38. One exception is Coulibaly, the exiled FN commander who died in a gunfight with soldiers loyal to Soro in the waning days of the 2011 battle of Abidjan.

39. Office Francais de Protection des Refugies et Apatrides, *L'armee ivoirienne depuis 2011*, 9.

40. Office Francais de Protection des Refugies et Apatrides, *L'armee ivoirienne depuis 2011*, 9; "ADO Livre Bataille au Désordre Militaire," Africa Intelligence, *La Lettre du Continent* n. 639, 12/07/2012.

41. Office Francais de Protection des Refugies et Apatrides, *L'armee ivoirienne depuis 2011*, 9.

42. Bakayoko was replaced as chief of staff of the army by Sékou Touré, a career FANCI officer who remained loyal to Gbagbo during the civil war, in January 2017. Touré was in turn replaced by Lassina Doumbia, another ex-FANCI officer and a former government prefect, in 2018.

5. Tracing Commander Embeddedness in Four Case Studies

1. On the use of the most similar case-selection method for causal inference, see Seawright and Gerring, "Case Selection Techniques in Case Study Research," 294–308; Mill, *System of Logic*.

2. Nielsen, "Case Selection via Matching," 573. For related discussions of the method, see Tarrow, "The Strategy of Paired Comparison," 239.

3. Fofana, *Côte d'Ivoire*, 41–52. Alassane Ouattara himself was born in the town of Kong, approximately 150 kilometers southeast of Korhogo. The former prime minister of Côte d'Ivoire, Amadou Gon Coulibaly, was a native of Korhogo.

4. On the history, migrations, and traditions of the Senoufo ethnic group, see Diamitani, "The Insider and Ethnography of Secrecy," 55–70.

5. Interview with former defense minister, Abidjan, October 2017.

6. Interview with former defense minister, Abidjan, October 2017. Ibrahim Coulibaly himself was born in Bouaké.

7. Interview with Ouahouri and Brahima, Korhogo, October 2017.

8. Interview with Ouahouri, Korhogo, October 2017.

9. Interview with Bakary, Korhogo, October 2017.

10. Interview with Tuo, Korhogo, October 2017.

11. Messamba was promoted to a ministerial position within the short-lived power-sharing government created by the Linas-Marcoussis peace agreement. He was initially appointed as head of the customs agency and later as the minister of War Victims, Displaced Persons, and Refugees.

12. Interview with Ouamar, Korhogo, October 2017. Interestingly, Diarrassouba would later resurrect his career after the fall of the Gbagbo government as a *proche* of Alassane Ouattara. In March 2019, he was promoted to the position of inspector general of the land army at the rank of colonel major.

13. In 2001, Fofié was arrested and imprisoned by the Gbagbo government for his suspected involvement in a conspiracy to overthrow the president, before escaping to Burkina Faso. This experience of imprisonment motivated his strong animus against the Gbagbo regime. During the civil war, Fofié renamed his own military unit the "Fansara 110," an homage to the cell number in the prison where he was held captive. In 2006, Fofié claimed that he joined the MPCI mutineers because he had been tortured for his suspected role in a 2001 coup plot. "Côte d'Ivoire: Interview with Sanctioned Rebel, Martin Kouakou Fofie," *IRIN News*, March 29, 2006, accessed November 13, 2023, https://reliefweb.int/report/c%C3%B4te-divoire/cote-divoire-interview-sanctioned-rebel-martin-kouakou-fofie.

14. Both Kanigui and Alphonse were former members of the Fédération Estudiantine et Scholaire de Côte d'Ivoire (FESCI) and members of the RDR party prior to the onset of the war. Both were close to Guillaume Soro.

15. Interview with Kanigui Soro, former civilian delegate of the FN, Korhogo zone, Abidjan, July 2017. The *cabinet civile* grew from a handful of individuals at the onset of the conflict to approximately twenty representatives in the Korhogo zone.

16. See Hellweg, "Encompassing the State," 3–28.

17. Interview with president of the *Confrérie des Dozos* and the secretary general to the president of the Confrérie, Korhogo, October 2017.

18. Interview with Sidibé, Korhogo, October 2017.

19. Interviews with Silué, Bakary, and Sidibé. Presumably, the FN were convinced to continue paying the salaries of civil servants in part because the issuance of birth certificates and citizenship paperwork had been a central political grievance of northerners over the previous decade.

20. Interview with Silué, Korhogo, October 2017.

21. As the deputy mayor of Korhogo explained, "The FN asked for our agents, and since I managed the municipal taxes, I put the list of agents at their disposition. Those who were called received a bit of money, they were given a small salary each month that I divided among the working agents." Interview with Silué, Korhogo, October 2017.

22. Interview with Brahima, Korhogo, October 2017.

23. Interview with Timité, Korhogo, October 2017.

24. Interview with Brahima, Korhogo, October 2017.

25. Interview with Sidibé and assistant, Korhogo, October 2017.

26. On the historical and colonial origins of the Senoufo chieftaincy system, see Förster, "The Invisible Social Body," 99–119.

27. Interview with Eric, Korhogo, October 2017.

28. Interview with Timité, Korhogo, October 2017.

29. Interview with Sidibé, Korhogo, October 2017.

30. Interview with Korhogo canton chief, Korhogo, October 2017.

31. Interview with Brahima, October 2017.

32. Interview with Brahima, October 2017.

33. Interview with Sidibé and assistant, Korhogo, October 2017.

34. Interview with Brahima, Korhogo, October 2017.

35. Interview with M. Yaya Soro, Korhogo, October 2017.

36. Koné, *Les Jeunes Patriotes*, 43–44.

37. The Armed Conflict Location Event Dataset estimated that 154 civilians were killed through one-sided violence in the fall of 2002 in Bouaké. Interviewees often placed the figure much higher.

38. "L'offensive des FANCI a commence: Bouaké bombardée depuis hier," *Le Nouveau Reveil*, October 7, 2002, National Library Archives, Abidjan.

39. "La télévision de Bouaké aux mains des assaillants," *Le Nouveau Reveil*, October 24, 2002, National Library Archives, Abidjan.

40. Interview with traditional leader, Bouaké, November 2016.

41. After the collapse of the Linas-Marcoussis government, Fozié became the head of the FN police and gendarmerie division.

42. Interview with former FN soldier, Bouaké, November 2016.

43. Interview with Ismaël, Bouaké, November 2016.
44. Interview with Ismaël, Bouaké, November 2016.
45. Interview with school director, Bouaké, November 2016.
46. Interview with interim director of regional health office, Bouaké, November 2017.
47. Interview with Ouattara Zawana, deputy mayor, Bouaké, November 2016.
48. Interview with Sidibé, Korhogo, October 2017.
49. Interview with Jule, church pastor, Bouaké, November 2016.
50. Interview with Zenedi, Bouaké, November 2016.
51. Interview with Ouattara Zawana, deputy mayor, Bouaké, November 2016.
52. Higonnet, *"My Heart is Cut."*
53. Interview with Father Achille, Bouaké, November 2016.
54. Interview with Father Achille, Bouaké, November 2016.
55. Interview with Father Maxime, Bouaké, November 2016.
56. Interview with chef de Tribune, Bouaké, November 2016. According to one anecdote that I heard repeated several times, Ousmane was once asked to provide security for a convoy carrying 150 million CFA. The convoy was attacked, and the money disappeared. After the convoy owner publicly accused Ousmane of the theft, the owner was fatally poisoned.
57. Data comes from the Political Transition and Inclusion survey, described in the appendix.
58. Responses are similar among respondents who identify with northern and non-northern ethnic groups.
59. Popineau, "Prendre la craie."
60. See the discussion of incentives for collaborative wartime rule in chapter 1.
61. In the second-round runoff ballot of the 2010 presidential elections, Laurent Gbagbo garnered only 14.3 percent of the vote in the Bouaké department. Source: Commision Electorale Indépendante (CEI): https://www.cei.ci/resultats-recents/. Moreover, Baoulé-majority localities in my dataset experienced, on average, a higher level of rebel goods provision compared to the average FN-ruled subprefecture. This suggests that the presence of Baoulé populations was not an impediment to collaborative FN rule in general.
62. The Coulibaly family's predominance was rooted in the period of colonial expansion. With the intensification of territorial warfare between Samori Turé's Wassoulou Empire and the French Colonial Empire in the late nineteenth century, Korhogo emerged as a significant source of recruits for Ture's slave (*sofa*) army. Supported by Turé, and later by the French colonial governor, the head of the Senoufo chieftaincy—Gbon Coulibaly—established his family's supremacy by subordinating other local chieftaincies and monopolizing control over the cotton cash-crop economy. Gbon Coulibaly's descendants in turn maintained a firm grip on regional power by aligning themselves with President Houphouët-Boigny and the ruling Parti Démocratique de Côte d'Ivoire (PDCI). See Gunderson, "Village Elders and Regional Intermediaries," 38; Speight, "Big-Men Coalitions and Political Order in Northern Cote d'Ivoire," 134–151.
63. Interview with traditional leader, Sokoura quartier, Bouaké, October 2016.
64. Many former employees of Bouaké's mayoral office also remained in exile until at least 2007. Interview with Ismael, Bouaké, November 2016. Interview with Koné, Bouaké, November 2016.
65. In an offensive in November 2004, for example, several of Bouaké's suburbs fell into the hands of loyalist soldiers before being recaptured by rebel forces.
66. Arjona, *Rebelocracy*, 53.
67. Interview with Traoré, Bouaké, November 2016.
68. Interview with Abel, Bouaké, November 2016.
69. Interview with Kanigui Soro, MP and former FN civilian delegate in Korhogo, Abidjan, July 2017.
70. David, "Why Are Institutions the 'Carriers of History?'" 205–220.
71. Lewis, *Conventions*, 41–42.
72. On path dependency in rebel governance, see Weinstein, *Inside Rebellion*, 169–171.
73. Later, Fofié was appointed as the deputy commander of the Second Regional Command in Daloa.

74. Vincent Duhem, "Les ex-comzones regnent-ils sur la Côte d'Ivoire?" *Jeune Afrique*, April 29, 2013.
75. Groga-Bada, "Côte d'Ivoire."
76. Interview with canton chief, Korhogo, October 2017; interview with Bakary, Korhogo, October 2017.
77. Interview with Sidibé, Korhogo, October 2017.
78. Interview with Senoufo canton chief, Korhogo, October 2017. Interview with dozo hunting association president, October 2017.
79. Interview with Sidibé, Korhogo, October 2017.
80. Interview with secretary general, subprefecture of Ferkéssedougou, October 2017.
81. Interview with Nagalourou, Korhogo, October 2017.
82. Interview with secretary general, subprefecture of Ferkéssedougou, October 2017.
83. Interview with executive secretary, secretary general, and deputy secretary general of Cellule 39, Korhogo, October 2017.
84. Interview with Eric, Korhogo, October 2017.
85. Interview with Sidibé, Korhogo, October 2017.
86. United Nations Security Council, "Final Report of the Group of Experts," 24–25.
87. UN Group of Experts committee member, email communication with the author, October 2016. See also "Les anciens com'zones dans l'armee Ivoirienne," Office Français de Protection des Réfugiés et Apatrides (OFPRA), 20–21.
88. United Nations Security Council, "Final Report of the Group of Experts," 30–31.
89. Interview with Sidibé, Korhogo, October 2017.
90. Interview with Issouf, Kignaman, and Touré, Korhogo, October 2017.
91. Interview with ONUCI security official, Abidjan, October 2016.
92. Interview with Sidibé, Korhogo, October 2017.
93. Interview with foreign embassy security official, Abidjan, Côte d'Ivoire, October 2016.
94. Interview with ONUCI SSR official, Abidjan, November 2016.
95. Serge Touré, "Des résidences du com'zone Fofié perquisitionnées," *Ivorian.net*, January 6, 2020.
96. Interview with Pere Maxime, Bouaké Cathedral, November 2016.
97. Interview with Adama, Bouaké, July 14, 2017; interview with Mamadou, Bouaké, July 2017.
98. Interview with former gendarmerie commander, Bouaké, July 2017.
99. Interview with Ismaël, Bouaké, November 2016.
100. Interview with Jule, church pastor, Bouaké, November 2016.
101. Diallo, "La Cellule 39 en Côte d'Ivoire," 173.
102. Interview with former FAFN soldier, Bouaké, November 2016.
103. United Nations Security Council, "Midterm Report of the Group of Experts."
104. Interview with local administrator, Bouaké, June 2017.
105. Interview with US embassy security attaché, Abidjan, October 2016.
106. Interview with US embassy security attaché, Abidjan, October 2016.
107. "Ivory Coast Promises to Pay Protesting Soldiers," *BBC News*, November 19, 2014, accessed November 13, 2023, https://www.bbc.com/news/world-africa-30113669.
108. Interview with Issiaka Ouattara, Abidjan, July 2017. See also "Les anciens com'zones dans l'armee Ivoirienne," OFPRA, 10.
109. Interview with Issiaka Ouattara, Abidjan, July 2017.
110. United Nations Security Council, "Midterm Report of the Group of Experts," 50.
111. The Yacouba comprise approximately 6 percent of the national Ivorian population. Ivorian National Institute of Statistics, *ENV 2015*.
112. Although not limited to this region, tensions between autochtone and allogène communities are most acute in the western coffee-growing region of Cote d'Ivoire. Since the 1930s, some migrant communities grew wealthy relative to the "firstcomer" inhabitants. When indigenous chiefs in the west began selling parcels of land to *nordiste* migrants in the 1960s and 1970s, these transactions sparked resentment from younger Ivorians who found themselves

increasingly shut out of land opportunities. Chauveau and Colin, "Customary Transfers and Land Sales in Cote d'Ivoire," 81–103; McGovern, *Making War in Côte d'Ivoire*.

113. Koné, *Les Jeunes Patriotes*, 10–11.

114. These included Krahn members of the Liberians United for Reconciliation and Democracy, a rebel group fighting against Charles Taylor's regime, as well as refugees driven into western Côte d'Ivoire by violence in Liberia since the onset of the Second Liberian Civil War in 1999. See Human Rights Watch, *Trapped Between Two Wars*, 29.

115. International Crisis Group, *Côte d'Ivoire*, 1–2. In January 2003, these groups merged with the MPCI to form the FN. Many Liberian mercenaries hired on the rebel side were later pushed out of the organization and drifted back into Liberia.

116. For a detailed chronology of events in this region, see Chelpi-den Hamer, *Militarized Youths in Western Côte d'Ivoire*, 89–91.

117. Liberian forces in Sangouiné were initially led by a commander who went by "Andre."

118. Interview with village chief, Sangouiné, November 2017.

119. Interview with village chief, Sangouiné, November 2017.

120. Interview with Ouahi, Mahapleu, November 2017.

121. Interview with village chief, Sangouiné, November 2017.

122. Fofana ("Loss," aka "Cobra") was a native of the central town of Mankono. A master corporal in the army prior to the war, he became zone commander of zone 6 (Man) on July 21, 2003.

123. Interviewees in Sangouiné and Mahapleu gave varied and sometimes conflicting names of early local commanders, all of whom operated under a nom de guerre. It was clear, however, that none of the local commanders who preceded Kassero, Rodrik, and Ondo were present in the area long enough to develop a lasting relationship with the community.

124. Heitz-Tokpa, "Trust and Distrust in Rebel-Held Côte d'Ivoire," 75.

125. Heitz-Tokpa, "Trust and Distrust in Rebel-Held Côte d'Ivoire," 67–68.

126. Interview with town mayor, Sangouiné, August 2017.

127. Interview with village chief, Sangouiné, November 2017.

128. Interview with Koh, Sangouiné, November 2017.

129. Interview with Celestin, Sangouiné, November 2017.

130. Interview with medical doctor, health clinic of Sangouiné, November 2017.

131. Interview with RDR branch official, Sangouiné, November 2017.

132. Interview with Koh, Sangouiné, November 2017.

133. Interview with village chief, Sangouiné, November 2017.

134. Interview with RDR branch official, Sangouiné, November 2017.

135. Interview with Celestin, Sangouiné, November 2017.

136. Interview with village chief, Sangouiné, November 2017.

137. Interview with Koh, Sangouiné, November 2017.

138. Interview with président des jeunes, Sangouiné, November 2017.

139. Interview with central village chief, village notables, and président des jeunes, Mahapleu, November 2017.

140. Interview with central village chief, Mahapleu, November 2017.

141. Interview with Ouahi, Mahapleu, November 2017.

142. Interview with Ouahi, Mahapleu, November 2017.

143. Interview with central village chief, village notables, and président des jeunes, Mahapleu, November 2017.

144. Interview with FPI branch member, Mahapleu, November 2017.

145. Interview with central village chief, village notables, and président des jeunes, Mahapleu, November 2017

146. Interview with Ouahi, Mahapleu, November 2017.

147. Interview with central village chief, village notables, and président des jeunes, Mahapleu, November 2017.

148. Another important source of resentment against the FN stemmed from numerous allegations of sexual assault committed by rebel elements in Mahapleu. Although interviewees

in my research generally refrained from providing details about such abuses (and I did not ask), evidence collected by an investigative research team from Amnesty International in 2011 documented several cases of rape by FN forces in Mahapleu, including by the rebel commanders themselves. Amnesty International, *Côte d'Ivoire Mission Report*, 3–4.

149. Top FN leaders—including the zone commander Fofana but also Guillaume Soro himself—distributed resources to commanders and FN commissars in the region to invest in development and gain local support. Heitz-Tokpa, "Trust and Distrust in Rebel-Held Côte d'Ivoire."

150. Blon Blaise acquired considerable personal wealth in the coffee and cocoa industry in the 1970s and 1980s before shifting into the political arena. He was a close associate of General Robert Gueï and one of the founding members of the Union Pour la Démocratie et la Paix en Côte d'Ivoire (UDPCI). He is sometimes nicknamed "the chameleon" or "the lizard" for his ability to adapt to shifts in national politics and remain aligned with the ruling regime. In 2017, Blon Blaise was promoted to third vice president of the National Assembly.

151. The variable *Block voting index*, a measure of the postwar strength of local institutions and social cohesion, shows that Sangouiné has stronger institutions (50.1) than Mahapleu (44.85).

152. Interview with Bernard, Man, November 2017; interview with Kathrin, Abidjan, November 2017.

153. Interview with Ouahi, Mahapleu, November 2017.

154. Interview with village chief, Sangouiné, November 2017.

155. Interview with Celestin, Sangouiné, November 2017.

156. Interview with Koh, Sangouiné, November 2017.

157. Interview with RDR branch member, Sangouiné, November 2017

158. Interview with Celestin, Sangouiné, November 2017.

159. Part of the reason for this reticence is likely due to the timing of my research visits in the summer and fall of 2017, only months after the outbreak of military mutinies and ex-combatant protests.

160. Interview with Koh, Sangouiné, November 2017.

161. Interview with Celestin, Sangouiné, November 2017.

162. Interview with Koh, Sangouiné, November 2017.

163. Interview with RDR branch member, Sangouiné, November 2017.

164. Schiel, Powell, and Faulkner, "Mutiny in Côte d'Ivoire," 110.

165. Interview with demobilized FAFN soldiers, Sangouiné, November 2017.

166. Interview with Djehe Claude, sous-prefét of Man, August 2017.

167. Interview with Djehe Claude, Man, August 2017; interview with Bernard, Man, November 2017.

168. Interview with village chief, Mahapleu, November 2017.

169. Interview with Bernard, Mahapleu, November 2017.

170. Interview with central village chief, village notables, and président des jeunes, Mahapleu, November 2017.

171. Interview with FPI branch members, Mahapleu, November 2017.

172. Interview with Ouahi, Mahapleu, November 2017.

173. Interview with Maurice, Mahapleu, November 2017.

174. Interview with Bernard, Mahapleu, November 2017.

175. Interview with Joseph, demobilized FAFN soldier, Mahapleu, November 2017.

176. Interview with Jonathan, demobilized FAFN soldier, Mahapleu, November 2017.

177. Interview with Djehe Claude, sous-prefét of Man, August 2017.

178. "Côte d'Ivoire: Interview with Sanctioned Rebel, Martin Kouakou Fofie," *IRIN News*, March 29, 2006, accessed November 13, 2023, https://reliefweb.int/report/c%C3%B4te-divoire/cote-divoire-interview-sanctioned-rebel-martin-kouakou-fofie.

179. If such a scenario seems far-fetched, one need only remember that when the army mutinies began in January 2017, several high-ranking ministers and businessmen in the country rushed to purchase flights out of the country, expecting the regime to fall within days. This story was recounted to me by several NGO workers and journalists.

180. Arjona, *Rebelocracy*, 144.
181. For a related argument, see Rubin, "Rebel Territorial Control"; and van Baalen, "Local Elites."

6. Commander Resistance after Rebel-Military Integration (1946–2019)

1. Toft, "Ending Civil Wars."
2. Glassmyer and Sambanis, "Rebel-Military Integration."
3. This definition follows Cunningham, Gleditsch, and Salehyan, "It Takes Two," 570–597.
4. For example, I exclude the 1980 coup d'état in Liberia against President William Tolbert, when a small group of Armed Forces of Libera (AFL) soldiers led by Samuel Doe entered the presidential palace, killed Tolbert and his bodyguards, and announced a new ruling junta. For similar reasons, I also exclude cases of regime change that were precipitated solely by a foreign military invasion with minimal local involvement, such as the US invasion of Iraq in 2003. However, domestic challenger groups that played a significant role in defeating incumbent regimes in partnership with foreign forces are included. For example, I include the United Islamic Front for the Salvation of Afghanistan due to the central role of its fighters in defeating the Taliban regime in 2001 alongside US and NATO forces.
5. Sambanis and Schulhofer-Wohl, "Civil War as Sovereignty Rupture."
6. Fortna, "A Lost Chance for Peace," 73.
7. For suggestive evidence along these lines, see Heywood, "Unita and Ethnic Nationalism in Angola," 47–66.
8. See also Weinstein, *Inside Rebellion*; and Arjona, *Rebelocracy*.
9. Huang, *Wartime Origins*.
10. Stewart, "Civil War as State-Making."
11. Licklider, "The Consequences of Negotiated Settlements"; Walter, "Bargaining Failures," 243–261.
12. Toft, *Securing the Peace*; Lyons, "The Importance of Winning."
13. Doyle and Sambanis, *Making War and Building Peace*; Fortna, *Does Peacekeeping Work?*; Walter, *Committing to Peace*.
14. Walter, "Critical Barrier"; Fortna, *Does Peacekeeping Work?*; Matanock, *Electing Peace*.
15. Doyle and Sambanis, *Making War and Building Peace*; Paris and Sisk, eds., *The Dilemmas of State-Building*.
16. Powell, "The Determinants of Attempting and Outcome of Coups d'État."
17. Banks and Wilson, "Cross-National Time-Series Data Archive."
18. Decalo, *Coups and Army Rule in Africa*; Harkness, "The Ethnic Army and the State," 587–616; Roessler, *Ethnic Politics and State Power in Africa*.
19. Harkness, *When Soldiers Rebel*; Roessler, *Ethnic Politics and State Power in Africa*.
20. De Bruin, *How to Prevent Coups d'État*.
21. Counterbalancing forces are security forces positioned near the capital city or presidential palace that can quickly interpose themselves between the regime and would-be coup plotters.
22. De Bruin, "Mapping Coercive Institutions."
23. Lindberg and Clark, "Does Democratization Reduce the Risk of Military Intervention in Politics in Africa?"
24. Svolik, "Power Sharing and Leadership Dynamics in Authoritarian Regimes."
25. Coppedge et al., "V-Dem [Country–Year/Country–Date] Dataset v11.1."
26. Doyle and Sambanis, *Making War and Building Peace*.
27. Levitsky and Way, "Beyond Patronage"; Balcells and Kalyvas, "Revolutionary Rebels and the Marxist Paradox."
28. Weinstein, *Inside Rebellion*.
29. For a discussion of the similarities and differences between these strands of revolutionary ideology, see Kalyvas, "Jihadi Rebels in Civil War," 36–47.

30. Reno, *Warfare in Independent Africa*, 37–41.

31. Process tracing in the case studies also confirmed that commander-regime splits often fell along ethnic fault lines. To take one example, when former guerrilla commanders in Guinea-Bissau mutinied against Louis Cabral's revolutionary African Party for the Independence of Guinea and Cape Verde and installed General João "Nino" Vieira, the impetus for antiregime mobilization rose in part out of military grievances about the dominant positions of the lighter-skinned "Cape Verdeans" in the regime leadership. Chabal, *Amilcar Cabral*, 162.

32. See Martin, "Insurgent Armies."

33. Stewart, *Governing for Revolution*.

34. Levitsky and Way, "Beyond Patronage"; Reno, *Warfare in Independent Africa*.

35. Antonio Giustozzi and Rasha Al Aqeedi, "Security and Governance in the Taliban's Emirate," *News Lines Institute*, November 24, 2021, accessed November 14, 2023, https://newlinesinstitute.org/political-systems/governance/security-and-governance-in-the-talibans-emirate/. Yacub Mujahid is the eldest son of Taliban founder Mohammad Omar.

36. Watkins, "An Assessment of Taliban Rule at Three Months," 6.

37. Giustozzi, "Hearts, Minds, and the Barrel of a Gun," 71–80; Ali, "One Land, Two Rules."

38. Ali, "One Land, Two Rules."

39. Ali, "One Land, Two Rules."

40. Taliban "hit teams" killed an estimated one thousand alleged collaborators each year. Giustozzi and Al Aqeedi, "Security and Governance in the Taliban's Emirate."

41. Giustozzi, "Hearts, Minds, and the Barrel of a Gun," 79.

42. Giustozzi, "Hearts, Minds, and the Barrell of a Gun," 79.

43. Semple, *Rhetoric, Ideology, and Organizational Structure of the Taliban Movement*, 30.

44. Giustozzi and Al Aqeedi, "Security and Governance in the Taliban's Emirate."

45. Giustozzi and Al Aqeedi, "Security and Governance in the Taliban's Emirate."

46. Giustozzi and Al Aqeedi, "Security and Governance in the Taliban's Emirate."

47. John Lee Anderson, "The Taliban Confront the Realities of Power," *New Yorker*, February 28, 2022.

48. Andrew Watkins, "What's Next for the Taliban's Leadership Amid Rising Dissent?" United States Institute of Peace, April 11, 2023, accessed November 14, 2023, https://www.usip.org/publications/2023/04/whats-next-talibans-leadership-amid-rising-dissent.

49. Joshua White, "Nonstate Threats in the Taliban's Afghanistan," Brookings Institute, February 1, 2022, accessed November 14, 2023, https://www.brookings.edu/articles/nonstate-threats-in-the-talibans-afghanistan/.

50. Watkins, "An Assessment of Taliban Rule at Three Months."

51. This section draws on Lombard, *State of Rebellion*; International Crisis Group, *Central African Republic: The Roots of Violence*; International Crisis Group, *Central African Republic: Anatomy of a Predator State*; and Spittaels et al., *Mapping Conflict Motives*.

52. In 2020, the FPRC announced it had joined a new rebel coalition, the Coalition of Patriots for Change (CPC), along with other groups like the Union for Peace in the Central African Republic (UPC) and the Central African Patriotic Movement (MPC). At this time, it is unclear whether the CPC remains a viable alliance.

53. International Crisis Group, *Managing Election Tensions in the Central African Republic*, 3.

54. Verjee, "A Faulty Prescription?"

55. Cassandra Vinograd, "Inside Ndele, FPRC's 'Peaceful' Parallel State," *Al Jazeera*, October 6, 2017, accessed November 14, 2023, https://www.aljazeera.com/news/2017/10/6/inside-ndele-fprcs-peaceful-parallel-state.

56. Spittaels et al., *Mapping Conflict Motives*, 38.

57. Vinograd, "Inside Ndele."

58. Control over roadblocks—and the power to tax and control movement of people that this entails—is probably the most consistently coercive element of rebel rule in CAR. But such forms of control pale in comparison to the coercive projects of groups like the Taliban, and roadblock control by armed gunmen is not necessarily seen by the population as a major aberration from the usual state of affairs. See Schouten, "Roadblock Politics in Central Africa," 937.

59. Lombard, "Denouncing Sovereignty," 1077.
60. Schouten, "Roadblock Politics in Central Africa," 931.
61. For a fascinating study of state strategies of cooperation and coexistence with nonstate armed groups, see Staniland, *Ordering Violence*.
62. Levitsky and Way, "Beyond Patronage"; Lyons, "The Importance of Winning"; Martin, "Insurgent Armies."
63. Gilligan and Stedman, "Where Do the Peacekeepers Go?"
64. De Bruin, "Preventing Coups d'état."

Conclusion: Field Commanders, War, and the State

1. Levitsky and Way, "Beyond Patronage"; Martin, "Insurgent Armies"; Meng and Paine, "Power Sharing and Authoritarian Stability."
2. Elections resulting in leadership turnover have been linked to preemptive military coups. See Harkness, *When Soldiers Rebel*.
3. Weinstein, *Inside Rebellion*. On rebel leadership ascension processes, see Cunningham and Sawyer, "Conflict Negotiations and Rebel Leader Selection."
4. Bauer et al., "Can War Foster Cooperation?" 249–274; Bateson, "Crime Victimization and Political Participation," 570–587; Blattman, "From Violence to Voting," 231–247; Gilligan, Pasquale, and Samii, "Civil War and Social Cohesion," 604–619. Important exceptions include Zukerman Daly, *Organized Violence after Civil War*; Huang, *Wartime Origins*; Kubota, "Imagined Statehood," 199–212; Martin, Piccolino, and Speight, "The Political Legacies of Rebel Rule"; Shenk, "Does Conflict Experience Affect Participatory Democracy after Civil War?"
5. Wood, "The Social Processes of Civil War," 539–561; Cheng, *Extralegal Groups in Post-Conflict Liberia*.
6. Blair and Kalmanovitz, "On the Rights of Warlords"; Malejacq, *Warlord Survival*; Martin, Piccolino, and Speight, "Ex-Rebel Authority after Civil War," 209–232.
7. For evidence that voters in post–civil war states engage in "security voting," see Zukerman Daly, "A Farewell to Arms?" 163–204.
8. Liu, "Control, Cooperation, and Cooptation," 37–76.
9. Zukerman Daly, Paler, and Samii, "Wartime Ties and the Social Logic of Crime," 536–550.
10. Blair et al., "Preventing Rebel Resurgence after Civil War."
11. Ake, *A Political Economy of Africa*; Herbst, *States and Power in Africa*; Migdal, *Strong Societies and Weak States*; Rabinowitz, *Coups, Rivals, and the Modern State*.
12. Huang, *Wartime Origins*; Toft, *Securing the Peace*.
13. Carter and Hassan, "Regional Governance in Divided Societies."
14. Bjarnesen and van Baalen, *Democratic Backsliding in Côte d'Ivoire*.
15. The discussion in this section draws on a working paper with Giulia Piccolino and Jeremy Speight.
16. Goldring and Matthews, "To Purge or Not to Purge?"; Sudduth, "Strategic Logic of Elite Purges in Dictatorships"; Boix and Svolik, "The Foundations of Limited Authoritarian Government."
17. Ricard, "Stability for Whom and for What?" 268; International Crisis Group, *Keeping Jihadists Out of Northern Côte d'Ivoire*.
18. Banegas and Popineau, "The 2020 Ivorian Election," 7–10.
19. Fearon, "Civil War and the Current International System," 20.
20. Lee, "International Statebuilding and the Domestic Politics of State Development," 5.
21. Lee, "International Statebuilding and the Domestic Politics of State Development," 10.
22. Driscoll, *Warlords and Coalition Politics*, 30; North, Wallis, and Weingast, *Violence and Social Orders*, 17.
23. Interview with Arthur Banga, University of Cocody, Abidjan, July 2017; interview with US embassy security attaché, Abidjan, October 2016.

24. Interview with Sidibé, Korhogo, October 2017.

25. United Nations Security Council, "Final Report of the Group of Experts on Côte d'Ivoire Pursuant to Paragraph 27 of Security Council Resolution 2219 (2015)," S/2016/254, March 17, 2016, 20–21.

26. "Ivory Coast to Clamp Down on Illegal Gold Mining," Reuters, March 23, 2015, accessed December 12, 2017, https://www.reuters.com/article/ivorycoast-gold/ivory-coast-to-clamp-down-on-illegal-gold-mining-idUSL6N0WP4F420150323.

27. "Former Ivory Coast PM Soro Goes on Trial on Coup-Plotting Charges," Reuters, May 19, 2021, accessed November 13, 2023, https://www.reuters.com/world/former-ivory-coast-pm-soro-goes-trial-coup-plotting-charges-2021-05-19/.

28. Benjamin Roger, "Côte d'Ivoire: How Much Influence Can Soro Wield Despite His Distance?" *Africa Report*, January 21, 2021, accessed November 14, 2023, https://www.theafricareport.com/60522/cote-divoire-how-much-influence-can-soro-wield-despite-his-distance/.

29. Interview with resource governance NGO employee, Abidjan, July 2017.

Bibliography

Archives

Materials for this book were collected from the following sites:
  Alassane Ouattara University Library, Bouaké, Côte d'Ivoire
  Centre de Recherche et d'Action pour la Paix (CERAP) Library and Archives, Abidjan, Côte d'Ivoire
  Cocody Library, Abidjan, Côte d'Ivoire
  Félix Houphouët-Boigny University Library, Abidjan, Côte d'Ivoire
  Harvard University Libraries, Cambridge, MA
  Institut Francais Library, Abidjan, Côte d'Ivoire
  Massachusetts Institute of Technology Libraries, Cambridge, MA
  National Library, Abidjan, Côte d'Ivoire

Primary and Secondary Sources

Ake, Claude. *A Political Economy of Africa*. Harlow: Longman, 1981.
Akindès, Francis. "Côte d'Ivoire: de la Stabilité Politique à la Crise. Vers une Politique de Réhabilitation Basée sur la Responsabilisation des Communautés à la Base." Abidjan: World Bank, 2007.
Akindès, Francis. "Côte d'Ivoire: Socio-political Crises, 'Ivoirité' and the Course of History." *African Sociological Review/Revue Africaine de Sociologie* 7, no. 2 (2003): 11–28.
Akindès, Francis, Moussa Fofana, and Gnangadjomon Koné. "Côte d'Ivoire: insurrection et contre-insurrection." *Alternatives Sud* 17 (2010): 93–97.
Akindes, Simon A. "Côte d'Ivoire: The Military, Ruling Elites, and Political Power." *Oxford Research Encyclopedia* (2021). Accessed November 13, 2023.

https://oxfordre.com/politics/view/10.1093/acrefore/9780190228637.001.0001/acrefore-9780190228637-e-1809.

Albrecht, Harold, and Dorothy Ohl. "Exit, Resistance, Loyalty: Military Behavior During Unrest in Authoritarian Regimes." *Perspectives on Politics* 14, no. 1 (2016): 38–52.

Albrecht, Peter, and Lars Buur. "An Uneasy Marriage: Non-state Actors and Police Reform." *Policing & Society* 19, no. 4 (2009): 390–405.

Ali, Obaid. "One Land, Two Rules: Delivering Public Services in Insurgency-Affected Dasht-e-Archi District in Kunduz Province." *Afghan Analysts Network*, February 26, 2019.

Allouche, Jeremy, and Patrick Anderson Zadi Zadi. "The Dynamics of Restraint in Côte d'Ivoire." *IDS Bulletin* 44, no. 1 (2013): 72–86.

Amnesty International. *Amnesty International Report 2001*. London: Amnesty International Publications, 2001.

Amnesty International. *Côte d'Ivoire Mission Report*. London: Amnesty International Publications, 2011.

Arjona, Ana. "Civilian Cooperation and Non-cooperation with Non-state Armed Groups: The Centrality of Obedience and Resistance." *Small Wars & Insurgencies* 28, nos. 4–5 (2017): 755–778.

Arjona, Ana. *Rebelocracy: Social Order in the Colombian Civil War*. New York: Cambridge University Press, 2016.

Arriola, Leonardo. *Multiethnic Coalitions in Africa: Business Financing of Opposition Election Campaigns*. Cambridge: Cambridge University Press, 2013.

Autesserre, Severine. *Peaceland: Conflict Resolution and the Everyday Politics of International Intervention*. New York: Cambridge University Press, 2014.

Axelrod, Robert, and Robert O. Keohane. "Achieving Cooperation Under Anarchy: Strategies and Institutions." In *Cooperation Under Anarchy*, edited by Kenneth Oye. Princeton, NJ: Princeton University Press, 1986.

Balcells, Laia. *Rivalry and Revenge: The Politics of Violence during Civil War*. Cambridge: Cambridge University Press, 2017.

Balcells, Laia, and Stathis Kalyvas. "Revolutionary Rebels and the Marxist Paradox." Unpublished manuscript.

Baldwin, Kate. "When Politicians Cede Control of Resources: Land, Chiefs, and Coalition-Building in Africa." *Comparative Politics* 43, no. 6 (2014): 253–271.

Baldwin, Kate. "Why Vote with the Chief? Political Connections and Public Goods Provision in Zambia." *American Journal of Political Science* 57, no. 4 (2013): 795–796.

Banégas, Richard, and Camille Popineau. "The 2020 Ivorian Election and the 'Third-term' Debate: A Crisis of 'Korocracy'?" *African Affairs* 120, no. 480 (2021): 461–477.

Banga, Arthur. *La coopération militaire entre la France et la Côte d'Ivoire*. Université Européenne, June 2014.

Banks, Arthur S., and Kenneth A. Wilson. "Cross-National Time-Series Data Archive." Databanks International. Accessed March 9, 2024. https://www.cntsdata.com/.

Barany, Zoltan. *The Soldier and the Changing State*. Princeton, NJ: Princeton University Press, 2012.

Barkey, Karen, and Sunita Parikh. "Comparative Perspectives on the State." *Annual Review of Sociology* 17, no. 1 (1991): 523–549.

Barma, Naazneen H. *The Peacebuilding Puzzle: Political Order in Post-conflict States*. New York: Cambridge University Press, 2016.

Bateson, Regina. "Crime Victimization and Political Participation." *American Political Science Review* 106, no. 3 (2012): 570–587.

Bauer, Michael, Christopher Blattman, Julie Chytilova, Joseph Henrich, Edward Miguel, and Tamar Mitts. "Can War Foster Cooperation?" *Journal of Economic Perspectives* 30, no. 3 (2016): 249–274.

Bayley, D. "The Police and Political Development in Europe." In *The Formation of National States in Western Europe*, edited by Charles Tilly. Princeton, NJ: Princeton University Press, 1975.

Beath, Andrew, Fotini Christia, and Ruben Enikolopov. "Winning Hearts and Minds through Development Aid: Evidence from a Field Experiment in Afghanistan." NES Working Paper, no. 166 (2011).

Beck, N., K. S. Gleditsch, and K. Beardsley. "Space Is More than Geography: Using Spatial Econometrics in the Study of Political Economy." *International Studies Quarterly* 50, no. 1 (2006): 27–44.

Beckley, Michael. "Economic Development and Military Effectiveness." *Journal of Strategic Studies* 33, no. 1 (2010): 43–79.

Belkin, Aaron, and Evan Schofer. "Coup Risk, Counterbalancing, and International Conflict." *Security Studies* 14, no. 1 (2005): 140–177.

Bellin, Eva. "Reconsidering the Robustness of Authoritarianism in the Middle East: Lessons from the Arab Spring." *Comparative Politics* 44, no. 2 (2012): 127–149.

Berman, Eli, Jacob Shapiro, and Joseph Felter. "Can Hearts and Minds Be Bought? The Economics of Counterinsurgency in Iraq." *Journal of Political Economy* 119, no. 4 (2011): 766–819.

Biddle, Stephen, Julia Macdonald, and Ryan Baker. "Small Footprint, Small Payoff: The Military Effectiveness of Security Force Assistance." *Journal of Strategic Studies* 41, no. 1–2 (2018): 89–142.

Bjarnesen, Jesper, and Sebastian van Baalen. *Democratic Backsliding in Côte D'Ivoire: Legislative Elections Tighten Ouattara's Grip on Power*. Nordiska Afrikainstitutet, 2021.

Blair, Robert A., and Pablo Kalmanovitz. "On the Rights of Warlords: Legitimate Authority and Basic Protection in War-Torn Societies." *American Political Science Review* 110, no. 3 (2016): 428–440.

Blair, Robert A., Sabrina M. Karim, and Benjamin S. Morse. "Establishing the Rule of Law in Weak and War-Torn States: Evidence from a Field Experiment with the Liberian National Police." *American Political Science Review* 113, no. 3 (2019): 641–657.

Blair, Robert A., Manuel Moscoso-Rojas, Andrés Vargas Castillo, and Michael Weintraub. "Preventing Rebel Resurgence after Civil War: A Field Experiment in Security and Justice Provision in Rural Colombia." *American Political Science Review* 116, no. 4 (2022): 1258–1277.

Blattman, Christopher. "From Violence to Voting: War and Political Participation in Uganda." *American Political Science Review* 103, no. 2 (2009): 231–247.

Blaydes, Lisa, and Eric Chaney. "The Feudal Revolution and Europe's Rise: Political Divergence of the Christian West and the Muslim World Before 1500 CE." *American Political Science Review* 107, no.1 (2013): 16–34.

Boix, Carles, and Milan W. Svolik. "The Foundations of Limited Authoritarian Government: Institutions, Commitment, and Power-Sharing in Dictatorships." *Journal of Politics* 75, no. 2 (2013): 300–316.

Boone, Catherine. "Africa's New Territorial Politics: Regionalism and the Open Economy in Côte d'Ivoire." *African Studies Review* 50, no. 1 (2007): 59–81.

Boone, Catherine. "Electoral Populism Where Property Rights are Weak: Land Politics in Contemporary Sub-Saharan Africa." *Comparative Politics* 41, no. 2 (2009): 183–201.

Boone, Catherine. *Political Topographies of the African State: Territorial Authority and Institutional Choice*. Cambridge: Cambridge University Press, 2003.

Bratton, Michael, and Nicolas Van de Walle. "Neopatrimonial Regimes and Political Transitions in Africa." *World Politics* 46, no. 4 (1994): 453–489.

Cammett, Melani Claire, and Lauren M. MacLean. "Introduction: The Political Consequences of Non-state Social Welfare in the Global South." *Studies in Comparative International Development* 46 (2011): 1–21.

Carey, Sabine C., Michael P. Colaresi, and Neil J. Mitchell. "Risk Mitigation, Regime Security, and Militias: Beyond Coup-Proofing." *International Studies Quarterly* 60, no. 1 (2016): 59–72.

Carreras, Miguel. "The Impact of Criminal Violence on Regime Legitimacy in Latin America." *Latin American Research Review* 48, no. 3 (2013): 85–107.

Carter, Brett L., and Mai Hassan. "Regional Governance in Divided Societies: Evidence from the Republic of Congo and Kenya." *Journal of Politics* 83, no. 1 (2021): 40–57.

Cederman, Lars-Erik, and Nils B. Weidmann. "Predicting Armed Conflict: Time to Adjust Our Expectations?" *Science* 355, no. 6324 (2017): 474–476.

Cederman, Lars-Erik, Andreas Wimmer, and Brian Min. "Why Do Ethnic Groups Rebel? New Data and Analysis." *World Politics* 62, no. 1 (2010): 87–119.

Centeno, Miguel. *Blood and Debt: War and the Nation-State in Latin America*. University Park, PA: University of Pennsylvania Press, 2002.

Chabal, Patrick. *Amilcar Cabral: Revolutionary Leadership and People's War*. Cambridge: Cambridge University Press, 1983.

Charbonneau, Bruno. "War and Peace in Côte d'Ivoire: Violence, Agency, and the Local/International Line." *International Peacekeeping* 19, no. 4 (2012): 508–524.

Chauveau, Jean-Pierre, and Jean-Philippe Colin. "Customary Transfers and Land Sales in Cote d'Ivoire: Revisiting the Embeddedness Issue." *Africa* 80, no. 1 (2010): 81–103.

Chelpi-den Hamer, Magali. *Militarized Youths in Western Côte d'Ivoire: Local Processes of Mobilization, Demobilization, and Related Humanitarian Interventions (2002–2007)*. Leiden: African Studies Centre, 2011.

Chelpi-den Hamer, Magali. "Militarized Youth in Western Côte d'Ivoire: Who Are They? Why Did They Fight?" In *Understanding Collective Political Violence*, edited by Yvan Guichaoua, 21–45. New York: Palgrave Macmillan, 2012.

Cheng, Christine. *Extralegal Groups in Post-conflict Liberia: How Trade Makes the State*. Oxford: Oxford University Press, 2018.

Chivvis, Christopher S., and Jeffrey Martini. *Libya after Qaddafi: Lessons and Implications for the Future*. Washington, DC: RAND, 2014.

Choi, Y. J. *La Crise Ivoirienne: Ce qu'il fallait comprendre*. Paris: Michel Lafon, 2015.

Christia, Fotini. *Alliance Formation in Civil Wars*. New York: Cambridge University Press, 2012.
Collier, Paul, V. L. Elliott, Håvard Hegre, Anke Hoeffler, Marta Reynal-Querol, and Nicholas Sambanis. *Breaking the Conflict Trap: Civil War and Development Policy, A World Bank Policy Research Report*. Washington, DC: World Bank, 2003.
Collier, Paul, and Anke Hoeffler. "Greed and Grievance in Civil War." *Oxford Economic Papers* 56, no. 4 (2004): 563–595.
Coppedge, Michael, John Gerring, Carl Henrik Knutsen, Staffan I. Lindberg, Jan Teorell, David Altman, Michael Bernhard, et al. "V-Dem [Country–Year/Country–Date] Dataset v11.1." Varieties of Democracy, 2021.
Crowder, Michael, ed. *West African Chiefs*. London: Hutchinson, 1970.
Cunningham, David E., Kristian Skrede Gleditsch, and Idean Salehyan. "It Takes Two: A Dyadic Analysis of Civil War Duration and Outcome." *Journal of Conflict Resolution* 53, no. 4 (2009): 570–597.
Cunningham, David E., Kristian Skrede Gleditsch, and Idean Salehyan. "Nonstate Actors in Civil Wars: A New Dataset." *Conflict Management and Peace Science* 30, no. 5 (2013): 516–531.
Cunningham, Kathleen Gallagher, and Katherine Sawyer. "Conflict Negotiations and Rebel Leader Selection." *Journal of Peace Research* 56, no. 5 (2019): 619–634.
Dahlum, Sirianne, and Tore Wig. "Chaos on Campus: Universities and Mass Political Protest." *Comparative Political Studies* 54, no. 1 (2021): 3–32.
David, Paul A. "Why Are Institutions the 'Carriers of History?': Path Dependence and the Evolution of Conventions, Organizations, and Institutions." *Structural Change and Economic Dynamics* 5, no. 2 (1994): 205–220.
De Bruin, Erica. *How to Prevent Coups d'État: Counterbalancing and Regime Survival*. Ithaca, NY: Cornell University Press, 2020.
De Bruin, Erica. "Mapping Coercive Institutions: The State Security Forces Dataset, 1960–2010." *Journal of Peace Research* 58, no. 2 (2021): 315–325.
De Bruin, Erica. "Preventing Coups d'état: How Counterbalancing Works." *Journal of Conflict Resolution* 62, no. 7 (2018): 1433–1458.
Decalo, Samuel. *Coups and Army Rule in Africa: Studies in Military Style*. New Haven, CT: Yale University Press, 1976.
DeRouen, Karl, Jr., Jenna Lea, and Peter Wallensteen. "The Duration of Civil War Peace Agreements." *Conflict Management and Peace Science* 26, no. 4 (2009): 367–387.
de Tessières, Savannah. "Enquête nationale sur les armes légères et de petit calibre en Côte d'Ivoire." Geneva: Small Arms Survey, 2012.
Diallo, Kamina. "La Cellule 39 en Côte d'Ivoire: Processus d'Identification et Mobilization d'un Groupe d'Ex-combattants." *Afrique contemporaine*, no. 263–264 (2017): 177–196.
Diamitani, Boureima T. "The Insider and Ethnography of Secrecy: Challenges of Collecting Data on the Fearful Komo of the Tagwa-Senufo." *African Archaeological Review* 28 (2011): 55–70.
Dow, David A. "Policing in a Post-conflict State: Evidence from Uganda." *Comparative Political Studies* 55, no. 9 (2022): 1595–1628.
Downes, Alexander B. "The Problem with Negotiated Settlements to Ethnic Civil Wars." *Security Studies* 13, no. 4 (2004): 230–279.

Doyle, Michael, and Nicholas Sambanis. *Making War and Building Peace: United Nations Peace Operations*. Princeton, NJ: Princeton University Press, 2006.

Driscoll, Jesse. *Warlords and Coalition Politics in Post-Soviet States*. New York: Cambridge University Press, 2015.

Dwyer, Maggie. "Tactical Communication: Mutiny as Dialogue in West and Central Africa." *Africa Spectrum* 50, no. 1 (2015): 5–23.

Evans, Peter. "The State as Problem and Solution: Predation, Embedded Autonomy, and Structural Change." In *The State: Critical Concepts*, edited by John Hall. London: Routledge, 1994.

Fearon, James D. "Civil War and the Current International System." *Daedelus* 146, no. 4 (Fall 2017): 18–32.

Fearon, James D. "Why Do Some Civil Wars Last So Much Longer than Others?" *Journal of Peace Research* 41, no. 3 (2004): 275–301.

"Final Report: International Election Observation Mission to Côte d'Ivoire, 2010 Presidential Elections and 2011 Legislative Elections." Atlanta: Carter Center, 2012.

Fofana, Lemassou. *Côte d'Ivoire: La Longue Marche du RDR*. Saint-Maur-des-Fosses: Sepia, 2009.

Fofana, Moussa. "Des Forces Nouvelles aux Forces Républicaines de Côte d'Ivoire." *Politique africaine* 2 (2011): 161–178.

Fofana, Moussa. "Ethnographie des Trajectoires Sociales des Jeunes Enrôlés dans la Rébellion en Côte d'Ivoire." PhD diss., Department of Anthropology and Sociology, Alassane Ouattara University, 2012.

Förster, Till. "Dialogue Direct: Rebel Governance and Civil Order in Northern Côte d'Ivoire." In *Rebel Governance in Civil War*, edited by Ana Arjona, Nelson Kasfir, and Zachariah Mampilly, 203–225. New York: Cambridge University Press, 2015.

Förster, Till. "Insurgent Nationalism: Political Imagination and Rupture in Côte d'Ivoire." *Africa Spectrum* 48, no. 3 (2013): 3–31.

Förster, Till. "The Invisible Social Body: Experience and Poro Ritual in Northern Côte d'Ivoire." *African Studies Review* 62, no. 1 (2019): 99–119.

Fortna, Virginia Page. *Does Peacekeeping Work? Shaping Belligerents' Choices after Civil War*. Cambridge: Cambridge University Press, 2008.

Fortna, Virginia Page. "A Lost Chance for Peace: The Bicesse Accords in Angola." *Georgetown Journal of International Affairs* 4 (2003): 73–79.

Fravel, M. Taylor. *Active Defense: China's Military Strategy since 1949*. Princeton, NJ: Princeton University Press, 2019.

Gilligan, Michael, Benjamin Pasquale, and Cyrus Samii. "Civil War and Social Cohesion: Lab-in-the-Field Evidence from Nepal." *Journal of Politics* 58, no. 3 (2014): 604–619.

Gilligan, Michael, and Stephen John Stedman. "Where Do the Peacekeepers Go?" *International Studies Review* 5, no. 4 (2003): 37–54.

Giustozzi, Antonio. "Hearts, Minds, and the Barrel of a Gun: The Taliban's Shadow Government." *Prism: A Journal of the Center for Complex Operations* 3, no. 2 (2012): 71–80.

Glassmyer, Katherine, and Nicholas Sambanis. "Rebel-Military Integration and Civil War Termination." *Journal of Peace Research* 45, no. 3 (2008): 365–384.

Goldring, Edward, and Austin S. Matthews. "To Purge or Not to Purge? An Individual-Level Quantitative Analysis of Elite Purges in Dictatorships." *British Journal of Political Science* 53, no. 2 (2023): 575–593.

Granovetter, Mark. "Economic Action and Social Structure: The Problem of Embeddedness." *American Journal of Sociology* 91, no. 3 (1985): 481–510.

Greitens, Sheena Chestnut. *Dictators and Their Secret Police: Coercive Institutions and State Violence*. New York: Cambridge University Press, 2016.

Groga-Bada, Malika. "Côte d'Ivoire: à Korhogo, l'adieu aux armes." *Jeune Afrique*, July 22, 2011.

Guevara, Che. *Guerrilla Warfare*. New York: Monthly Review Press, 1961.

Guichauoua, Yvan, and Jake Lomax. "Fleeing, Staying Put, Working With Rebel Rulers." Brighton, UK: Institute for Development Studies, 2013.

Gunderson, William Charles. "Village Elders and Regional Intermediaries: Differing Responses to Change in the Korhogo Region of the Ivory Coast." PhD diss., Department of Political Science, Indiana University, 1975.

Hamm, Joseph A., Rick Trinkner, and James D. Carr. "Fair Process, Trust, and Cooperation: Moving Toward an Integrated Framework of Police Legitimacy." *Criminal Justice and Behavior* 44, no. 9 (2017): 1183–1212.

Harkness, Kristen A. "The Ethnic Army and the State: Explaining Coup Traps and the Difficulties of Democratization in Africa." *Journal of Conflict Resolution* 60, no. 4 (2016): 587–616.

Harkness, Kristen A. *When Soldiers Rebel: Ethnic Armies and Political Instability in Africa*. Cambridge: Cambridge University Press, 2018.

Hartzell, Caroline, and Matthew Hoddie. *Crafting Peace: Power-Sharing Institutions and the Negotiated Settlement of Civil Wars*. University Park: Pennsylvania State University Press, 2007.

Hartzell, Caroline, and Matthew Hoddie. "Institutionalizing Peace: Power Sharing and Post–Civil War Conflict Management." *American Journal of Political Science* 47, no. 2 (2003): 318–332.

Hecht, Robert M. "The Ivory Coast Economic 'Miracle': What Benefits for Peasant Farmers?" *Journal of Modern African Studies* 21, no. 1 (1983): 25–53.

Heitz-Tokpa, Kathrin. "The Onset of War as a Novel Experience: Dislocation and Familiarization in Côte d'Ivoire, Late 2002." *Social Anthropology* 24, no. 4 (2016): 419–432.

Heitz-Tokpa, Kathrin. "Power-Sharing in the Local Arena: Man—A Rebel-Held Town in Western Côte d'Ivoire." *Africa Spectrum* 44, no. 3 (2009): 109–131.

Heitz-Tokpa, Kathrin. "Trust and Distrust in Rebel-Held Côte d'Ivoire." PhD diss., Institute for Social Anthropology, University of Basel, 2013.

Hellweg, Joseph. "Encompassing the State: Sacrifice and Security in the Hunters' Movement of Cote d'Ivoire." *Africa Today* 50, no. 4 (2004): 3–28.

Hellweg, Joseph. *Hunting the Ethical State: The Benkadi Movement of Côte d'Ivoire*. Chicago: University of Chicago Press, 2011.

Herbst, Jeffrey. *States and Power in Africa: Comparative Lessons in Authority and Control*. Princeton, NJ: Princeton University Press, 2000.

Heywood, Linda M. "Unita and Ethnic Nationalism in Angola." *Journal of Modern African Studies* 27, no.1 (1989): 47–66.

Higonnet, Etelle. *"My Heart is Cut": Sexual Violence by Rebels and Pro-Government Forces in Cote d'Ivoire.* New York: Human Rights Watch, 2007.

Hillebrecht, Courtney, and Scott Straus. "Who Pursues the Perpetrators? State Cooperation with the ICC." *Human Rights Quarterly* 39, no. 1 (2017): 162–188.

Hintze, Otto. *The Historical Essays of Otto Hintze.* New York: Oxford University Press, 1975.

Hoffman, Danny. "The City as Barracks: Freetown, Monrovia, and the Organization of Violence in Postcolonial African Cities." *Cultural Anthropology* 22, no. 3 (2007): 400–428.

Horowitz, Donald. *Ethnic Groups in Conflict.* Berkeley: University of California Press, 1985.

Huang, Reyko. *The Wartime Origins of Democratization: Civil War, Rebel Governance, and Political Regimes.* Cambridge: Cambridge University Press, 2016.

Human Rights Watch. *Trapped Between Two Wars: Violence Against Civilians in Western Côte d'Ivoire.* New York: Human Rights Watch, 2003.

Humphreys, Macartan, and Jeremy M. Weinstein. "Demobilization and Reintegration." *Journal of Conflict Resolution* 51, no. 4 (2007): 531–567.

Humphreys, Macartan, and Jeremy Weinstein. "Handling and Manhandling Civilians in Civil War." *American Political Science Review* 100, no. 3 (2006): 429–447.

Huntington, Samuel. *Political Order in Changing Societies.* New Haven, CT: Yale University Press, 1968.

International Crisis Group. *Central African Republic: Anatomy of a Predator State.* Brussels: International Crisis Group, 2007.

International Crisis Group. *Central African Republic: The Roots of Violence.* Brussels: International Crisis Group, 2015.

International Crisis Group. *Côte d'Ivoire: "The War is Not Yet Over."* Freetown: International Crisis Group, 2003.

International Crisis Group. *A Critical Period for Ensuring Stability in Côte d'Ivoire.* Brussels: International Crisis Group, 2011.

International Crisis Group. *Keeping Jihadists Out of Northern Côte d'Ivoire.* Abidjan: International Crisis Group, 2023.

International Crisis Group. *Managing Election Tensions in the Central African Republic.* Brussels: International Crisis Group, 2020.

Ivorian National Institute of Statistics. *Enquete Sur le Niveau de Vie des Ménages en Côte d'Ivoire (ENV 2002).* Abidjan: National Institute of Statistics, 2002.

Ivorian National Institute of Statistics. *Enquete Sur le Niveau de Vie des Ménages en Côte d'Ivoire (ENV 2008).* Abidjan: National Institute of Statistics, 2008.

Ivorian National Institute of Statistics. *Enquete Sur le Niveau de Vie des Ménages en Côte d'Ivoire (ENV 2015).* Abidjan: National Institute of Statistics, 2015.

Jackson, Jonathan, and Ben Bradford. "Measuring Public Attitudes towards the Police." Ottawa: Public Safety Canada, 2019.

Jarstad, Anna, and Desireé Nilsson. "From Words to Deeds: The Implementation of Power-Sharing Pacts in Peace Accords." *Conflict Management and Peace Science* 25, no. 3 (2008): 206–223.

Jervis, Robert. *Perception and Misperception in International Politics.* Princeton, NJ: Princeton University Press, 1976.

Jowell, Marco. "Cohesion Through Socialization: Liberation, Tradition and Modernity in the Forging of the Rwanda Defence Force (RDF)." *Journal of East African Studies* 8, no. 2 (2014): 278–293.

Kalyvas, Stathis N. "Jihadi Rebels in Civil War." *Daedalus* 147, no. 1 (Winter 2018): 36–47.

Kalyvas, Stathis N. *The Logic of Violence in Civil War*. Cambridge: Cambridge University Press, 2006.

Kalyvas, Stathis N. "'New' and 'Old' Civil Wars: A Valid Distinction?" *World Politics* 54, no. 1 (October 2001): 99–118.

Kaplan, Oliver, and Enzo Nussio. "Community Counts: The Social Reintegration of Ex-combatants in Colombia." *Conflict Management and Peace Science* 35, no. 2 (2018): 132–153.

Karaman, K. Kivanc, and Sevket Pamuk. "Different Paths to the Modern State in Europe: The Interaction Between Warfare, Economic Structure, and Political Regime." *American Political Science Review* 107, no. 3 (2013): 603–626.

Klein, Herbert. *A Concise History of Bolivia*. New York: Cambridge University Press, 2011.

Kleinfeld, Rachel. *Fragility and Security Sector Reform*. Washington, DC: Carnegie Endowment for International Peace, 2016.

Koné, Gnangadjomon. *Les Jeunes Patriotes: Ou La Revanche des Porteurs de Chaises en Côte d'Ivoire*. Abidjan: Les Classiques Ivoiriens, 2015.

Krebs, Ronald R., and Roy Licklider. "United They Fall: Why the International Community Should Not Promote Military Integration after Civil War." *International Security* 40, no. 3 (2015): 93–138.

Kriger, Norma J. *Guerrilla Veterans in Post-war Zimbabwe*. Cambridge: Cambridge University Press, 2003.

Kriger, Norma J. *Zimbabwe's Guerrilla War: Peasant Voices*. Cambridge: Cambridge University Press, 1991.

Kubota, Y. "Imagined Statehood: Wartime Rebel Governance and Post-war Subnational Identity in Sri Lanka." *World Development* 90 (2017): 199–212.

Kydd, Andrew. "Game Theory and the Spiral Model." *World Politics* 49, no. 3 (1997): 371–400.

Lake, David A. "Rightful Rulers: Authority, Order and the Foundations of Global Governance." *International Studies Quarterly* 54, no. 3 (2010): 587–613.

Landau-Wells, Marika. "High Stakes and Low Bars: How International Recognition Shapes the Conduct of Civil Wars." *International Security* 43, no. 1 (2018): 100–137.

Langer, Arnim. "Horizontal Inequalities and Violent Group Mobilization in Côte d'Ivoire." *Oxford Development Studies* 33, no. 1 (2005): 24–44.

Leboeuf, Aline. *La réforme du secteur de sécurité à 'Ivoirienne*. Institut français des relations internationales, March 2016.

Lee, Melissa M. "International Statebuilding and the Domestic Politics of State Development." *Annual Review of Political Science* 25, no. 11 (2021): 1–11.

Le Pape, Marc, and Claudine Vidal. *Côte d'Ivoire. L'année Terrible, 1999–2000*. Paris: Karthala, 2002.

"Les anciens com'zones dans l'armee Ivoirienne: Trafics, corruption et zones d'influence." Paris: Office Français de Protection des Réfugiés et Apatrides

(OFPRA), Division de l'Information, de la Documentation et des Recherches (DIDR), September 11, 2017.

Levi, Margaret. "The Predatory Theory of Rule." *Politics & Society* 10, no. 4 (1981): 431–465.

Levitsky, Steven, and Lucan Way. "Beyond Patronage: Violent Struggle, Ruling Party Cohesion, and Authoritarian Durability." *Perspectives on Politics* 10, no. 4 (2012): 869–889.

Lewis, D. *Conventions: A Philosophical Inquiry.* Cambridge, MA: Harvard University Press, 1969.

Licklider, Roy. "The Consequences of Negotiated Settlements in Civil Wars, 1945–1993." *American Political Science Review* 89, no. 3 (September 1995): 681–690.

Licklider, Roy, ed. *New Armies from Old: Merging Competing Military Forces after Civil Wars.* Washington, DC: Georgetown University Press, 2015.

Lilja, Jannie, and Lisa Hultman. "Intraethnic Dominance and Control: Violence Against Co-Ethnics in the Early Sri Lankan Civil War." *Security Studies* 20, no. 2 (2011): 171–197.

Lindberg, Staffan, and John F. Clark. "Does Democratization Reduce the Risk of Military Intervention in Politics in Africa?" *Democratization* 15, no. 1 (2008): 86–105.

Liu, Shelley X. "Control, Cooperation, and Cooptation: How Rebels Govern after Winning Civil War." *World Politics* 74, no. 1 (2022): 37–76.

Lombard, Louisa. "Denouncing Sovereignty: Claims to Liberty in Northeastern Central African Republic." *Comparative Studies in Society and History* 60, no. 4 (2018): 1066–1095.

Lombard, Louisa. *State of Rebellion: Violence and Intervention in the Central African Republic.* London: Zed Books, 2016.

Lyons, Terrence. "The Importance of Winning: Victorious Insurgent Groups and Authoritarian Politics." *Comparative Politics* 48, no. 2 (2016): 167–184.

MacLean, Lauren. "Constructing a Social Safety Net in Africa: An Institutionalist Analysis of Colonial Rule and State Social Policies in Ghana and Côte d'Ivoire." *Studies in Comparative International Development* 37, no. 3 (2002): 64–90.

MacLean, Lauren. *Informal Institutions and Citizenship in Rural Africa: Risk and Reciprocity in Ghana and Côte d'Ivoire.* Cambridge: Cambridge University Press, 2010.

Malejacq, Romain. *Warlord Survival: The Delusion of State Building in Afghanistan.* Ithaca, NY: Cornell University Press, 2020.

Mampilly, Zachariah. *Rebel Rulers: Insurgent Governance and Civilian Life During War.* Ithaca, NY: Cornell University Press, 2011.

Mampilly, Zachariah, and Megan Stewart. "A Typology of Rebel Political Institutional Arrangements." *Journal of Conflict Resolution* 65, no. 1 (2021): 15–45.

Mann, Michael. *States, War, and Capitalism.* New York: Blackwell, 1988.

Manning, Robert A. "Whatever Happened to 'Marxist Terrorist' Mugabe? So Far, So Fair in Zimbabwe." *New Republic*, April 4, 1981.

Mao, Zedong. *On Guerrilla Warfare.* Chicago: University of Illinois Press, 2000.

Marten, Kimberly. *Warlords: Strong-Arm Brokers in Weak States.* Ithaca, NY: Cornell University Press, 2012.

Martin, Philip A. "Commander-Community Ties After Civil War." *Journal of Peace Research* 58, no. 4 (2021): 778–793.

Martin, Philip A. "Insurgent Armies: Military Obedience and State Formation after Rebel Victory." *International Security* 46, no. 3 (2021): 87–127.

Martin, Philip A. "Why Zimbabwe's Military Abandoned Mugabe: The Blood Brotherhood Sticks Together." *Foreign Affairs*, November 17, 2017.

Martin, Philip A., Giulia Piccolino, and Jeremy S. Speight. "Ex-Rebel Authority after Civil War: Theory and Evidence from Côte d'Ivoire." *Comparative Politics* 53, no. 2 (2021): 209–232.

Martin, Philip A., Giulia Piccolino, and Jeremy S. Speight. "The Political Legacies of Rebel Rule: Evidence from a Natural Experiment in Côte d'Ivoire." *Comparative Political Studies* 55, no. 9 (2022): 1439–1470.

Mason, David T., Mehmet Gurses, Patrick T. Brandt, and Jason Michael Quinn. "When Civil Wars Recur: Conditions for Durable Peace after Civil Wars." *International Studies Perspectives* 12, no. 2 (2011): 171–189.

Matanock, Aila M. *Electing Peace: From Civil Conflict to Political Participation*. Cambridge: Cambridge University Press, 2017.

Matanock, Aila M., and Adam Lichtenheld. "How Does International Intervention Work to Secure Peace Settlements After Civil Conflicts?" *British Journal of Political Science* 52, no. 4 (2022): 1810–1830.

McCarthy, John, and Mayer N. Zald. "Resource Mobilization and Social Movements: A Partial Theory." *American Journal of Sociology* 82, no. 6 (1977): 1212–1241.

McGovern, Mike. *Making War in Côte d'Ivoire*. Chicago: University of Chicago Press, 2011.

McLaughlin, Theodore. "Loyalty Strategies and Military Defection in Rebellion." *Comparative Politics* 42, no. 3 (2010): 333–350.

McMahon, R. Blake, and Branislav L. Slantchev. "The Guardianship Dilemma: Regime Security through and from the Armed Forces." *American Political Science Review* 109, no. 2 (2015): 297–313.

McNerney, Michael, Angela O'Mahony, Thomas S. Szayna, Derek Eaton, Caroline Baxter, Colin P. Clarke, Emma Cutrufello, et al. *Assessing Security Cooperation as a Preventive Tool*. Santa Monica, CA: Rand, 2014.

Meng, Anne, and Jack Paine. "Power Sharing and Authoritarian Stability: How Rebel Regimes Solve the Guardianship Dilemma." *American Political Science Review* 116, no. 4 (2022): 1208–1225.

Metelits, Claire. *Inside Insurgency: Violence, Civilians, and Revolutionary Group Behavior*. New York: New York University Press, 2010.

Migdal, Joel S. *Strong Societies and Weak States: State-Society Relations and State Capabilities in the Third World*. Princeton, NJ: Princeton University Press, 1986.

Mill, John Stuart. *System of Logic*, 8th ed. London: Longmans, Green, 1872.

Moody, Jessica. "Ex-combatants Thinking Differently: Attitudes to Threatening the State in Post-conflict Côte d'Ivoire." *Conflict, Security & Development* 20, no. 6 (2020): 732–734.

Moody, Jessica. "Reaching for the Impossible? Coordinating DDR and Transitional Justice in Post-conflict Côte d'Ivoire." *International Peacekeeping* 28, no. 1 (2021): 110–133.

Mukhopadhyay, Dipali. *Warlords, Strongman Governors, and the State in Afghanistan*. New York: Cambridge University Press, 2014.

Nielsen, Rich. "Case Selection via Matching." *Sociological Methods and Research* 45, no. 3 (2016): 569–597.

Nordlinger, Eric A. *Soldiers in Politics: Military Coups and Government*. Englewood Cliffs, NJ: Prentice-Hall.

North, Douglass, John Wallis, and Barry Weingast. *Violence and Social Orders: A Conceptual Framework for Interpreting Recorded Human History*. New York: Cambridge University Press, 2009.

O'Donnell, Guillermo, and Philippe C. Schmitter. *Transitions from Authoritarian Rule: Tentative Conclusions about Uncertain Democracies*. Baltimore: Johns Hopkins University Press, 1988.

Office Francais de Protection des Refugies et Apatrides (OFPRA). *L'armee ivoirienne depuis 2011*. Paris: OFPRA, Division de l'Information, de la Documentation, et des Recherches, October 4, 2017.

Ogwang, Tom. "The Root Causes of the Conflict in Ivory Coast." *Africa Portal Backgrounder Series*, no. 5 (April 2011).

Olson, Mancur. "Dictatorship, Democracy, and Development." *American Political Science Review* 87, no. 3 (1993): 567–576.

Organization for Economic Cooperation and Development (OECD). "Development Aid at a Glance: Statistics by Region: 2. Africa." OECD, 2018. Accessed November 14, 2023. https://www.oecd.org/dac/financing-sustainable-development/development-finance-data/Africa-Development-Aid-at-a-Glance-2018.pdf.

Ostrom, Elinor. "Crossing the Great Divide: Coproduction, Synergy, and Development." *World Development* 24, no. 6 (1996): 1073–1087.

Paine, Jack. "Reframing the Guardianship Dilemma: How the Military's Dual Disloyalty Options Imperil Dictators." *American Political Science Review* 116, no. 4 (2022): 1425–1442.

Paris, Roland, and Timothy D. Sisk, eds. *The Dilemmas of State-Building: Confronting the Contradictions of Postwar Peace Operations*. London: Routledge, 2009.

Pérez, Orlando J. "Democratic Legitimacy and Public Insecurity: Crime and Democracy in El Salvador and Guatemala." *Political Science Quarterly* 118, no. 4 (2003): 627–644.

Piccolino, Giulia. "David against Goliath in Côte d'Ivoire? Laurent Gbagbo's War against global Governance." *African Affairs* 111, no. 442 (January 2012): 1–23.

Piccolino, Giulia. "Peacebuilding and Statebuilding in Post-2011 Côte d'Ivoire: A Victor's Peace?" *African Affairs* 117, no. 468 (2018): 485–508.

Pigeaud, Fanny. *France Côte d'Ivoire: une histoire tronquée*. Paris: Vent d'ailleurs, 2015.

Popineau, Camille. "Prendre la craie: La mobilisation des enseignants rebelles dans le Nord de la Côte d'Ivoire (2002–2011)." *Politique Africaine* 4, no. 148 (2017): 27–48.

Powell, Jonathan. "The Determinants of Attempting and Outcome of Coups d'État." *Journal of Conflict Resolution* 56, no. 6 (2012): 1017–1040.

Powell, Robert. "War as a Commitment Problem." *International Organization* 60, no. 1 (2006): 169–203.

Quinlivan, James T. "Coup-Proofing: Its Practice and Consequences in the Middle East." *International Security* 24, no. 2 (Fall 1999): 131–165.

Rabinowitz, Beth S. *Coups, Rivals, and the Modern State: Why Rural Coalitions Matter in Sub-Saharan Africa*. Cambridge: Cambridge University Press, 2018.

Raleigh, Clionadh, and Kars De Bruijne. "Where Rebels Dare to Tread: A Study of Conflict Geography and Co-option of Local Power in Sierra Leone." *Journal of Conflict Resolution* 61, no. 6 (2017): 1230–1260.

Reese, Roger R. *The Soviet Military Experience: A History of the Soviet Army, 1917–1991*. Routledge: London, 2000.

Reno, William. *Warfare in Independent Africa*. Cambridge: Cambridge University Press, 2011.

Reno, William. *Warlord Politics and African States*. Boulder: Lynne Rienner, 1999.

Ricard, Maxime. "Faire de 'l'ordre': la fabrique sociopolitique de la pluralisation de l'activité policière en Côte d'Ivoire." PhD diss., Political Science Department, Université du Québec à Montréal, 2020.

Ricard, Maxime. "Stability for Whom and for What?: The Ivorian Peacebuilding Experience under Alassane Ouattara." In *Routledge Handbook of African Peacebuilding*, 260–273. London: Routledge, 2022.

Rickard, Kit, and Kristin M. Bakke. "Legacies of Wartime Order: Punishment Attacks and Social Control in Northern Ireland." *Security Studies* 30, no. 4 (2021): 603–636.

Roessler, Philip. "The Enemy Within: Personal Rule, Coups, and Civil War in Africa." *World Politics* 63, no. 2 (2011): 300–346.

Roessler, Philip. *Ethnic Politics and State Power in Africa: The Logic of the Coup-Civil War Trap*. Cambridge: Cambridge University Press, 2016.

Rothchild, Donald. "Hegemonial Exchange: An Alternative Model for Managing Conflict in Middle Africa." In *Ethnicity, Politics and Development*, edited by Dennis Thomson and Dov Ronen, 65–104. Boulder: Lynne Rienner, 1986.

Rubin, Michael. "Rebel Territorial Control and Civilian Collective Action in Civil War: Evidence from the Communist Insurgency in the Philippines." *Journal of Conflict Resolution* 64, no. 2–3 (2020): 459–489.

Sambanis, Nicholas, and Katherine Glassmeyer. "Rebel—Military Integration and Civil War Termination." *Journal of Peace Research* 45, no. 3 (2008): 365–384.

Sambanis, Nicholas, and Jonah Schulhofer-Wohl. "Civil War as Sovereignty Rupture: Coding Intra-State Conflict, 1945–2015." *Journal of Conflict Resolution* 63, no. 6 (2019): 1542–1578.

Schelling, Thomas. *The Strategy of Conflict*. Cambridge, MA: Harvard University Press, 1960.

Schiel, Rebecca, Jonathan Powell, and Christopher Faulkner. "Mutiny in Africa, 1950–2018." *Conflict Management and Peace Science* 38, no. 4 (2021): 481–499.

Schiel, Rebecca, Jonathan Powell, and Christopher Faulkner. "Mutiny in Côte d'Ivoire." *Africa Spectrum* 52, no. 2 (2017): 103–115.

Schouten, Peer. "Roadblock Politics in Central Africa." *EPD: Society and Space* 37, no. 5 (2019): 924–941.

Seawright, Jason, and John Gerring. "Case Selection Techniques in Case Study Research: A Menu of Qualitative and Quantitative Options." *Political Research Quarterly* 61, no. 2 (2008): 294–308.

Security Assistance Monitor. "Côte d'Ivoire." Accessed November 14, 2023. https://securityassistance.org/data.

Semple, Michael. *Rhetoric, Ideology, and Organizational Structure of the Taliban Movement*. Washington, DC: United States Institute of Peace, 2014.

Shenk, Jaimie. "Does Conflict Experience Affect Participatory Democracy after Civil War? Evidence from Colombia." *Journal of Peace Research* 60, no. 6 (2022): 985–1001.

Simmons, Beth A., and Daniel J. Hopkins. "The Constraining Power of International Treaties: Theory and Methods." *American Political Science Review* 99, no. 4 (2005): 623–631.

Skocpol, Theda. "Review Article: What Makes Peasants Revolutionary?" *Comparative Politics*, 14, no. 3 (April 1982): 351–375.

Slater, Dan. *Ordering Power: Contentious Politics and Authoritarian Leviathans in Southeast Asia*. Cambridge: Cambridge University Press, 2010.

Snyder, Richard. "Explaining Transitions from Neopatrimonial Dictatorships." *Comparative Politics* 24, no. 4 (1992): 379–399.

Soro, Guillaume. *Pourquoi je suis devenu un rebelle: La Côte d'Ivoire au bord du gouffre*. Paris: Hachette Literature, 2005.

Speight, Jeremy S. "Big-Men Coalitions and Political Order in Northern Côte d'Ivoire (2002–2013)." PhD diss., Department of Political Science, Concordia University, 2016.

Speight, Jeremy S. "Rebel Organization and Local Politics: Evidence from Bouna (Northern Côte d'Ivoire, 2002–10)." *Civil Wars* 15, no. 2 (2013): 210–241.

Speight, Jeremy S., and Katrin Wittig. "Pathways from Rebellion: Rebel-Party Configurations in Côte d'Ivoire and Burundi." *African Affairs* 117, no. 466 (2018): 21–43.

Spittaels, Steven, Filip Hilger, Lotte Hoex, and Yannick Weyns. *Mapping Conflict Motives: The Central African Republic*. Antwerp: International Peace Information Service, 2014.

Staniland, Paul. *Networks of Rebellion: Explaining Insurgent Cohesion and Collapse*. Ithaca, NY: Cornell University Press, 2014.

Staniland, Paul. *Ordering Violence: Explaining Armed Group-State Relations from Conflict to Cooperation*. Ithaca, NY: Cornell University Press, 2021.

Stewart, Megan. "Civil War as State-Making: Strategic Governance in Civil War." *International Organization* 72, no. 1 (2018): 205–226.

Stewart, Megan. *Governing for Revolution: Social Transformation in Civil War*. New York: Cambridge University Press, 2021.

Stewart, Megan. "Rebel Governance: Military Boon or Bust?" *Conflict Management and Peace Science* 37, no. 1 (2020): 16–38.

Stokes, Susan C., Thad Dunning, Marcelo Nazareno, and Valeria Busco. *Brokers, Voters, and Clientelism: The Puzzle of Distributive Politics*. Cambridge: Cambridge University Press, 2013.

Straus, Scott. "'It's Sheer Horror Here': Patterns of Violence during the First Four Months of Côte d'Ivoire's Post-electoral Crisis." *African Affairs* 110, no. 440 (2011): 481–489.

Straus, Scott. *Making and Unmaking Nations: War, Leadership, and Genocide in Modern Africa*. Ithaca, NY: Cornell University Press, 2015.

Straus, Scott, and Lars Waldorf, eds. *Remaking Rwanda: State Building and Human Rights after Mass Violence*. Madison: University of Wisconsin Press, 2011.

Sudduth, Jun Koga. "Strategic Logic of Elite Purges in Dictatorships." *Comparative Political Studies* 50, no. 13 (2017): 1768–1801.

Svolik, Milan. "Power Sharing and Leadership Dynamics in Authoritarian Regimes." *American Journal of Political Science* 53, no. 2 (2009): 477–494.

Tajima, Yuhki. "When Do Communities Accept or Aid Former Combatants? A Theoretical Framework with Evidence from Postwar Aceh, Indonesia." Unpublished manuscript, 2018.

Talmadge, Caitlin. *The Dictator's Army: Battlefield Effectiveness in Authoritarian Regimes*. Ithaca, NY: Cornell University Press, 2015.
Tarrow, Sidney. "The Strategy of Paired Comparison: Toward a Theory of Practice." *Comparative Political Studies* 43, no. 2 (2010): 230–259.
Thaler, Kai M. "From Insurgent to Incumbent: Statebuilding and Service Provision after Rebel Victory in Civil Wars." PhD diss., Harvard University, 2018.
Themnér, Anders. "Former Military Networks and the Micro-Politics of Violence and State-building in Liberia." *Comparative Politics* 47, no. 3 (April 2015): 334–353.
Themnér, Anders. "Wealth in Ex-Combatants: Examining the Resilience of Ex-Command Structures in Postwar Liberia." *Journal of Global Security Studies* 4, no. 4 (October 2019): 526–544.
Themnér, Anders, and Mats Utas. "Governance through Brokerage: Informal Governance in Post–Civil War Societies." *Civil Wars* 18, no. 3 (2016): 256–257.
Thompson, William. *Grievances of Military Coup-Makers*. Beverly Hills, CA: Sage, 1973.
Tilly, Charles. *Coercion, Capital, and European States, AD 990–1992*. Oxford: Blackwell, 1992.
Tilly, Charles. *The Formation of National States in Western Europe*. Princeton, NJ: Princeton University Press, 1975.
Tilly, Charles. *From Mobilization to Revolution*. Reading, MA: Addison-Wesley, 1978.
Toft, Monica Duffy. "Ending Civil Wars: The Case for Rebel Victory?" *International Security* 34, no. 4 (2010): 7–36.
Toft, Monica Duffy. *Securing the Peace: The Durable Settlement of Civil Wars*. Princeton, NJ: Princeton University Press, 2009.
Tremblay, Marc-Adelard. "The Key Informant Technique: A Nonethnographic Application." *American Anthropologist* 59, no. 4 (August 1957): 688–701.
Trotsky, Leon. *My Life: An Attempt at an Autobiography*. New York: Pathfinder Press, 1970.
Tsai, Lily. "Solidary Groups, Informal Accountability, and Local Public Goods Provision in Rural China." *American Political Science Review* 101, no. 2 (2007): 355–372.
United Nations Security Council. "Final Report of the Group of Experts on Côte d'Ivoire Pursuant to Paragraph 27 of Security Council Resolution 2153 (2014)." New York: UN Headquarters, 2015.
United Nations Security Council. "Letter Dated 15 March 2016 from the Chair of the Security Council Committee Established Pursuant to Resolution 1572 (2004) Concerning Côte d'Ivoire Addressed to the President of the Security Council." New York: UN Headquarters, 2016.
United Nations Security Council. "Midterm Report of the Group of Experts on Côte d'Ivoire Pursuant to Paragraph 19 of Security Council Resolution 2101 (2013)." New York: UN Headquarters, 2013.
Uppsala Conflict Data Program. "UCDP Conflict Encyclopedia." Uppsala University. Accessed April 17, 2024. https://ucdp.uu.se/.
van Baalen, Sebastian. "Guns and Governance: Local Elites and Rebel Governance in Côte d'Ivoire." PhD diss., Uppsala University, 2020.
van Baalen, Sebastian. "Local Elites, Civil Resistance, and the Responsiveness of Rebel Governance in Côte d'Ivoire." *Journal of Peace Research* 58, no. 5 (2021): 930–944.

Verjee, Aly. "A Faulty Prescription? Critiquing Joint Security Units after Peace Agreements in Sudan, South Sudan, and the Central African Republic." *African Security* 15, no. 2 (2022): 91–110.

Vu, Tuong. *Paths to Development in Asia: South Korea, Vietnam, China, and Indonesia.* New York: Cambridge University Press, 2010.

Wagner, Robert Harrison. "The Causes of Peace." In *Stopping the Killing: How Civil Wars End*, edited by Roy Licklider, 235–268. New York: New York University Press, 1993.

Walter, Barbara F. "Bargaining Failures and Civil War." *Annual Review of Political Science* 12 (2009): 243–261.

Walter, Barbara F. *Committing to Peace: The Successful Settlement of Civil Wars.* Princeton, NJ: Princeton University Press, 2002.

Walter, Barbara F. "The Critical Barrier to Civil War Settlement." *International Organization* 51, no. 3 (1997): 335–364.

Walter, Barbara F. "Why Bad Governance Leads to Repeat Civil War." *Journal of Conflict Resolution* 59, no. 7 (2015): 1242–1272.

Watkins, Andrew. "An Assessment of Taliban Rule at Three Months." *CTC Sentinel* 14, no. 9 (2021): 1–14.

Watts, Stephen, Trevor Johnston, Matthew Lane, Sean Mann, Michael J. McNerney, and Andrew Brooks. *Building Security in Africa: An Evaluation of U.S. Security Sector Assistance in Africa from the Cold War to the Present.* Washington, DC: RAND, 2018.

Way, Lucan A., and Steven Levitsky. "The Dynamics of Autocratic Coercion after the Cold War." *Communist and Post-Communist Studies* 39, no. 3 (2006): 387–410.

Weingast, Barry, and Douglass C. North. "Constitutions and Commitment: The Evolution of Institutional Governing Public Choice in Seventeenth-Century England." *Journal of Economic History* 49, no. 4 (1989): 803–832.

Weinstein, Jeremy. "Autonomous Recovery and International Intervention in Comparative Perspective." *Center for Global Development*, Working Paper, no. 57 (2005).

Weinstein, Jeremy. *Inside Rebellion: The Politics of Insurgent Violence.* New York: Cambridge University Press, 2006.

White, Peter B. "The Perils of Peace: Civil War Peace Agreements and Military Coups." *Journal of Politics* 82, no. 1 (January 2020): 104–118.

Wickham-Crowley, Timothy. *Guerrillas and Revolution in Latin America: A Comparative Study of Insurgents and Regimes since 1956.* Princeton, NJ: Princeton University Press, 1991.

Wimmer, Andreas. *Waves of War: Nationalism, State Formation, and Ethnic Exclusion in the Modern World.* New York: Cambridge University Press, 2013.

Woldense, Josef. "The Ruler's Game of Musical Chairs: Shuffling During the Reign of Ethiopia's Last Emperor." *Social Networks* 52 (2018): 154–166.

Wollenberg, Eric. *The Red Army: A Study of the Growth of Soviet Imperialism.* New York: Transatlantic, 1941.

Wood, Elisabeth. "The Social Processes of Civil War: The Wartime Transformation of Social Networks." *Annual Review of Political Science* 11 (2008): 539–561.

Wyss, Marco. "The Gendarme Stay in Africa: France's Military Role in Côte d'Ivoire." *African Conflict and Peacebuilding Review* 3, no. 1 (2013): 81–111.

Zedong, Mao. *On Guerrilla Warfare*. New York: Anchor Press, 1978.
Zolberg, Aristide R. *Creating Political Order: The Party-States of West Africa*. Chicago: University of Chicago Press, 1966.
Zolberg, Aristide R. *One-Party Government in the Ivory Coast*. Princeton, NJ: Princeton University Press, 1964.
Zukerman Daly, Sarah. "A Farewell to Arms? Election Results and Lasting Peace after Civil Wars." *International Security* 46, no. 3 (2022): 163–204.
Zukerman Daly, Sarah. "Organizational Legacies of Violence: Conditions Favoring Insurgency Onset in Colombia, 1964–1984." *Journal of Peace Research* 49, no. 3 (2012): 473–491.
Zukerman Daly, Sarah. *Organized Violence after Civil War: The Geography of Recruitment in Latin America*. Cambridge: Cambridge University Press, 2016.
Zukerman Daly, Sarah, Laura Paler, and Cyrus Samii. "Wartime Ties and the Social Logic of Crime." *Journal of Peace Research* 57, no. 4 (2020): 536–550.

Index

Page numbers followed by an *f* indicates a figure and by a *t* indicates a table.

Afghanistan, Islamic Emirate of, 5, 152–53
Africa Research Bulletin, 90
anticolonial war, 146–47, 150, 156
Arjona, Ana, 28, 205n32
Armed Forces of Liberia (AFL), 221n4
Authority for Disarmament, Demobilization, and Reintegration (ADDR), 88

Bakayoko, Soumaïla, 70, 102, 117, 168, 212n21, 215n42, 224n27
Bamba, Affousy, 210n52
Beardsley, Kyle, 95
Beck, Nathaniel, 95
Bedié, Henry Konan, 47–48
Blaydes, Lisa, 203n2
Blon Blaise, Siki (aka "The Bulldozer"), 126, 220n150
Boone, Catherine, 38
Bouaké: community-police relations, 119; description of, 110; FN commanders in, 57; FN power sharing in, 112; FN rebels and, 73, 102, 110–11; French Licorne troops and, 50; mayoral office exiles, 217n64; mutinies and protests in, 52, 94, 131; predatory rule in, 110, 130; rebel capital, 64. *See also* Korhogo or Bouaké
Bozizé, Francois, 139
Burkina Faso, 48, 107, 122, 210n52, 216n13

Cabral, Louis, 222n31
Campaoré, Blaise, 48
Cape Verde, 222n31
Central African Republic (CAR): civil conflict in, 153; Coalition of Patriots for Change (CPC), 222n52; Front Populaire pour la Renaissance de la Centrafrique (FPRC), 154–55, 222n52; rebel coercive elements, 162, 222n58; rebel-military integration, 7, 151, 153–54; Russian Wagner Group, 154; Séléka (rebel group), 153–54; UN peacekeeping mission, 154
Chaney, Eric, 203n2
chefferie system and patrimony, 54, 61, 109–10, 112–14, 116, 124–26
Chirac, Jacques, 49
Choi, Young-Jin, 211n4
civil-military relations: attempted coups and, 16, 37; coup-proofing and, 13; domestic power brokers and, 165; dysfunction and, 168; ethnic cleavages and, 144, 147; former FN forces and, 86–87; rebel military victories and, 7; regime leaders and, 35; regime survival and, 101–2; regime types and, 145; understanding of, 12; in weak states, 163
Clark, John F., 145
collaborative rule: alternative terms, 205nn30–32; commander-community ties in, 75–76, 78, 80–81, 99, 133; commander

243

INDEX

collaborative rule *(continued)*
  embeddedness, 19, 23, 32, 41, 85, 104; definition of, 8; ex-rebel commanders, 146, 155–56; ex-rebel commanders and, 33–34; FN goods and civilian control survey, 61–65; FN rebels and, 39, 46, 96–97; informal alliances and, 91; innovation and, 205n33; military mutinies and, 86, 93f, 95; or predatory rule, 29, 31, 37; rebel governance and, 91–92, 114, 130, 137, 157
collaborative rule variables: coercion, 76, 80; coethnic areas and, 80; commander native resident, 77; ethnicity northern, 77, 79; mining site, 76, 79; organized meetings, 76, 80; wartime services quality, 82–83. *See also* rebel goods provision
Colombia, 206n38
Côte d'Ivoire: administrative divisions of, 207n3, 210n56; *chefferie* system and patrimony, 54, 61; civil war causes, 46–47, 51, 208n5, 209n38; election and two presidents (2010), 69, 211nn5–6, 211n9; FN and FRCI coup, 45; military ethnic polarization, 47; military junta, 47–48; presidential elections (1995), 47; rebel rule variations, 45–46. *See also* Gbagbo, Laurent and Gbagbo regime; Ouattara, Alassane and Ouattara regime
Côte d'Ivoire (northern): Dioula (Muslims), 208n12; failed putsch in Abidjan, 52; FN-controlled localities surveys, 58, 211n83, 211n86; FN goods and civilian control, 53–54, 60–63; FN rebels and local elites, 38–39, 41, 52, 54–56, 64–65, 86; FN rebels and power sharing, 56–58; institution building in, 46; insurgent governance in, 11, 18, 51–52; north south cleavage, 208n12. *See also* Gbagbo, Laurent and Gbagbo regime
Côte d'Ivoire Association for the Demobilized (ADCI), 119
Coulibaly, Amadou Gon, 215n3
Coulibaly, Gbon, 217n62
Coulibaly, Ibrahim ("IB"): in Bouaké, 111; and Bouaké, 215n6; FN commander, 48, 52, 212n9; "Invisible Commandos," 211n9; killing by FRCI forces, 213n29, 215n38; from Korhogo, 107; military junta and exiled soldiers, 48, 52; and Soro, 108, 203n60, 210n52
Coulibaly, Ibrahima Gon ("Goz"), 102
Coulibaly, Ousmane, 57
counterbalancing, 144, 147–48, 150, 221n21

Dacoury-Tabley, Louis-André, 210n52
Daly, Sarah Zukerman, 31, 206n38
De Bruin, Erica, 145

defections: definition of, 137; goods provisions and postwar regime, 138; locally embedded commanders and, 157–58. *See also* dichotomous variables
defections, alternative explanations. *See* anticolonial war; counterbalancing; democracy; ethnic cleavages; ideology; military resources; military victory or intense war; regime type; third-party intervention
demobilized combatants (démos), 89, 115–17, 119, 127–29, 131, 220n159
democracy, 145, 148–49
Diarrassouba, Zoumana, 107–8, 215n12
dichotomous variables, 82, 92, 140–41, 144–46
disarmament and demobilization (DDR) programs, 30, 73, 88–89, 155, 166, 214n9
Doe, Samuel, 221n4
Douanier, Coulibaly Drissa, 109
Doumbia, Lassina, 102, 215n42, 224n27

Ecole Pour Tous, 113
Economic Community of West African States (ECOWAS), 209n33
embedded authoritarianism, 163
Eritrea, 162
Eritrean People's Liberation Front (EPLF), 140, 156, 163
Ethiopia, 37, 162
ethnic cleavages, 13–14, 21, 49, 138, 143–44, 147–50, 222n31
ethnic issues, 39, 47–49, 55, 63
ex-FN forces: autonomy of, 7, 164; community leaders and, 19; coordinated armed attacks (2017), 4; demobilization of, 6, 71; and FRCI, 88, 106; military mutinies by, 86, 88, 90, 95, 117, 203n60; and Ouattara, 14, 70, 101, 128, 131; purges of, 213n29; in Sangouiné, 67
ex-rebel commanders: ambition and, 82, 159; commander visits, 74–75; community leaders and commanders, 72–73; cooperation or resistance, 26, 89, 137–38; efforts to isolate and contain, 168; embedded and non-embedded commanders, 35, 73–74, 132; embeddedness, 4, 23, 28–31, 33–34, 68, 84–86, 91, 100–101, 162, 206n38, 206n45, 213n44; grievances against the government, 34, 100–101; local elite and, 161; local legitimacy and positions, 31, 72–73, 75, 77; material support, 75; mixed motivation of, 22–23, 25–26; mobilization power, 30, 167; networks or independence of, 95; Ouattara regime and, 6–7, 14, 19, 71; postwar commander influence, 75–76, 78f–79f, 80–82, 84, 160–61; predatory rule, 205n28; rebel-ruled communities and,

27–28, 30–32, 36, 72, 206n49; regime leaders and, 27; statebuilding and, 25, 34, 40–41, 96, 157–58, 204n10; war-to-peace transition, 33. *See also* Forces Nouvelles; military mutinies and demobilized rebel protests
external interveners, 14–15, 50, 155, 165–66

Faulkner, Christopher, 90
Fédération Estudiantine et Scholaire de Côte d'Ivoire (FESCI), 52, 210n52, 216n14
field commanders: autonomous capacity of, 36, 207n60; centralized authority and, 157; parallel armed networks, 204n21; predatory rule and, 36; rebel governance and, 160, 205n35
Fofana, Losseni, 54, 122–24, 128–29, 219n122, 220n149
Fofana, Moussa, 56
Fofié, Martin Kouakou: arrest of, 216n13; arsenal of, 116; community ties and, 127; independent power base of, 5–6; influential elites and, 131, 133; and Korhogo, 106, 108–10, 113, 115–16, 118; northern politicians and, 132; and Ouattara government, 117; and Ousmane, 119; Second Regional Command (Daloa), 217n73; Third Regional Command (FRCI), 116; and transfer to Daloa, 117–18, 120; UN sanctions and, 212n28; zone commander, 3
Forces Armées des Forces Nouvelles (FAFN): and Bouaké, 111; demobilized checkpoints and, 72; demobilized rebel events and, 90; ethnic groups of, 210n72; FN military wing, 52; Fofié and, 212n28; and Kassero, 67, 123; in Korhogo, 108; military mutinies and demobilized rebel protests, 120; naming of, 201n1; zone and sector commands in, 53
Forces Armées du Nord (FAN), 140
Forces Armées Nationales de Côte d'Ivoire (FANCI): anti-Gbagbo rebels and, 48; and Bouaké, 110–11; civil war clashes in Korhogo, 107, 114; civil war in western Côte d'Ivoire, 122; defections to FRCI, 69; embedded commanders and, 132; mercenaries and, 49; officers of, 215n42, 224n27; Ouattara-Soro coalition, 70–71; zone and sector commands in FN, 53
Forces Nouvelles (FN): in Abidjan, 45; anti-Gbagbo militias, 208nn25–26; army integration and, 3; and Cellule 39 (FN veterans), 115–17, 119; civilian and soldiers balance, 51; com'zones, 82, 89, 95; disbanded (2011), 169; merger with MJP and MPIGO, 49; merger with RDR party, 70; military junta and, 48; naming of, 201n1; nature resources and funding, 64; origins of, 46; Ouattara government and,
164; political-military coalition, 45; postwar embeddedness, 85; postwar grievances, 88; prewar ethnic or partisan identities of, 39, 49; progovernment sympathies and, 123; rebel ruled localities and, 104; reorganization into three divisions, 52–53; in Sangouiné, 124; warfare against Gbago regime, 49–51
Forces Républicaines de Côte d'Ivoire (FRCI): in Abidjan, 45; and Coulibaly, 213n29; FN field commanders and, 6; FN rebranding and integration, 69, 94, 102, 104, 106, 115; and Fofié clash, 116–18; and ICC, 71; and Kassero, 67, 126–27; Letoh and, 212n21; loyalty to Ouattara, 120; military mutinies and, 86, 88–90, 95, 128; naming of, 201n1; and Ondo, 68; relieved of command, 168; strength after Ouattara-Soro coalition, 70. *See also* Ouattara, Alassane and Ouattara regime
Forces Spéciales, 102
Fozié, Tuo, 48, 70, 111, 216n41
France: foreign aid to Côte d'Ivoire, 212n17; French colonialism, 46, 48, 217n62; French interposition force (Operation Licorne), 49–51, 209n33; Ouattara-Soro coalition and, 70
Fraternité Matin, 90
Front Populaire Ivoirien (FPI), 48, 69, 124–25, 211n89. *See also* Gbagbo, Laurent and Gbagbo regime

Gaddafi, Muammar, 5, 204n16
Gbagbo, Laurent and Gbagbo regime: anti-Gbagbo militias and FN, 208n25; arrest of and government collapse, 45, 51, 212n21, 213n29; civil war clashes in Korhogo, 107, 114; civil war in western Côte d'Ivoire, 122; civil war loss, 115; civil war losses in Mahapleu, 128; election loss (2010), 69, 72, 211n5, 217n61; election of (2000), 48; ethnic non-support in Bouaké, 113; and Fofié, 216n13; former supporters in government, 102; FPI party on Kassero, 124; government official of, 215n42, 224n27; indicted by ICC, 17, 71, 115; intervention forces bias, 50; Korhogo or Bouaké alternatives, 106; local elite distain for, 55; military defeat of, 6, 19; military support to defeat, 88; nonembedded commanders and, 132; northerners and, 65; and Ouattara, 53; ouster of and foreign powers, 70; pro-Gbagbo militia in Bouaké, 110–11; response to FN success in north, 49; retreat from north, 52; time in government, 208n7; western Côte d'Ivoire support for, 123. *See also* Forces Armées Nationales de Côte d'Ivoire

INDEX

Glassmyer, Katherine, 139, 201n11
Gleditsch, Kristian, 95
Groupement de Sécurité de la Présidence de la République de Côte d'Ivoire (GSPR), 102, 115, 119
Gueï, Robert, 47–48, 108, 111, 220n150
Guinea, 222n31
Guinea-Bissau, 7, 222n31

Habré, Hissen, 140
Heitz-Tokpa, Kathrin, 52–54, 122–23
Houphouët- Boigny, Félix and regime, 46–47, 49, 54, 96, 107, 164, 209n38, 217n62
Houthi rebellion (Yemen), 139
Huang, Reyko, 11, 141
Humphreys, Macartan, 206n50
hypotheses: alternative explanations, 79, 94–95, 132, 143–44, 147; collaborative rule and ex-rebel power (H1), 33, 41, 68, 78, 81, 130, 133; rebel rule and commander resistance (H2), 37, 41, 91, 93, 132–33

ideology, 145–48, 150–52, 158
International Criminal Court (ICC), 17, 71, 88, 115
Ismael, 119
ivoirité and ethnic-cultural distinctiveness, 47–48, 51, 55, 208n7
Ivorian civil war (2002-2011): causes of, 46–47; coup-civil war trap, 51; elections at end of civil war (2010), 69; FN and, 18, 50–51, 121; FN field commanders after, 88; local rule variations, 17, 41; low combat and deaths during, 50, 209n40; military mutinies and, 86; north south partition after, 50; rebel-military integration after, 68; stalemate, 114

La Jeunesse Forces Nouvelles (JFN), 56

Kagame, Paul, 13, 70
Kassero, 67–68, 123–24, 126–28, 131–32, 219n123
Katiola (northern town), 73
Kofi, Paul Kofi, 117
Konaté, Sidiki, 210n52
Koné, Amadou, 210n52
Koné, Gnangadjomon, 49
Koné, Lanciné, 115
Koné, Mamadou, 210n52
Korhogo: autonomous mobilization power, 132; *cabinet civile*, 216n15; civil war experience, 107–8; collaborative rule in, 108–9, 130; commander-community ties in, 118; community-police relations, 99; *dozoton* hunting group, 54, 108; *état civil* service, 108–9, 216n19, 216n21; ex-FN forces rebellion, 4; local governing elites in, 133; rebel control of, 3, 67, 108–10, 116. *See also* Fofié, Martin Kouakou
Korhogo or Bouaké: collaborative wartime rule in, 20; commander embeddedness in, 104–5, 105t; comparisons of, 106; and FN commanders and, 52, 54; FN governance in, 111–13, 118; institutional path dependency, 114; MPCI and, 49; optimal counterfactuals, 105; proximity to hostile government forces, 114; and RDR politicians, 106; similarities of, 113; strong local elites in Korhogo, 113–14
Kosovo Liberation Army (KLA), 140
Kurds (Iraq), 139

Lagos Accords (1979, Chad), 140
Leboeuf, Aline, 95
Lenin, Vladimir, 204n11
Le Patriote, 90
Letoh, Fermin Detoh, 212n21
Levi, Margaret, 22, 34
Liberians United for Reconciliation and Democracy, 219n114
Libya, 14–15, 27, 204n16
Libyan National Liberation Army, 5
Linas-Marcoussis peace accords, 111, 215n11
Lindberg, Staffan, 145
Lyons, Terrence, 11

Mahapleu, 124–26, 129–31, 219n148. *See also* Sangouiné or Mahapleu
Mampilly, Zachariah, 28, 205n33
Mangou, Philippe, 212n21
Marten, Kimberly, 15
Massemba, 215n11
Médecins Sans Frontières (MSF), 54, 112
mercenary class, 204n19
Messamba, Koné, 107
Migdal, Joel, 11
military mutinies and demobilized rebel protests: alternative explanations, 94–95; coercive bargaining tactic, 86; collaborative wartime governance and, 92–94, 103; community ties and, 127–28; ex-rebel commanders and, 41, 86–88, 168; FN rebels and, 19, 89, 117, 203n60, 214n25; FN soldier payouts, 102; in Korhogo, 106; likelihood of mutinies, 91, 95; Ondo and, 129; rebel-civilian relations, 20; regime survival and, 101; spatial autocorrelation in, 95; uniformed FRCI soldiers and, 90
military resources, 144, 147–48
military victory or intense war, 39, 143, 145–46, 148, 149f, 150, 156, 159
Mourlaye, Dao, 102

INDEX

Mouvement Patriotique de Côte d'Ivoire (MPCI), 49–50, 107, 111, 121–22, 201n1, 203n60, 209n26, 216n13, 219n115
Mouvement Populaire Ivoirien du Grand Ouest (MPIGO), 49, 122, 209n26. *See also* Forces Nouvelles
Movement for Justice and Peace (MJP), 49, 122, 209n26. *See also* Forces Nouvelles
Mugabe, Robert, 6, 202n15, 204n18

National Movement for the Liberation of Azawad (MNLA) Mali, 139
National Union for the Total Independence of Angola (UNITA), 141
nonstate armed groups, 4, 22, 51, 138–39, 141, 154, 160, 221n4. *See also* ex-rebel commanders
Nord-Sud, 90
North Atlantic Treaty Organization (NATO), 151–52, 221n4

Ondo, 67–68, 124–26, 128–29, 131–32, 219n123
Ouahi, 122, 124
Ouattara, Alassane and Ouattara regime: anti-Gbagbo militias and FN, 209n25; background of, 215n3; and Bakayoko, 70; border security aid, 164; candidate Ouattara banned from election, 211n89; coup-proofing tactics of, 102; current status of, 168; and Diarrassouba, 215n12; election of (2010), 69, 211nn5–6; ex-rebel commanders and, 72, 74, 167; FN disbanding and mutinies, 85–86, 117; FN grievances with, 89–90, 128–29; FN resistance to statebuilding, 105; FN soldier payouts, 102; and Fofié, 3, 132; and Gbagbo arrest, 45; head of FN la Centrale, 52; and ICC, 71; junta leadership and, 48; Korhogo and Fofié conflict, 106; and Mangou, 212n21; military mutinies and protests, 88; military mutinies and protests against, 101; political patronage networks of, 38; presidential elections (1995), 47; protests against (2017), 4; and Soro, 118; statebuilding and, 119–20; victory over Gbagbo regime (2011), 115. *See also* Ouattara-Soro coalition
Ouattara, Alassane and Ouattara regime and, 163
Ouattara, Issiaka ("Wattao"), 70, 120
Ouattara-Soro coalition, 69–71, 73–74, 118, 133, 220n179
Oueddei, Goukouni, 140
Ousmane, Chérif (aka Papa Guépard): in Bouaké, 112, 114; Compagnie Guépard, 111; continued influence lacking, 132; demobilized rebel protests and, 131; and FAFN, 70; Groupement de Sécurité de la Présidence de la République de Côte d'Ivoire (GSPR), 115; military coup (1999) role, 111; military junta and, 48; Republican Guard commander, 102; theft and poisoning, 217n56; weak local postwar ties, 106, 118–19; willingness to obey regime orders, 120–21

Parti Démocratique de Côte d'Ivoire (PDCI), 47–48, 52, 55, 217n62
Patassé, Félix, 139
peacebuilding and statebuilding, 4–5, 16, 21, 24, 68, 84, 143, 155, 161, 165–67
peacekeeping forces, external, 46, 50–51, 64, 69
People's Liberation Army (China), 159, 163
Piccolino, Giulia, 82
police-citizen relations, 87, 96–101, 215n33
political rulers and domestic violence, 203n2
postwar commander-community ties: centralized statebuilding and, 18, 41, 95; civilian welfare and, 19, 73, 96, 161; commander specific attributes, 82; endurance or declining, 62, 65, 68, 85, 96; military mutinies and, 93; quantitative evidence of, 58; rebel rule and, 11–12, 27, 29, 75, 77–78, 84, 163, 169
Powell, Jonathan, 90
predatory governance, 104–5
predatory rule: alternative providers and, 160; in Bouaké, 106, 110, 115; civilians and resources, 38–39, 62; commander-community ties in, 75, 104, 133; consequences of, 32–33, 206n50; declining local ties, 85, 160; distinction with collaborative rule, 28; ex-rebel commanders and, 46, 68, 81, 91; and field commanders, 8–9, 23, 29, 35, 206n52; FN goods and civilian control survey, 61–63; Mahapleu and, 74; military mutinies and, 92, 95; Outtara regime and, 20; postwar statebuilding and, 37, 41; predictions of, 66; reasons for, 63; rebel rule and, 5, 130, 137; regime leaders and, 86; revolutionary ideology and, 40; Taliban and, 152; wartime rule, 58
"Predatory Theory of Rule, The" (Levi), 22
Prospe, 164
Prosper, Oulaï Tiémoko, 126

Rassemblement des Républicains (RDR) party, 52, 56, 70, 101, 106, 115, 164, 210n52, 211n89, 216n14

INDEX

rationalist models, 204n19
rebel goods provision, 53–54, 60, 76, 80, 93, 141–43, 146–51, 156, 158, 217n61
rebel governance: battlefield conditions, 39; ethnic and partisan identities, 39; existing social structures, 38; ideological orientation, 40; local elite and, 46, 159–60; occupied civilians and, 38–39, 157, 207n62; selection of, 37
rebel-military integration: in Côte d'Ivoire, 71–72; FN field commanders and, 3, 6, 24–25, 88, 159; in Libya and South Sudan, 27; limits to external intervenors, 165–66; local social ties and, 14; regime leaders and, 24–27; renewed conflict and, 7–8; Rwanda and Côte d'Ivoire, 12–13; security force loyalty and, 85; settlements and, 140–41; threat to peace, 4, 15; variation in, 13; weak state example, 22–23, 27, 32–33, 35–37; Zimbabwe and Côte d'Ivoire, 6
Red Army, 205n22
regime leaders: coup-proofing, 13, 35, 102; and embedded and non-embedded commanders, 10, 23, 34–36; ethnic group exclusion, 207n56; and field commanders, 6, 8–9, 11, 19–21, 25, 27, 36, 40; foreign audience and, 26, 35; funding and, 12; loyalty to, 5; military mutinies and protests, 87–88; national militaries and, 22, 24; and rebel-military integration, 36, 204n11; statebuilding and, 26, 33
regime type, 138, 143, 145, 148
Resistência Nacional Moçambicana (RENAMO), 5
Rodrik, 124–26, 128, 219n123
Roessler, Philip, 51, 204n4
Rwanda, 13, 16, 37, 51, 70, 163, 212n13
Rwandan Patriotic Front (RPF), 7, 13, 26, 37, 159

Sambanis, Nicholas, 139, 201n11, 208n5
Sangouiné: autonomous mobilization power, 132; collaborative rule in, 130; commander–community ties in, 124; ex-combatants and Kassero, 127; ex-rebel networks protests, 131; kinship-based ties, 56; local governing elites in, 126, 133; mutinies in, 128. See also Kassero
Sangouiné or Mahapleu: civil war in western Côte d'Ivoire, 121–22; coffee and cocoa cultivation, 121; collaborative rule and, 130; commander-community ties in, 74, 128–29; commander embeddedness in, 104–5, 105t, 121, 126–27; comparisons of, 20, 121, 125–26; descriptions of, 67; early commanders, 219n123; ex-rebel commanders and, 68; "firstcomer"

(*autochtone*) and "newcomer" (*allogène*) residents, 121, 218n112; FN control of, 121–23; local elites and, 126; MPIGO militia and Liberian mercenaries, 122; optimal counterfactuals, 105; rebel-civilian relations in, 123; similarities of, 132; stronger institutions per block voting index, 126
Savimbi, Jonas, 141
Schiel, Rebecca, 90
Schulhofer-Wohl, Jonah, 208n5
security-sector reform (SSR), 4, 14, 27, 34, 36, 73, 85, 131, 156, 158, 165, 167
Sidibé, 112
Sierra Leone, 206n50
Skocpol, Theda, 11
Snyder, Richard, 207n60
Soro, Alphonse, 108, 216n14
Soro, Guillaume Kigbafori: Catholic Christians and, 208n12; and Coulibaly, 107; délégué civiles, political commissars, 52; deteriorating alliance with Ouattara, 101; ex-FN allies purged, 213n29; FN leadership and, 52, 102, 210n52; FN merger announcement, 70; and Fofié, 118; Ivorian national student union leader, 48; and MPCI, 203n60; and Ouattara, 89; and Ouattara government, 168; prime minister and minister of defense, 69; purge of pro-Coulibaly officers, 108; resources for local support, 220n149
Soro, Kanigui, 108, 210n52, 216n14
South Sudan, 14–15, 27, 162
Speight, Jeremy, 82
Stewart, Megan, 28, 142, 151, 205n33
Straus, Scott, 209n38
Sudan People's Liberation Army / Movement (SPLA/M), 140
surveys and studies: Afghanistan and Central African Republic security, 138; Armed Conflict Location Event Dataset (ACLED), 90, 216n37; Block voting index, 126, 220n151; case-selection strategy, 105, 130; civil war termination dataset (Toft), 139; collaborative rule scale or index, 63, 211n89; community informant survey (2017), 58, 60–63, 74, 91, 94, 99, 119, 132; data collection methodology, 17, 58, 87–88, 90–94, 97, 130–31, 138–40, 214nn19–20, 215n34; Enquête niveau de vie des ménages (ENV) household socioeconomic surveys, 58, 63, 80, 98–99; Ethnic Power Relations (EPR) dataset, 208n7; ex-rebel commander defections, 138; Insurgent Social Service Provision Dataset, 142–43; patterns of wartime rebel rule, 58–65, 209n40; Political Transition and Inclusion Survey, 96–97, 215n31;

INDEX

Rebel Governance Dataset, 142–43;
rebel-military integration dataset, 138;
research design in Côte d'Ivoire, 158;
State Security Forces Dataset, 145; UCDP
Conflict Termination Dataset, 139, 145;
United States Agency for International
Development (USAID), 58, 80, 82;
Varieties of Democracy (V-Dem)
dataset, 145
Svolik, Milan, 145

Taliban, 5, 138, 151–53, 155, 221n4, 222n40
Taylor, Charles, 219n114
Themnér, Anders, 12
third-party intervention, 15, 24, 143–44, 147–48, 149f, 156
Tigray People's Liberation Front (TPLF), 37, 156
Tilly, Charles, 157
Timité, 109
Toft, Monica, 139
Tolbert, William, 221n4
Touadéra, Faustin-Archange, 154
Touré, Herve ("Vetcho"), 73
Touré, Sékou, 215n42, 224n27
Turé, Samori, 217n62

Uganda, 51
Ugandan National Resistance Movement, 5
Union Pour la Démocratie et la Paix en Côte d'Ivoire (UDPCI), 126, 220n150
Unité d'Intervention, 102
United Islamic Front, 221n4
United Nations Children's Fund (UNICEF), 112

United Nations Mission in Côte d'Ivoire (MINUCI), 50–51, 209n35
United Nations Operation in Côte d'Ivoire (ONUCI), 4, 53–54, 209n35, 212n28
United Somali Congress (USC) (Somalia), 139
United States, 15, 70, 212n17
United Tajik Opposition (UTO), 5
United Wa State Army (UWSA) (Myanmar), 139
UN mission in Côte d'Ivoire, 211n4
US Agency for International Development (USAID), 58, 80, 82

van Baalen, Sebastian, 38, 54, 56–57
Vieira, João "Nino," 222n31
Vietnam, 7
Voroshilov, Klim, 205n22

wartime institutions, 5, 10, 104, 133, 162
war veterans, 88, 214n8
Watkins, Andrew, 153
weak states, 163, 204n4. *See also* rebel-military integration
Weinstein, Jeremy, 28, 205n31, 206n50
Wood, Elizabeth, 206n49

Yacouba people, 67, 121–23, 125, 218n111
Yacub Mujahid, Mohammad, 152, 222n35

Zimbabwe, 16, 51, 163, 204n18
Zimbabwe Defence Forces (ZDF), 6
Zimbabwe National African Union (ZANU), 6, 26, 202n15, 204n18
Zimbabwe National African Union–Patriotic Front (ZANU–PF), 6–7